JOURNAL

OF

A RESIDENCE ON A

GEORGIAN PLANTATION

IN 1838—1839.

By FRANCES ANNE KEMBLE.

SLAVERY THE CHIEF CORNER STONE.

'This stone (Slavery), which was rejected by the first builders, is become the chief stone of the corner in our new edifice.'—*Speech of* ALEXANDER H. STEPHENS, *Vice-President of the Confederate States: delivered March 21, 1861.*

Foreword by Jean-Louis Brindamour

AFRO-AM PRESS
DIVISION OF AFRO-AM. BOOKS, INC.
CHICAGO
1969

The original edition of this work was published in
New York by Harper & Brothers in 1864. The copy
from which this reprint edition was made was loaned
to Afro-Am Press from the Special Collection on the
History and Literature of the Negro, George Cleveland
Hall Branch, The Chicago Public Library

Manufactured in the United States of America by
RCS Press, Inc., Chicago

FOREWORD

"... Abraham the cook, in speaking of his brother's theft at the rice-island, said 'it was a shame even for a colored man to do such things.' I labor hard, whenever any such observation is made, to explain to them that the question is one of moral and mental culture — not the color of an integument — and assure them, much to my own comfort, whatever it may be to theirs, that white people are as dirty and as dishonest as colored folks, when they have suffered the same lack of decent training. If I could but find one of these women on whose mind the idea had dawned that she was neither more nor less than my equal, I think I should embrace her in an ecstacy of hopefulness."[1]

So wrote a young white English lady, age 29 years, who had never before encountered slavery in any

[1] *Page 256.*

form. She had been educated in convents in France before she made her first public appearance as Juliet under her father's management at Covent Garden in 1829 — though she had not been formally trained for the stage and always said she acutely disliked the profession of acting. In 1834, after two gloriously successful years of touring the United States theatre circuit with her father, she married Pierce Butler of Philadelphia. Her husband owned an estate of rice and cotton plantations, in the islands at the entrance of the Altamaha, on the coast of Georgia. In 1838-39 the Butlers, with their two little daughters, took up residence on the Georgia estate. This work is the journal kept by "Fanny" Kemble during that year.

Journal of a Residence on a Georgian Plantation is unique in its reportage because the author clearly sees the evils of slavery for *both* slaves and slave holders; her pity is directed at both. The *Journal* is a highly rational, yet highly emotional document; sensitive, literate, engrossing.

There is constant juxtaposition throughout the entries of the author's horror of slavery and its evils with her love of the beauties and serenity of nature. The break which later came with her husband is clearly heralded in these pages: ". . . in temperament she had never had much in common with her husband; in taste she was beginning to have even less."[2] Her husband, on a charge of abandonment, was granted a divorce in 1849.

The *Journal* was not published until 1863, and was published only then in an effort to influence British opinion during the Civil War. Throughout the work one encounters humanity as only a noble spirit can see it: pure, devoid of trappings, joyous and pathetic. There is not an area of slavery that is not touched here in microcosm: religion, health, familial ties, miscegenation, discipline. The descriptions of the hospital, the interviews with the slave population of the estate,

[2] *see Fanny Kemble by Dorothie Bobbe (1931), page 143.*

the visits to the slave "homes," and on an estate which was a model of the "progressive" southern attitude toward slavery, often bring tears to the readers' eyes. Man's inhumanity to man — and in a situation in which an enlightened white woman can do no more than beg her plantation-owner husband for leniency toward his slaves and then cry out her agony for the situation to an unheeding God and nature when he refuses her requests and accuses her of undermining the basic tenets upon which southern slavery was founded — is pictured in this unforgettable narrative.

The "Letter to the Editor of the *Times*" and the "Letter to C.G., Esq." clearly render a picture of what we are finally seeing in our own era: a "revolution" by black and white alike against the final vestiges of hypocrisy in a society in which all men *are* equal. Her predictions in these letters are amazingly accurate. There is not a man in our country today who could not benefit by absorbing the extraordinary record kept by this gentlewoman so many years ago.

JEAN-LOUIS BRINDAMOUR
Chicago
1969

TO

ELIZABETH DWIGHT SEDGWICK,

THIS JOURNAL,

ORIGINALLY KEPT FOR HER,

IS

MOST AFFECTIONATELY

Dedicated.

PREFACE.

THE following diary was kept in the winter and spring of 1838-9, on an estate consisting of rice and cotton plantations, in the islands at the entrance of the Altamaha, on the coast of Georgia.

The slaves in whom I then had an unfortunate interest were sold some years ago. The islands themselves are at present in the power of the Northern troops. The record contained in the following pages is a picture of conditions of human existence which I hope and believe have passed away.

LONDON, *January* 16, 1863.

JOURNAL.

Philadelphia, December, 1838.

MY DEAR E——,—I return you Mr. ——'s letter. I do not think it answers any of the questions debated in our last conversation at all satisfactorily: the *right* one man has to enslave another, he has not the hardihood to assert; but in the reasons he adduces to defend that act of injustice, the contradictory statements he makes appear to me to refute each other. He says, that to the Continental European protesting against the abstract iniquity of slavery, his answer would be, "The slaves are infinitely better off than half the Continental peasantry." To the Englishman, "They are happy compared with the miserable Irish." But supposing that this answered the question of original injustice, which it does not, it is not a true reply. Though the negroes are fed, clothed, and housed, and though the Irish peasant is starved, naked, and roofless, the bare name of freemen—the lordship over his own person, the power to choose and will—are blessings beyond food, raiment, or shelter; possessing which, the want of every comfort of life is yet more tolerable than their fullest enjoyment without them. Ask the thousands of ragged destitutes who yearly land upon these shores to seek the means of existence — ask the friendless, penniless foreign emigrant if he will give up his present misery, his future uncertainty, his doubtful and difficult struggle for life at once, for the secure, and, as it is called, fortunate dependence of the slave: the indignation with which he would spurn the offer will prove that he possesses one good beyond all others, and that his birthright as a man is more precious to him yet than the mess of pottage for which he is told to exchange it because he is starving.

Of course the reverse alternative can not be offered to the slaves, for at the very word the riches of those who own them would make themselves wings and flee away. But I do not admit the comparison between your slaves and even the lowest class of European free laborers, for the former are *allowed* the exercise of no faculties but those which they enjoy in common with the brutes that perish. The just comparison is between the slaves and the useful animals to whose level your laws reduce them; and I will acknowledge that the slaves of a kind owner may be as well cared for, and as happy, as the dogs and horses of a merciful master; but the latter condition—*i. e.*, that of happiness—must again depend upon the complete perfection of their moral and mental degradation. Mr. ——, in his letter, maintains that they *are* an inferior race, and, compared with the whites, "*animals*, incapable of mental culture and moral improvement:" to this I can only reply, that if they are incapable of profiting by instruction, I do not see the necessity for laws inflicting heavy penalties on those who offer it to them. If they really are brutish, witless, dull, and devoid of capacity for progress, where lies the *danger* which is constantly insisted upon of offering them that of which they are incapable. We have no laws forbidding us to teach our dogs and horses as much as they can comprehend; nobody is fined or imprisoned for reasoning upon knowledge and liberty to the beasts of the field, for they are incapable of such truths. But these themes are forbidden to slaves, not because they can not, but because they can and would seize on them with avidity — receive them gladly, comprehend them quickly; and the masters' power over them would be annihilated at once and forever. But I have more frequently heard not that they were incapable of receiving instruction, but something much nearer the truth —that knowledge only makes them miserable: the moment they are in any degree enlightened, they become unhappy. In the letter I return to you Mr. —— says that the very slightest amount of education, merely teaching them to read, "impairs their value as slaves, for it instantly destroys their contentedness, and, since you do not contemplate changing their condition, it is surely doing them an ill service to destroy their acquiescence in it;" but this is a very different ground of argument from the other. The discontent they evince upon the mere dawn of an advance in intelligence proves not only that they can acquire, but combine ideas, a process to which it is very difficult to assign a limit; and there indeed the whole question lies, and there and nowhere else the shoe really pinches. A slave is ignorant; he eats, drinks, sleeps, labors, and is happy. He learns to read; he feels, thinks, reflects, and becomes miserable. He discovers himself to be one of a debased and degraded race, deprived of the elementary rights which God has granted to all men alike; every action is controlled, every word noted; he may not stir beyond his appointed bounds, to the right hand or to the left, at his own will, but at the will of another he may be sent miles and miles of weary journeying—tethered, yoked, collared, and fettered—away from whatever he may know as home, severed from all those ties of blood and affection which he alone of all human, of all living creatures on the face of the earth, may neither enjoy in peace nor defend when they are outraged. If he is well treated, if his master be tolerably humane or even understand his own interest tolerably, this is probably *all* he may have to endure: it is only to the consciousness of these evils that knowledge and reflection awaken him. But how is it if

A 2

his master be severe, harsh, cruel—or even only careless
—leaving his creatures to the delegated dominion of some
overseer or agent, whose love of power, or other evil dispositions, are checked by no considerations of personal
interest? Imagination shrinks from the possible result
of such a state of things; nor must you, or Mr. ——, tell
me that the horrors thus suggested exist only in imagination. The Southern newspapers, with their advertisements of negro sales and personal descriptions of fugitive
slaves, supply details of misery that it would be difficult
for imagination to exceed. Scorn, derision, insult, menace
—the handcuff, the lash — the tearing away of children
from parents, of husbands from wives—the weary trudg-
ing in droves along the common highways, the labor of
body, the despair of mind, the sickness of heart — these
are the realities which belong to the system, and form the
rule, rather than the exception, in the slave's experience.
And this system exists here in this country of yours,
which boasts itself the asylum of the oppressed, the home
of freedom, the one place in all the world where all men
may find enfranchisement from all thraldoms of mind, soul,
or body—the land elect of liberty.

Mr. —— lays great stress, as a proof of the natural inferiority of the blacks, on the little comparative progress
they have made in those states where they enjoy their
freedom, and the fact that, whatever quickness of parts
they may exhibit while very young, on attaining maturity
they invariably sink again into inferiority, or at least me-
diocrity, and indolence. But surely there are other causes
to account for this besides natural deficiency, which must,
I think, be obvious to any unprejudiced person observing
the condition of the free blacks in your Northern communities. If, in the early portion of their life, they escape
the contempt and derision of their white associates—if
the blessed unconsciousness and ignorance of childhood

keeps them for a few years unaware of the conventional proscription under which their whole race is placed (and it is difficult to walk your streets, and mark the tone of insolent superiority assumed by even the gutter-urchins over their dusky contemporaries, and imagine this possible)—as soon as they acquire the first rudiments of knowledge, as soon as they begin to grow up and pass from infancy to youth, as soon as they cast the first observing glance upon the world by which they are surrounded, and the society of which they are members, they must become conscious that they are marked as the Hebrew lepers of old, and are condemned to sit, like those unfortunates, without the gates of every human and social sympathy. From their own sable color, a pall falls over the whole of God's universe to them, and they find themselves stamped with a badge of infamy of Nature's own devising, at sight of which all natural kindliness of man to man seems to recoil from them. They are not slaves indeed, but they are pariahs; debarred from all fellowship save with their own despised race—scorned by the lowest white ruffian in your streets, not tolerated as companions even by the foreign menials in your kitchen. They are free certainly, but they are also degraded, rejected, the offscum and the offscouring of the very dregs of your society; they are free from the chain, the whip, the enforced task and unpaid toil of slavery; but they are not the less under a ban. Their kinship with slaves forever bars them from a full share of the freeman's inheritance of equal rights, and equal consideration and respect. All hands are extended to thrust them out, all fingers point at their dusky skin, all tongues—the most vulgar, as well as the self-styled most refined—have learned to turn the very name of their race into an insult and a reproach. How, in the name of all that is natural, probable, possible, should the spirit and energy of any human creature support itself under such an accumulation of injustice and obloquy? Where shall any mass of men be found with power of character and mind sufficient to bear up against such a weight of prejudice? Why, if one individual rarely gifted by heaven were to raise himself out of such a slough of despond, he would be a miracle; and what would be his reward? Would he be admitted to an equal share in your political rights? would he ever be allowed to cross the threshold of your doors? would any of you give your daughter to his son, or your son to his daughter? would you, in any one particular, admit him to the footing of equality which any man with a white skin would claim, whose ability and worth had so raised him from the lower degrees of the social scale? You would turn from such propositions with abhorrence, and the servants in your kitchen and stable— the ignorant and boorish refuse of foreign populations, in whose countries no such prejudice exists, imbibing it with the very air they breathe here—would shrink from eating at the same table with such a man, or holding out the hand of common fellowship to him. Under the species of social proscription in which the blacks in your Northern cities exist, if they preserved energy of mind, enterprise of spirit, or any of the best attributes and powers of free men, they would prove themselves, instead of the lowest and least of human races, the highest and first, not only of all that do exist, but of all that ever have existed; for they alone would seek and cultivate knowledge, goodness, truth, science, art, refinement, and all improvement, purely for the sake of their own excellence, and without one of those incentives of honor, power, and fortune, which are found to be the chief, too often the only, inducements which lead white men to the pursuit of the same objects.

You know very well, dear E——, that in speaking of the free blacks of the North I here state nothing but what is true, and of daily experience. Only last week I heard

in this very town of Philadelphia of a family of strict
probity and honor, highly principled, intelligent, well-edu-
cated, and accomplished, and (to speak in the world's language) respectable in every way—i. e., *rich*. Upon an
English lady's stating it to be her intention to visit these
persons when she came to Philadelphia, she was told that
if she did nobody else would visit *her;* and she probably
would excite a malevolent feeling, which might find vent
in some violent demonstration against this family. All
that I have now said of course bears only upon the condition of the free colored population of the North, with
which I am familiar enough to speak confidently of it. As
for the slaves, and their capacity for progress, I can say
nothing, for I have never been among them to judge what
faculties their unhappy social position leaves to them un-
impaired. ˉ But it seems to me that no experiment on a
sufficiently large scale can have been tried for a sufficient
length of time to determine the question of their incurable
inferiority. Physiologists say that three successive generations appear to be necessary to produce an effectual
change of constitution (bodily and mental), be it for health
or disease. There are positive physical defects which
produce positive mental ones; the diseases of the muscu-
lar and nervous systems descend from father to son. Upon
the agency of one corporal power how much that is not
corporal depends; from generation to generation internal
disease and external deformity, vices, virtues, talents, and
deficiencies are transmitted, and by the action of the same
law it must be long indeed before the offspring of slaves
—creatures begotten of a race debased and degraded to
the lowest degree, themselves born in slavery, and whose
progenitors have eaten the bread and drawn the breath
of slavery for years—can be measured, with any show of
justice, by even the least favored descendants of European nations, whose qualities have been for centuries devel-

oping themselves under the beneficent influences of freedom, and the progress it inspires.

I am rather surprised at the outbreak of violent disgust
which Mr. —— indulges in on the subject of amalgamation, as that formed no part of our discussion, and seems
to me a curious subject for abstract argument. I should
think the intermarrying between blacks and whites a matter to be as little insisted upon if repugnant, as prevented
if agreeable to the majority of the two races. At the
same time, I can not help being astonished at the furious
and ungoverned execration which all reference to the possibility of a fusion of the races draws down upon those
who suggest it, because nobody pretends to deny that,
throughout the South, a large proportion of the population
is the offspring of white men and colored women. In
New Orleans, a class of unhappy females exists whose
mingled blood does not prevent their being remarkable
for their beauty, and with whom no man, no *gentleman*,
in that city shrinks from associating; and while the slaveowners of the Southern States insist vehemently upon the
mental and physical inferiority of the blacks, they are be-
nevolently doing their best, in one way at least, to raise
and improve the degraded race, and the bastard population which forms so ominous an element in the social safety of their cities certainly exhibit in their forms and features the benefit they derive from their white progenitors.
It is hard to conceive that some mental improvement does
not accompany this physical change. Already the finer
forms of the European races are cast in these dusky
moulds: the outward configuration can hardly thus improve without corresponding progress in the inward capacities. The white man's blood and bones have begotten this bronze race, and bequeathed to it, in some degree,
qualities, tendencies, capabilities, such as are the inheritance of the highest order of human animals. Mr. ——

(and many others) speaks as if there were a natural repugnance in all whites to any alliance with the black race; and yet it is notorious, that almost every Southern planter has a family more or less numerous of illegitimate colored children. Most certainly, few people would like to assert that such connections are formed because it is the *interest* of these planters to increase the number of their human property, and that they add to their revenue by the closest intimacy with creatures that they loathe, in order to reckon among their wealth the children of their body. Surely that is a monstrous and unnatural supposition, and utterly unworthy of belief. That such connections exist commonly is a sufficient proof that they are not abhorrent to nature; but it seems, indeed, as if marriage (and not concubinage) was the horrible enormity which can not be tolerated, and against which, moreover, it has been deemed expedient to enact laws. Now it appears very evident that there is no law in the white man's nature which prevents him from making a colored woman the mother of his children, but there *is* a law on his statute-books forbidding him to make her his wife; and if we are to admit the theory that the mixing of the races is a monstrosity, it seems almost as curious that laws should be enacted to prevent men marrying women toward whom they have an invincible natural repugnance, as that education should by law be prohibited to creatures incapable of receiving it. As for the exhortation with which Mr. —— closes his letter, that I will not "go down to my husband's plantation prejudiced against what I am to find there," I know not well how to answer it. Assuredly I *am* going prejudiced against slavery, for I am an Englishwoman, in whom the absence of such a prejudice would be disgraceful. Nevertheless, I go prepared to find many mitigations in the practice to the general injustice and cruelty of the system —much kindness on the part of the masters, much content

on that of the slaves; and I feel very sure that you may
rely upon the carefulness of my observation, and the accuracy of my report, of every detail of the working of the
thing that comes under my notice; and certainly, on the
plantation to which I am going, it will be more likely that
I should some things extenuate, than set down aught in
malice.   Yours ever faithfully.

Darien, Georgia.

DEAR E——,—Minuteness of detail, and fidelity in the
account of my daily doings, will hardly, I fear, render my
letters very interesting to you now; but, cut off as I am
here from all the usual resources and amusements of civilized existence, I shall find but little to communicate to
you that is not furnished by my observations on the novel
appearance of external nature, and the moral and physical
condition of Mr. ——'s people. The latter subject is, I
know, one sufficiently interesting in itself to you, and I
shall not scruple to impart all the reflections which may
occur to me relative to their state during my stay here,
where inquiry into their mode of existence will form my
chief occupation, and, necessarily also, the staple commod-
ity of my letters. I purpose, while I reside here, keeping
a sort of journal, such as Monk Lewis wrote during his
visit to his West India plantations. I wish I had any
prospect of rendering my diary as interesting and amusing to you as his was to me.

In taking my first walk on the island, I directed my
steps toward the rice mill, a large building on the banks
of the river, within a few yards of the house we occupy.
Is it not rather curious that Miss Martineau should have
mentioned the erection of a steam mill for threshing rice
somewhere in the vicinity of Charleston as a singular novelty, likely to form an era in Southern agriculture, and to

produce the most desirable changes in the system of labor
by which it is carried on? Now on this estate alone there
are three threshing mills—one worked by steam, one by
the tide, and one by horses; there are two private steam
mills on plantations adjacent to ours, and a public one at
Savannah, where the planters who have none on their own
estates are in the habit of sending their rice to be threshed at a certain percentage; these have all been in operation for some years, and I therefore am at a loss to understand what made her hail the erection of the one at
Charleston as likely to produce such immediate and happy results. By-the-by — of the misstatements, or rather
mistakes, for they are such, in her books, with regard to
certain facts — her only disadvantage in acquiring information was not by any means that natural infirmity on
which the periodical press, both here and in England,
has commented with so much brutality. She had the
misfortune to possess, too, that unsuspecting reliance upon
the truth of others which they are apt to feel who themselves hold truth most sacred; and this was a sore disadvantage to her in a country where I have heard it myself
repeatedly asserted—and, what is more, much gloried in
—that she was purposely misled by the persons to whom
she addressed her inquiries, who did not scruple to disgrace themselves by imposing in the grossest manner upon
her credulity and anxiety to obtain information. It is a
knowledge of this very shameful proceeding which has
made me most especially anxious to avoid *fact hunting*.
I might fill my letters to you with accounts received from
others, but, as I am aware of the risk which I run in so doing, I shall furnish you with no details but those which
come under my own immediate observation. To return
to the rice mill: it is worked by a steam-engine of thirty
horse power, and, besides threshing great part of our own
rice, is kept constantly employed by the neighboring plant-

ers, who send their grain to it in preference to the more distant mill at Savannah, paying, of course, the same percentage, which makes it a very profitable addition to the estate. Immediately opposite to this building is a small shed, which they call the cook's shop, and where the daily allowance of rice and corn grits of the people is boiled and distributed to them by an old woman, whose special business this is. There are four settlements or villages (or, as the negroes call them, camps) on the island, consisting of from ten to twenty houses, and to each settlement is annexed a cook's shop with capacious caldrons, and the oldest wife of the settlement for officiating priestess. Pursuing my walk along the river's bank, upon an artificial dike, sufficiently high and broad to protect the fields from inundation by the ordinary rising of the tide—for the whole island is below high-water mark—I passed the blacksmith's and cooper's shops. At the first all the common iron implements of husbandry or household use for the estate are made, and at the latter all the rice barrels necessary for the crop, besides tubs and buckets, large and small, for the use of the people, and cedar tubs, of noble dimensions and exceedingly neat workmanship, for our own household purposes. The fragrance of these when they are first made, as well as their ample size, renders them preferable as dressing-room furniture, in my opinion, to all the china foot-tubs that ever came out of Staffordshire. After this I got out of the vicinity of the settlement, and pursued my way along a narrow dike—the river on the one hand, and, on the other, a slimy, poisonous-looking swamp, all rattling with sedges of enormous height, in which one might lose one's way as effectually as in a forest of oaks. Beyond this, the low rice-fields, all clothed in their rugged stubble, divided by dikes into monotonous squares, a species of prospect by no means beautiful to the mere lover of the picturesque. The only thing that I met with to attract my attention was a most beautiful species of ivy, the leaf longer and more graceful than that of the common English creeper, glittering with the highest varnish, delicately veined, and of a rich brown-green, growing in profuse garlands from branch to branch of some stunted evergreen bushes which border the dike, and which the people call salt-water bush. My walks are rather circumscribed, inasmuch as the dikes are the only promenades. On all sides of these lie either the marshy rice-fields, the brimming river, or the swampy patches of yet unreclaimed forest, where the hugh cypress-trees and exquisite evergreen undergrowth spring up from a stagnant sweltering pool, that effectually forbids the foot of the explorer.

As I skirted one of these thickets to-day, I stood still to admire the beauty of the shrubbery. Every shade of green, every variety of form, every degree of varnish, and all in full leaf and beauty in the very depth of winter. The stunted dark-colored oak; the magnolia bay (like our own culinary and fragrant bay), which grows to a very great size; the wild myrtle, a beautiful and profuse shrub, rising to a height of six, eight, and ten feet, and branching on all sides in luxuriant tufted fullness; most beautiful of all, that pride of the South, the magnolia grandiflora, whose lustrous dark green perfect foliage would alone render it an object of admiration, without the queenly blossom whose color, size, and perfume are unrivaled in the whole vegetable kingdom. This last magnificent creature grows to the size of a forest tree in these swamps, but seldom adorns a high or dry soil, or suffers itself to be successfully transplanted. Under all these the spiked palmetto forms an impenetrable covert, and from glittering graceful branch to branch hang garlands of evergreen creepers, on which the mocking-birds are swinging and singing even now; while I, bethinking me of the pinching cold that is at this hour tyrannizing over your region, look

·ound on this strange scene—on these green woods, this
unfettered river, and sunny sky—and feel very much like
one in another planet from yourself.

The profusion of birds here is one thing that strikes me
as curious, coming from the vicinity of Philadelphia, where
even the robin redbreast, held sacred by the humanity of
all other Christian people, is not safe from the *gunning*
prowess of the unlicensed sportsmen of your free country.
The negroes (of course) are not allowed the use of fire-
arms, and their very simply constructed traps do not do
much havoc among the feathered hordes that haunt their
rice-fields. Their case is rather a hard one, as partridges,
snipes, and the most delicious wild ducks abound here,
and their allowance of rice and Indian meal would not be
the worse for such additions. No day passes that I do
not, in the course of my walk, put up a number of the
land birds, and startle from among the gigantic sedges
the long-necked water-fowl by dozens. It arouses the killing propensity in me most dreadfully, and I really entertain serious thoughts of learning to use a gun, for the mere
pleasure of destroying these pretty birds as they whirr
from their secret coverts close beside my path. How
strong an instinct of animal *humanity* this is, and how
strange if one be more strange than another. Reflection
rebukes it almost instantaneously, and yet for the life of
me I can not help wishing I had a fowling-piece whenever I put up a covey of these creatures; though I suppose,
if one were brought bleeding and maimed to me, I should
begin to cry, and be very pathetic, after the fashion of
Jacques. However, one must live, you know; and here
our living consists very mainly of wild ducks, wild geese,
wild turkeys, and venison. Now, perhaps, can one imagine the universal doom overtaking a creature with less
misery than in the case of the bird who, in the very moment of his triumphant soaring, is brought dead to the

ground. I should like to bargain for such a finis myself amazingly, I know, and have always thought that the death I should prefer would be to break my neck off the back of my horse at a full gallop on a fine day. Of course a bad shot should be hung—a man who shatters his birds' wings and legs; if I undertook the trade, I would learn of some Southern duelist, and always shoot my bird through the head or heart—as an expert murderer knows how. Besides these birds of which we make our prey, there are others that prey upon their own fraternity. Hawks of every sort and size wheel their steady rounds above the rice-fields; and the great turkey-buzzards—those most unsightly carrion birds—spread their broad black wings, and soar over the river like so many mock eagles. I do not know that I ever saw any winged creature of so forbidding an aspect as these same turkey-buzzards; their heavy flight, their awkward gait, their bald-looking head and neck, and their devotion to every species of foul and detestable food, render them almost abhorrent to me. They abound in the South, and in Charleston are held in especial veneration for their scavenger-like propensities, killing one of them being, I believe, a finable offense by the city police regulations. Among the Brobdignagian sedges that in some parts of the island fringe the Altamaha, the nightshade (apparently the same as the European creeper) weaves a perfect matting of its poisonous garlands, and my remembrance of its prevalence in the woods and hedges of England did not reconcile me to its appearance here. How much of this is mere association I can not tell; but, whether the wild duck makes its nest under its green arches, or the alligators and snakes of the Altamaha have their secret bowers there, it is an evil-looking weed, and I shall have every leaf of it cleared away.

I must inform you of a curious conversation which took place between my little girl and the woman who performs

for us the offices of chambermaid here—of course one of
Mr. ——'s slaves. What suggested it to the child, or
whence indeed she gathered her information, I know not;
but children are made of eyes and ears, and nothing, however minute, escapes their microscopic observation. She
suddenly began addressing this woman. "Mary, some
persons are free and some are not (the woman made no
reply). I am a free person (of a little more than three
years old). I say, I am a free person, Mary—do you know
that?" "Yes, missis." "Some persons are free and some
are not—do you know that, Mary?" "Yes, missis, *here*,"
was the reply; "I know it is so here, in this world." Here
my child's white nurse, my dear Margery, who had hitherto been silent, interfered, saying, "Oh, then you think it
will not always be so?" "Me hope not, missis." I am
afraid, E——, this woman actually imagines that there
will be no slaves in heaven; isn't that preposterous, now,
when, by the account of most of the Southerners, slavery
itself must be heaven, or something uncommonly like it?
Oh, if you could imagine how this title "Missis," addressed
to me and to my children, shocks all my feelings! Several
times I have exclaimed, "For God's sake do not call me
that!" and only been awakened, by the stupid amazement
of the poor creatures I was addressing, to the perfect use-
lessness of my thus expostulating with them; once or
twice, indeed, I have done more — I have explained to
them, and they appeared to comprehend me well, that I
had no ownership over them, for that I held such ownership sinful, and that, though I was the wife of the man
who pretends to own them, I was, in truth, no more their
mistress than they were mine. Some of them I know understood me, more of them did not.

Our servants—those who have been selected to wait
upon us in the house—consist of a man, who is quite a tolerable cook (I believe this is a natural gift with them, as

with Frenchmen); a dairy-woman, who churns for us; a laundry-woman; her daughter, our housemaid, the aforesaid Mary; and two young lads of from fifteen to twenty, who wait upon us in the capacity of footmen. As, however, the latter are perfectly filthy in their persons and clothes—their faces, hands, and naked feet being literally incrusted with dirt—their attendance at our meals is not, as you may suppose, particularly agreeable to me, and I dispense with it as often as possible. Mary, too, is so intolerably offensive in her person that it is impossible to endure her proximity, and the consequence is that, among Mr. ——'s slaves, I wait upon myself more than I have ever done in my life before. About this same personal offensiveness, the Southerners, you know, insist that it is inherent with the race, and it is one of their most cogent reasons for keeping them as slaves. But, as this very disagreeable peculiarity does not prevent Southern women from hanging their infants at the breasts of negresses, nor almost every planter's wife and daughter from having one or more little pet blacks sleeping like puppy-dogs in their very bedchamber, nor almost every planter from admitting one or several of his female slaves to the still closer intimacy of his bed, it seems to me that this objection to doing them right is not very valid. I can not imagine that they would smell much worse if they were free, or come in much closer contact with the delicate organs of their white fellow-countrymen; indeed, inasmuch as good deeds are spoken of as having a sweet savor before God, it might be supposed that the freeing of the blacks might prove rather an odoriferous process than the contrary. However this may be, I must tell you that this potent reason for enslaving a whole race of people is no more potent with me than most of the others adduced to support the system, inasmuch as, from observation and some experience, I am strongly inclined to believe that peculiar igno-

rance of the laws of health and the habits of decent cleanliness are the real and only causes of this disagreeable
characteristic of the race, thorough ablutions and change
of linen, when tried, having been perfectly successful in
removing all such objections; and if ever you have come
into any thing like neighborly proximity with a low Irishman or woman, I think you will allow that the same causes
produce very nearly the same effects. The stench in an
Irish, Scotch, Italian, or French hovel are quite as intolerable as any I ever found in our negro houses, and the filth
and vermin which abound about the clothes and persons
of the lower peasantry of any of those countries as abominable as the same conditions in the black population of
the United States. A total absence of self-respect begets
these hateful physical results, and in proportion as moral
influences are remote, physical evils will abound. Well-
being, freedom, and industry induce self-respect, self-respect induces cleanliness and personal attention, so that
slavery is answerable for all the evils that exhibit themselves where it exists—from lying, thieving, and adultery,
to dirty houses, ragged clothes, and foul smells.

But to return to our Ganymedes. One of them—the
eldest son of our laundry-woman, and Mary's brother, a
boy of the name of Aleck (Alexander)—is uncommonly
bright and intelligent; he performs all the offices of a
well-instructed waiter with great efficiency, and any where
out of slave land would be able to earn fourteen or fifteen
dollars a month for himself; he is remarkably good tem-
pered and well disposed. The other poor boy is so stupid
that he appears sullen from absolute darkness of intellect;
instead of being a little lower than the angels, he is scarce
ly a little higher than the brutes, and to this condition are
reduced the majority of his kind by the institutions under
which they live. I should tell you that Aleck's parents
and kindred have always been about the house of the

overseer, and in daily habits of intercourse with him and his wife; and wherever this is the case the effect of involuntary education is evident in the improved intelligence of the degraded race. In a conversation which Mr. —— had this evening with Mr. O——, the overseer, the latter mentioned that two of our carpenters had in their leisure time made a boat, which they had disposed of to some neighboring planter for sixty dollars.

Now, E——, I have no intention of telling you a one-sided story, or concealing from you what are cited as the advantages which these poor people possess; you, who know that no indulgence is worth simple justice, either to him who gives or him who receives, will not thence conclude that their situation thus mitigated is, therefore, what it should be. On this matter of the sixty dollars earned by Mr. ——'s two men much stress was laid by him and his overseer. I look at it thus: If these men were industrious enough, out of their scanty leisure, to earn sixty dollars, how much more of remuneration, of comfort, of improvement might they not have achieved were the price of their daily labor duly paid them, instead of being unjustly withheld to support an idle young man and his idle family—i. e., myself and my children.

And here it may be well to inform you that the slaves on this plantation are divided into field-hands and mechanics or artisans. The former, the great majority, are the more stupid and brutish of the tribe; the others, who are regularly taught their trades, are not only exceedingly expert at them, but exhibit a greater general activity of intellect, which must necessarily result from even a partial degree of cultivation. There are here a gang (for that is the honorable term) of coopers, of blacksmiths, of bricklayers, of carpenters, all well acquainted with their peculiar trades. The latter constructed the wash-hand stands, clothes-presses, sofas, tables, etc., with which our house is

B

furnished, and they are very neat pieces of workmanship
—neither veneered or polished indeed, nor of very costly
materials, but of the white pine wood planed as smooth
as marble—a species of furniture not very luxurious perhaps, but all the better adapted therefore to the house itself, which is certainly rather more devoid of the conveniences and adornments of modern existence than any thing
I ever took up my abode in before. It consists of three
small rooms, and three still smaller, which would be more
appropriately designated as closets, a wooden recess by
way of pantry, and a kitchen detached from the dwelling
—a mere wooden out-house, with no floor but the bare
earth, and for furniture a congregation of filthy negroes,
who lounge in and out of it like hungry hounds at all hours
of the day and night, picking up such scraps of food as
they can find about, which they discuss squatting down
upon their hams, in which interesting position and occupation I generally find a number of them whenever I have
sufficient hardihood to venture within those precincts, the
sight of which and its tenants is enough to slacken the
appetite of the hungriest hunter that ever lost all nice regards in the mere animal desire for food. Of our three
apartments, one is our sitting, eating, and *living* room,
and is sixteen feet by fifteen. The walls are plastered indeed, but neither painted nor papered; it is divided from
our bedroom (a similarly elegant and comfortable chamber) by a dingy wooden partition covered all over with
hooks, pegs, and nails, to which hats, caps, keys, etc., etc.,
are suspended in graceful irregularity. The doors open
by wooden latches, raised by means of small bits of pack-
thread—I imagine, the same primitive order of fastening
celebrated in the touching chronicle of Red Riding Hood;
how they shut I will not attempt to describe, as the shut-
ting of a door is a process of extremely rare occurrence
throughout the whole Southern country. The third room,

a chamber with sloping ceiling, immediátely over our sitting-room and under the roof, is appropriated to the nurse
and my two babies. Of the closets, one is Mr. ——, the
overseer's, bedroom, the other his office or place of business; and the third, adjoining our bedroom, and opening
immediately out of doors, is Mr. ——'s dressing-room and
cabinet d'affaires, where he gives audiences to the negroes,
redresses grievances, distributes red woolen caps (a singular gratification to a slave), shaves himself, and performs the other offices of his toilet. Such being our abode,
I think you will allow there is little danger of my being
dazzled by the luxurious splendors of a Southern slave
residence. Our sole mode of summoning our attendants
is by a pack-thread bell-rope suspended in the sitting-
room. From the bedrooms we have to raise the windows
and our voices, and bring them by power of lungs, or help
ourselves—which, I thank God, was never yet a hardship
to me.

I mentioned to you just now that two of the carpenters
had made a boat in their leisure time. I must explain
this to you, and this will involve the mention of another
of Miss Martineau's mistakes with regard to slave labor,
at least in many parts of the Southern States. She mentions that on one estate of which she knew, the proprietor
had made the experiment, and very successfully, of ap-
pointing to each of his slaves a certain task to be performed in the day, which once accomplished, no matter
how early, the rest of the four-and-twenty hours were allowed to the laborer to employ as he pleased. She mentions this as a single experiment, and rejoices over it as
a decided amelioration in the condition of the slave, and
one deserving of general adoption. But in the part of
Georgia where this estate is situated, the custom of task
labor is universal, and it prevails, I believe, throughout
Georgia, South Carolina, and parts of North Carolina; in

other parts of the latter state, however—as I was informed by our overseer, who is a native of that state—the estates are small, rather deserving the name of farms, and
the laborers are much upon the same footing as the laboring men at the North, working from sunrise to sunset in
the fields with the farmer and his sons, and coming in with
them to their meals, which they take immediately after
the rest of the family.   In Louisiana and the new southwestern slave states, I believe, task labor does not prevail;
but it is in those that the condition of the poor human
cattle is most deplorable, as you know it was there that
the humane calculation was not only made, but openly and
unhesitatingly avowed, that the planters found it, upon
the whole, their most profitable plan to work off (kill with
labor) their whole number of slaves about once in seven
years, and renew the whole stock.   By-the-by, the Jewish institution of slavery is much insisted upon by the
Southern upholders of the system; perhaps this is their
notion of the Jewish jubilee, when the slaves were by Mo-
ses's strict enactment to be all set free.   Well, this task
system is pursued on this estate; and thus it is that the
two carpenters were enabled to make the boat they sold
for sixty dollars.   These tasks, of course, profess to be
graduated according to the sex, age, and strength of the
laborer; but in many instances this is not the case, as I
think you will agree when I tell you that on Mr. ——'s
first visit to his estates he found that the men and the
women who labored in the fields had the same task to
perform.   This was a noble admission of female equality,
was it not?—and thus it had been on the estate for many
years past.   Mr. ——, of course, altered the distribution
of the work, diminishing the quantity done by the women.

I had a most ludicrous visit this morning from the
midwife of the estate—rather an important personage
both to master and slave, as to her unassisted skill and

science the ushering of all the young negroes into their
existence of bondage is intrusted. I heard a great deal
of conversation in the dressing-room adjoining mine while
performing my own toilet, and presently Mr. —— opened
my room door, ushering in a dirty, fat, good-humored
looking old negress, saying, " The midwife, Rose, wants to
make your acquaintance." " Oh massa!" shrieked out the
old creature, in a paroxysm of admiration, " where you get
this lilly alabaster baby!" For a moment I looked round
to see if she was speaking of my baby; but no, my dear,
this superlative apostrophe was elicited by the fairness of
my skin: so much for degrees of comparison. Now I
suppose that if I chose to walk arm in arm with the din-
giest mulatto through the streets of Philadelphia, nobody
could possibly tell by my complexion that I was not his
sister, so that the mere quality of mistress must have had
a most miraculous effect upon my skin in the eyes of poor
Rose. But this species of outrageous flattery is as usual
with these people as with the low Irish, and arises from
the ignorant desire, common to both the races, of propi-
tiating at all costs the fellow-creature who is to them as a
Providence — or rather, I should say, a fate — for 'tis a
heathen and no Christian relationship. Soon after this
visit, I was summoned into the wooden porch or piazza
of the house, to see a poor woman who desired to speak
to me. This was none other than the tall, emaciated-
looking negress who, on the day of our arrival, had embraced me and my nurse with such irresistible zeal. She
appeared very ill to-day, and presently unfolded to me a
most distressing history of bodily afflictions. She was
the mother of a very large family, and complained to me
that, what with childbearing and hard field labor, her
back was almost broken in two. With an almost savage
vehemence of gesticulation, she suddenly tore up her
scanty clothing, and exhibited a spectacle with which I

was inconceivably shocked and sickened.   The facts, without any of her corroborating statements, bore tolerable witness to the hardships of her existence.   I promised to attend to her ailments and give her proper remedies; but these are natural results, inevitable and irremediable ones, of improper treatment of the female 'frame; and, though there may be alleviation, there can not be any cure when once the beautiful and wonderful structure has been thus made the victim of ignorance, folly, and wickedness.

After the departure of this poor woman, I walked down the settlement toward the Infirmary or hospital, calling in at one or two of the houses along the row. These cabins consist of one room, about twelve feet by fifteen, with a couple of closets smaller and closer than the state-rooms of a ship, divided off from the main room and each other by rough wooden partitions, in which the inhabitants sleep.   They have almost all of them a rude bedstead, with the gray moss of the forests for mattress, and filthy, pestilential-looking blankets for covering. Two families (sometimes eight and ten in number) reside in one of these huts, which are mere wooden frames pinned, as it were, to the earth by a brick chimney outside, whose enormous aperture within pours down a flood of air, but little counteracted by the miserable spark of fire, which hardly sends an attenuated thread of lingering smoke up its huge throat.   A wide ditch runs immediately at the back of these dwellings, which is filled and emptied daily by the tide.   Attached to each hovel is a small scrap of ground for a garden, which, however, is for the most part untended and uncultivated.   Such of these dwellings as I visited to-day were filthy and wretched in the extreme, and exhibited that most deplorable consequence of ignorance and an abject condition, the inability of the inhabitants to secure and improve even such pitiful comfort as might yet be achieved by them.   Instead of

the order, neatness, and ingenuity which might convert
even these miserable hovels into tolerable residences,
there was the careless, reckless, filthy indolence which
even the brutes do not exhibit in their lairs and nests,
and which seemed incapable of applying to the uses of
existence the few miserable means of comfort yet within
their reach. Firewood and shavings lay littered about
the floors, while the half-naked children were cowering
round two or three smouldering cinders.   The moss with
which the chinks and crannies of their ill-protecting
dwellings might have been stuffed was trailing in dirt
and dust about the ground, while the back door of the
huts, opening upon a most unsightly ditch, was left wide
open for the fowls and ducks, which they are allowed to
raise, to travel in and out, increasing the filth of the
cabin by what they brought and left in every direction.
In the midst of the floor, or squatting round the cold
hearth, would be four or five little children from four to
ten years old, the latter all with babies in their arms, the
care of the infants being taken from the mothers (who
are driven afield as soon as they recover from child labor),
and devolved upon these poor little nurses, as they are
called, whose business it is to watch the infant, and carry
it to its mother whenever it may require nourishment.
To these hardly human little beings I addressed my remonstrances about the filth, cold, and unnecessary wretchedness of their room, bidding the elder boys and girls
kindle up the fire, sweep the floor, and expel the poultry.
For a long time my very words seemed unintelligible to
them, till, when I began to sweep and make up the fire,
etc., they first fell to laughing, and then imitating me.
The incrustations of dirt on their hands, feet, and faces
were my next object of attack, and the stupid negro practice (by-the-by, but a short time since nearly universal in
enlightened Europe) of keeping the babies with their feet

bare, and their heads, already well capped by nature with their woolly hair, wrapped in half a dozen hot, filthy coverings. Thus I traveled down the " street," in every dwelling endeavoring to awaken a new perception, that of cleanliness, sighing, as I went, over the futility of my own exertions, for how can slaves be improved? Nathless, thought I, let what can be done; for it may be that, the two being incompatible, improvement may yet expel slavery; and so it might, and surely would, if, instead of beginning at the end, I could but begin at the beginning of my task. If the mind and soul were awakened, instead of mere physical good attempted, the physical good would result, and the great curse vanish away; but my hands are tied fast, and this corner of the work is all that I may do. Yet it can not be but, from my words and actions, some revelations should reach these poor people; and going in and out among them perpetually, I shall teach, and they learn involuntarily a thousand things of deepest import. They must learn, and who can tell the fruit of that knowledge alone, that there are beings in the world, even with skins of a different color from their own, who have sympathy for their misfortunes, love for their virtues, and respect for their common nature—but oh! my heart is full almost to bursting as I walk among these most poor creatures.

The Infirmary is a large two-story building, terminating the broad orange-planted space between the two rows of houses which form the first settlement; it is built of whitewashed wood, and contains four large-sized rooms. But how shall I describe to you the spectacle which was presented to me on entering the first of these? But half the casements, of which there were six, were glazed, and these were obscured with dirt, almost as much as the other windowless ones were darkened by the dingy shutters, which the shivering inmates had fastened to in order to protect themselves from the cold. In the enormous chimney glimmered the powerless embers of a few sticks of wood, round which, however, as many of the sick women as could approach were cowering, some on wooden settles, most of them on the ground, excluding those who were too ill to rise; and these last poor wretches lay prostrate on the floor, without bed, mattress, or pillow, buried in tattered and filthy blankets, which, huddled round them as they lay strewed about, left hardly space to move upon the floor. And here, in their hour of sickness and suffering, lay those whose health and strength are spent in unrequited labor for us—those who, perhaps even yesterday, were being urged on to their unpaid task—those whose husbands, fathers, brothers, and sons were even at that hour sweating over the earth, whose produce was to buy for us all the luxuries which health can revel in, all the comforts which can alleviate sickness. I stood in the midst of them, perfectly unable to speak, the tears pouring from my eyes at this sad spectacle of their misery, myself and my emotion alike strange and incomprehensible to them. Here lay women expecting every hour the terrors and agonies of childbirth, others who had just brought their doomed offspring into the world, others who were groaning over the anguish and bitter disappointment of miscarriages— here lay some burning with fever, others chilled with cold and aching with rheumatism, upon the hard cold ground, the draughts and dampness of the atmosphere increasing their sufferings, and dirt, noise, and stench, and every aggravation of which sickness is capable, combined in their condition—here they lay like brute beasts, absorbed in physical suffering; unvisited by any of those Divine influences which may ennoble the dispensations of pain and illness, forsaken, as it seemed to me, of all good; and yet, O God, Thou surely hadst not forsaken them! Now pray take notice that this is the hospital of an estate where the

B 2

owners are supposed to be humane, the overseer efficient and kind, and the negroes remarkably well cared for and comfortable. As soon as I recovered from my dismay, I addressed old Rose the midwife, who had charge of this room, bidding her open the shutters of such windows as were glazed, and let in the light. I next proceeded to make up the fire; but, upon my lifting a log for that purpose, there was one universal outcry of horror, and old Rose, attempting to snatch it from me, exclaimed, "Let alone, missis—let be; what for you lift wood? you have nigger enough, missis, to do it!" I hereupon had to explain to them my view of the purposes for which hands and arms were appended to our bodies, and forthwith began making Rose tidy up the miserable apartment, removing all the filth and rubbish from the floor that could be removed, folding up in piles the blankets of the patients who were not using them, and placing, in rather more sheltered and comfortable positions, those who were unable to rise. It was all that I could do, and having enforced upon them all my earnest desire that they should keep their room swept, and as tidy as possible, I passed on to the other room on the ground floor, and to the two above, one of which is appropriated to the use of the men who are ill. They were all in the same deplorable condition, the upper rooms being rather the more miserable, inasmuch as none of the windows were glazed at all, and they had, therefore, only the alternative of utter darkness, or killing draughts of air from the unsheltered casements. In all, filth, disorder, and misery abounded; the floor was the only bed, and scanty begrimed rags of blankets the only covering. I left this refuge for Mr. ——'s sick dependents with my clothes covered with dust, and full of vermin, and with a heart heavy enough, as you will well believe. My morning's work had fatigued me not a little, and I was glad to return to the house, where I gave vent to my indignation and regret at the scene I had just witnessed to Mr. —— and his overseer, who, here, is a member of our family. The latter told me that the condition of the hospital had appeared to him, from his first entering upon his situation (only within the last year), to require a reform, and that he had proposed it to the former manager, Mr. K——, and Mr. ——'s brother, who is part proprietor of the estate, but, receiving no encouragement from them, had supposed that it was a matter of indifference to the owners, and had left it in the condition in which he had found it, in which condition it has been for the last nineteen years and upward.

This new overseer of ours has lived fourteen years with an old Scotch gentleman, who owns an estate adjoining Mr. ——'s, on the island of St. Simon's, upon which estate, from every thing I can gather, and from what I know of the proprietor's character, the slaves are probably treated with as much humanity as is consistent with slavery at all, and where the management and comfort of the hospital in particular had been most carefully and judiciously attended to. With regard to the indifference of our former manager upon the subject of the accommodation for the sick, he was an excellent overseer, *videlicet* the estate returned a full income under his management, and such men have nothing to do with sick slaves: they are tools, to be mended only if they can be made available again; if not, to be flung by as useless, without farther expense of money, time, or trouble.

I am learning to row here, for circumscribed, as my walks necessarily are, impossible as it is to resort to my favorite exercise on horseback upon these narrow dikes, I must do something to prevent my blood from stagnating; and this broad brimming river, and the beautiful light canoes which lie moored at the steps, are very inviting persuaders to this species of exercise. My first attempt

was confined to pulling an oar across the stream, for
which I rejoiced in sundry aches and pains altogether
novel, letting alone a delightful row of blisters on each of
my hands.

I forgot to tell you that in the hospital were several
sick babies, whose mothers were permitted to suspend
their field labor in order to nurse them. Upon addressing some remonstrances to one of these, who, besides having a sick child, was ill herself, about the horribly dirty
condition of her baby, she assured me that it was impossible for them to keep their children clean; that they
went out to work at daybreak, and did not get their tasks
done till evening, and that then they were too tired and
worn out to do any thing but throw themselves down
and sleep. This statement of hers I mentioned on my
return from the hospital, and the overseer appeared extremely annoyed by it, and assured me repeatedly that it
was not true.

In the evening Mr. ——, who had been over to Darien,
mentioned that one of the storekeepers there had told
him that, in the course of a few years, he had paid the
negroes of this estate several thousand dollars for moss,
which is a very profitable article of traffic with them:
they collect it from the trees, dry and pick it, and then
sell it to the people in Darien for mattresses, sofas, and
all sorts of stuffing purposes, which, in my opinion, it answers better than any other material whatever that I am
acquainted with, being as light as horse-hair, as springy
and elastic, and a great deal less harsh and rigid. It is
now bedtime, dear E——, and I doubt not it has been
sleepy time with you over this letter long ere you came
thus far. There is a preliminary to my repose, however,
in this agreeable residence, which I rather dread, namely,
the hunting for, or discovering without hunting, in fine
relief upon the whitewashed walls of my bedroom, a most

hideous and detestable species of *reptile* called centipedes, which come out of the cracks and crevices of the walls, and fill my very heart with dismay. They are from an inch to two inches long, and appear to have not a hundred, but a thousand legs. I can not ascertain very certainly from the negroes whether they sting or not, but they look exceedingly as if they might, and I visit my babies every night in fear and trembling, lest I should find one or more of these hateful creatures mounting guard over them. Good-night; you are well to be free from centipedes—better to be free from slaves.

DEAR E——, —This morning I paid my second visit to the Infirmary, and found there had been some faint attempt at sweeping and cleaning, in compliance with my entreaties. The poor woman Harriet, however, whose statement with regard to the impossibility of their attending properly to their children had been so vehemently denied by the overseer, was crying bitterly. I asked her what ailed her, when, more by signs and dumb show than words, she and old Rose informed me that Mr. O—— had flogged her that morning for having told me that the women had not time to keep their children clean. It is part of the regular duty of every overseer to visit the Infirmary at least once a day, which he generally does in the morning, and Mr. O——'s visit had preceded mine but a short time only, or I might have been edified by seeing a man horsewhip a woman. I again and again made her repeat her story, and she again and again affirmed that she had been flogged for what she told me, none of the whole company in the room denying it or contradicting her. I left the room because I was so disgusted and indignant that I could hardly restrain my feelings, and to express them could have produced no single good result. In the next ward, stretched upon the ground, apparently either asleep or so overcome with sickness as to be incapable of moving, lay an immense woman; her stature, as she cumbered the earth, must have been, I should think, five feet seven or eight, and her bulk enormous. She was wrapped in filthy rags, and lay with her face on the floor. As I approached, and stooped to see what ailed her, she suddenly threw out her arms, and, seized with violent convulsions, rolled over and over upon the floor, beating her head violently upon the ground, and throwing her enormous limbs about in a horrible manner. Immediately upon the occurrence of this fit, four or five women threw themselves literally upon her, and held her down by main force; they even proceeded to bind her legs and arms together, to prevent her dashing herself about; but this violent coercion and tight bandaging seemed to me, in my profound igno-rance, more likely to increase her illness by impeding her breathing and the circulation of her blood, and I bade them desist, and unfasten all the strings and ligatures not only that they had put round her limbs, but which, by tighten-ing her clothes round her body, caused any obstruction. How much I wished that, instead of music, and dancing, and such stuff, I had learned something of sickness and health, of the conditions and liabilities of the human body, that I might have known how to assist this poor creature, and to direct her ignorant and helpless nurses! The fit presently subsided, and was succeeded by the most deplorable prostration and weakness of nerves, the tears streaming down the poor woman's cheeks in show-ers, without, however, her uttering a single word, though she moaned incessantly. After bathing her forehead, hands, and chest with vinegar, we raised her up, and I sent to the house for a chair with a back (there was no such thing in the hospital), and we contrived to place her in it. I have seldom seen finer women than this poor creature and her younger sister, an immense strapping lass called Chloe — tall, straight, and extremely well made—who was assisting her sister, and whom I had remarked, for the extreme delight and merriment which my cleansing propensities seemed to give her, on my last visit to the hospital. She was here taking care of a sick baby, and helping to nurse her sister Molly, who, it seems, is subject to those fits, about which I spoke to our physician here—an intelligent man residing in Darien, who visits the estate whenever medical assistance is required. He seemed to attribute them to nervous disorder, brought on by frequent childbearing. This woman is young, I suppose at the outside not thirty, and her sister informed me that she had had ten children—ten children, E——! Fits and hard labor in the fields, unpaid labor, labor exacted with stripes—how do you fancy that? I wonder if my mere narration can make your blood boil as the facts did mine? Among the patients in this room was a young girl, apparently from fourteen to fifteen, whose hands and feet were literally rotting away piecemeal, from the effect of a horrible disease, to which the negroes are subject here, and I believe in the West Indies, and when it attacks the joints of the toes and fingers, the pieces absolutely decay and come off, leaving the limb a maimed and horrible stump! I believe no cure is known for this disgusting malady, which seems confined to these poor creatures. Another disease, of which they complained much, and which, of course, I was utterly incapable of accounting for, was a species of lock-jaw, to which their babies very frequently fall victims in the first or second week after their birth, refusing the breast, and the mouth gradually losing the power of opening itself. The horrible diseased state of head, common among their babies, is a mere result of filth and confinement, and therefore, though

I never any where saw such distressing and disgusting objects as some of these poor little woolly skulls presented,
the cause was sufficiently obvious. Pleurisy, or a tendency to it, seems very common among them; also peripneumonia, or inflammation of the lungs, which is terribly
prevalent, and generally fatal. Rheumatism is almost
universal; and as it proceeds from exposure, and want of
knowledge and care, attacks indiscriminately the young
and old. A great number of the women are victims to
falling of the womb and weakness in the spine; but these
are necessary results of their laborious existence, and do
not belong either to climate or constitution.

I have ingeniously contrived to introduce bribery, cor-
ruption, and pauperism, all in a breath, upon this island,
which, until my advent, was as innocent of these pollu-
tions, I suppose, as Prospero's isle of refuge. Wishing,
however, to appeal to some perception, perhaps a little
less dim in their minds than the abstract loveliness of
cleanliness, I have proclaimed to all the little baby nurses
that I will give a cent to every little boy or girl whose
baby's face shall be clean, and one to every individual with
clean face and hands of their own. My appeal was fully
comprehended by the majority, it seems, for this morning I was surrounded, as soon as I came out, by a swarm
of children carrying their little charges on their backs
and in their arms, the shining, and, in many instances, wet
faces and hands of the latter bearing ample testimony to
the ablutions which had been inflicted upon them. How
they will curse me and the copper cause of all their woes
in their baby bosoms! Do you know that, little as grown
negroes are admirable for their personal beauty (in my
opinion, at least), the black babies of a year or two old
are very pretty; they have, for the most part, beautiful
eyes and eyelashes, the pearly perfect teeth, which they
retain after their other juvenile graces have left them;

their skins are all (I mean of blacks generally) infinitely finer and softer than the skins of white people. Perhaps you are not aware that among the white race the *finest grained* skins generally belong to persons of dark complexion. This, as a characteristic of the black race, I think might be accepted as some compensation for the coarse woolly hair. The nose and mouth, which are so peculiarly displeasing in their conformation in the face of a negro man or woman, being the features least developed in a baby's countenance, do not at first present the ugliness which they assume as they become more marked; and when the very unusual operation of washing has been performed, the blood shines through the fine texture of the skin, giving life and richness to the dingy color, and displaying a species of beauty which I think scarcely any body who observed it would fail to acknowledge. I have seen many babies on this plantation who were quite as pretty as white children, and this very day stooped to kiss a little sleeping creature that lay on its mother's knees in the Infirmary—as beautiful a specimen of a sleeping infant as I ever saw. The caress excited the irrepressible delight of all the women present—poor creatures! who seem-ed to forget that I was a woman, and had children myself, and bore a woman's and a mother's heart toward them and theirs; but, indeed, the Honorable Mr. Slumkey could not have achieved more popularity by his performances in that line than I by this exhibition of feeling; and, had the question been my election, I am very sure nobody else would have had a chance of a vote through the island. But wisely is it said that use is second nature, and the contempt and neglect to which these poor people are used make the commonest expression of human sympathy appear a boon and gracious condescension. While I am speaking of the negro countenance, there is another beauty which is not at all unfrequent among those I see here

—a finely-shaped oval face—and those who know (as all
painters and sculptors, all who understand beauty do) how
much expression there is in the outline of the head, and
how very rare it is to see a well-formed face, will be apt
to consider this a higher matter than any coloring, of
which, indeed, the red and white one so often admired is
by no means the most rich, picturesque, or expressive.
At first the dark color confounded all features to my eye,
and I could hardly tell one face from another. Becoming, however, accustomed to the complexion, I now perceive all the variety among these black countenances that
there is among our own race, and as much difference in
features and in expression as among the same number of
whites. There is another peculiarity which I have remarked among the women here—very considerable beauty in the make of the hands; their feet are very generally
ill made, which must be a natural, and not an acquired de-
fect, as they seldom injure their feet by wearing shoes.
The figures of some of the women are handsome, and their
carriage, from the absence of any confining or tighten-
ing clothing, and the habit' they have of balancing great
weights on their heads, erect and good.

At the upper end of the row of houses, and nearest to
our overseer's residence, is the hut of the head driver.
Let me explain, by the way, his office. The negroes, as I
before told you, are divided into troops or gangs, as they
are called; at the head of each gang is a driver, who stands
over them, whip in hand, while they perform their daily
task, who renders an account of each individual slave and
his work every evening to the overseer, and receives from
him directions for their next day's tasks. Each driver is
allowed to inflict a dozen lashes upon any refractory slave
in the field, and at the time of the offense; they may not,
however, extend the chastisement, and if it is found ineffectual, their remedy lies in reporting the unmanageable

individual either to the head driver or the overseer, the former of whom has power to inflict three dozen lashes at his own discretion, and the latter as many as he himself sees fit, within the number of fifty; which limit, however, I must tell you, is an arbitrary one on this plantation, appointed by the founder of the estate, Major ——, Mr. ——'s grandfather, many of whose regulations, indeed I believe most of them, are still observed in the government of the plantation. Limits of this sort, however, to the power of either driver, head driver, or overseer, may or may not exist elsewhere; they are, to a certain degree, a check upon the power of these individuals; but in the absence of the master, the overseer may confine himself within the limit or not, as he chooses; and as for the master himself, where is his limit? He may, if he likes, flog a slave to death, for the laws which pretend that he may not are a mere pretense, inasmuch as the testimony of a black is never taken against a white; and upon this plantation of ours, and a thousand more, the overseer is the *only* white man, so whence should come the testimony to any crime of his? With regard to the oft-repeated statement that it is not the owner's interest to destroy his human property, it answers nothing; the instances in which men, to gratify the immediate impulse of passion, sacrifice not only their eternal, but their evident, palpable, positive worldly interest, are infinite. Nothing is commoner than for a man under the transient influence of anger to disregard his worldly advantage; and the black slave, whose preservation is indeed supposed to be his owner's interest, may be, will be, and is occasionally sacrificed to the blind impulse of passion.

To return to our head driver, or, as he is familiarly called, head man, Frank—he is second in authority only to the overseer, and exercises rule alike over the drivers and the gangs in the absence of the sovereign white man

from the estate, which happens whenever Mr. O—— visits
the other two plantations at Woodville and St. Simon's.
He is sole master and governor of the island, appoints the
work, pronounces punishments, gives permission to the
men to leave the island (without it they never may do so),
and exercises all functions of undisputed mastery over his
fellow-slaves, for you will observe that all this while he is
just as much a slave as any of the rest.   Trustworthy,
upright, intelligent, he may be flogged to-morrow if Mr.
O—— or Mr. —— so please it, and sold the next day, like
a cart-horse, at the will of the latter.   Besides his various
other responsibilities, he has the key of all the stores, and
gives out the people's rations weekly; nor is it only the
people's provisions that are put under his charge—meat,
which is only given out to them occasionally, and provisions for the use of the family, are also intrusted to his
care.   Thus you see, among these *inferior* creatures, their
own masters yet look to find, surviving all their best efforts to destroy them, good sense, honesty, self-denial, and
all the qualities, mental and moral, that make one man
worthy to be trusted by another.   From the impercepti-
ble but inevitable effect of the sympathies and influences
of human creatures toward and over each other, Frank's
intelligence has become uncommonly developed by intimate communion in the discharge of his duty with the
former overseer, a very intelligent man, who has only just
left the estate, after managing it for nineteen years; the
effect of this intercourse, and of the trust and responsibility laid upon the man, are that he is clear-headed, well
judging, active, intelligent, extremely well mannered, and,
being respected, he respects himself.   He is as ignorant
as the rest of the slaves; but he is always clean and tidy
in his person, with a courteousness of demeanor far removed from servility, and exhibits a strong instance of
the intolerable and wicked injustice of the system under

which he lives, having advanced thus far toward improvement, in spite of all the bars it puts to progress; and here
being arrested, not by want of energy, want of sense, or
any want of his own, but by being held as another man's
property, who can only thus hold him by forbidding him
farther improvement.   When I see that man, who keeps
himself a good deal aloof from the rest, in his leisure hours
looking, with a countenance of deep thought, as I did to-
day, over the broad river, which is to him as a prison wall,
to the fields and forest beyond, not one inch or branch of
which his utmost industry can conquer as his own, or acquire and leave an independent heritage to his children, I
marvél what the thoughts of such a man may be.   I was
in his house to-day, and the same superiority in cleanliness, comfort, and propriety exhibited itself in his dwelling as in his own personal appearance and that of his wife
—a most active, trustworthy, excellent woman, daughter
of the oldest, and probably most highly respected of all
Mr. ——'s slaves.   To the excellent conduct of this woman, and, indeed, every member of her family, both the present and the last overseer bear unqualified testimony.

As I was returning toward the house after my long
morning's lounge, a man rushed out of the blacksmith's
shop, and, catching me by the skirt of my gown, poured
forth a torrent of self-gratulations on having at length
found the "right missis."   They have no idea, of course,
of a white person performing any of the offices of a servant, and as throughout the whole Southern country the
owner's children are nursed and tended, and sometimes
suckled by their slaves (I wonder how this inferior milk
agrees with the lordly *white* babies?), the appearance of
M—— with my two children had immediately suggested
the idea that she must be the missis.   Many of the poor
negroes flocked to her, paying their profound homage
under this impression; and when she explained to them

that she was not their owner's wife, the confusion in their minds seemed very great—Heaven only knows whether they did not conclude that they had two mistresses, and Mr.—— two wives; for the privileged race must seem, in their eyes, to have such absolute masterdom on earth, that perhaps they thought polygamy might be one of the sovereign white men's numerous indulgences. The ecstasy of the blacksmith on discovering the "right missis" at last was very funny, and was expressed with such extraordinary grimaces, contortions, and gesticulations, that I thought I should have died of laughing at this rapturous identification of my most melancholy relation to the poor fellow.

Having at length extricated myself from the group which forms round me whenever I stop but for a few minutes, I pursued my voyage of discovery by peeping into the kitchen garden. I dared do no more; the aspect of the place would have rejoiced the very soul of Solomon's sluggard of old—a few cabbages and weeds innumerable filled the neglected-looking inclosure, and I ventured no farther than the entrance into its most uninviting precincts. You are to understand that upon this swamp island of ours we have quite a large stock of cattle, cows, sheep, pigs, and poultry in the most enormous and inconvenient abundance. The cows are pretty miserably off for pasture, the banks and pathways of the dikes being their only grazing ground, which the sheep perambulate also, in earnest search of a nibble of fresh herbage; both the cows and sheep are fed with rice flour in great abundance, and are pretty often carried down for change of air and more sufficient grazing to Hampton, Mr. ——'s estate, on the island of St. Simon's, fifteen miles from this place, farther down the river—or rather, indeed, I should say in the sea, for 'tis salt water all round, and one end of the island has a noble beach open to the vast Atlantic.

The pigs thrive admirably here, and attain very great perfection of size and flavor, the rice flour upon which they are chiefly fed tending to make them very delicate. As for the poultry, it being one of the few privileges of the poor blacks to raise as many as they can, their abundance is literally a nuisance—ducks, fowls, pigeons, turkeys (the two latter species, by-the-by, are exclusively the master's property), cluck, scream, gabble, gobble, crow, cackle fight, fly, and flutter in all directions, and to their immense concourse, and the perfect freedom with which they intrude themselves even into the piazza of the house the pantry, and kitchen, I partly attribute the swarms of fleas, and other still less agreeable vermin, with which we are most horribly pestered.

My walk lay to-day along the bank of a canal, which has been dug through nearly the whole length of the island, to render more direct and easy the transportation of the rice from one end of the estate to another, or from the various distant fields to the principal mill at Settlement No. 1. It is of considerable width and depth, and opens by various locks into the river. It has, unfortunately, no trees on its banks, but a good foot-path renders it, in spite of that deficiency, about the best walk on the island. I passed again to-day one of those beautiful evergreen thickets, which I described to you in my last letter; it is called a reserve, and is kept uncleared and uncultivated in its natural swampy condition, to allow of the people's procuring their firewood from it. I can not get accustomed, so as to be indifferent to this exquisite natural ornamental growth, and think, as I contemplate the various and beautiful foliage of these watery woods, how many of our finest English parks and gardens owe their chiefest adornments to plantations of these shrubs, procured at immense cost, reared with infinite pains and care, which are here basking in the winter's sunshine, waiting to be cut down for firewood! These little groves are peopled with wild pigeons and birds, which they designate here as black-birds. These sometimes rise from the rice fields with a whirr of multitudinous wings that is almost startling, and positively overshadow the ground beneath like a cloud.

I had a conversation that interested me a good deal, during my walk to-day, with my peculiar slave Jack. This lad, whom Mr. —— has appointed to attend me in my roamings about the island, and rowing expeditions on the river, is the son of the last head driver, a man of very extraordinary intelligence and faithfulness—such, at least, is the account given of him by his employers (in the buri-al-ground of the negroes is a stone dedicated to his mem-ory, a mark of distinction accorded by his masters, which his son never failed to point out to me when we passed that way). Jack appears to inherit his quickness of ap-prehension; his questions, like those of an intelligent child, are absolutely inexhaustible; his curiosity about all things beyond this island, the prison-house of his exist-ence, is perfectly intense; his countenance is very pleas-ing, mild, and not otherwise than thoughtful; he is, in common with the rest of them, a stupendous flatterer, and, like the rest of them, also seems devoid of physical and moral courage. To-day, in the midst of his torrent of in-quiries about places and things, I suddenly asked him if he would like to be free. A gleam of light absolutely shot over his whole countenance, like the vivid and in-stantaneous lightning; he stammered, hesitated, became excessively confused, and at length replied, "Free, missis! what for me wish to be free? Oh no, missis, me no wish to be free, if massa only let we keep pig!" The fear of offending by uttering that forbidden wish—the dread of admitting, by its expression, the slightest discontent with his present situation—the desire to conciliate my favor, even at the expense of strangling the intense natural long-

ing that absolutely glowed in his every feature—it was a
sad spectacle, and I repented my question. As for the
pitiful request, which he reiterated several times, adding,
" No, missis, me no want to be free; me work till me
die for missis and massa," with increased emphasis; it
amounted only to this, that negroes once were, but no
longer are, permitted to keep pigs. The increase of filth
and foul smells consequent upon their being raised is, of
course, very great; and, moreover, Mr. —— told me,
when I preferred poor Jack's request to him, that their
allowance was no more than would suffice their own necessity, and that they had not the means of feeding the
animals. With a little good management they might
very easily obtain them, however; their little " kail-yard"
alone would suffice to it, and the pork and bacon would
prove a most welcome addition to their farinaceous diet.
You perceive at once (or, if you could have seen the boy's
face, you would have perceived at once) that his situation
was no mystery to him; that his value to Mr. ——, and, as
he supposed, to me, was perfectly well known to him, and
that he comprehended immediately that his expressing
even the desire to be free might be construed by me into
an offense, and sought, by eager protestations of his delighted acquiescence in slavery, to conceal his soul's natural yearning, lest I should resent it. 'Twas a sad passage between us, and sent me home full of the most painful thoughts. I told Mr. ——, with much indignation, of
poor Harriet's flogging, and represented that if the people were to be chastised for any thing they said to me, I
must leave the place, as I could not but hear their complaints, and endeavor, by all my miserable limited means,
to better their condition while I was here. He said he
would ask Mr. O—— about it, assuring me, at the same
time, that it was impossible to believe a single word any
of these people said. At dinner, accordingly, the inquiry

C

was made as to the cause of her punishment, and Mr. O—— then said it was not at all for what she had told me that he had flogged her, but for having answered him impertinently; that he had ordered her into the field, whereupon she had said she was ill and could not work; that he retorted he knew better, and bade her get up and go to work; she replied, "Very well, I'll go, but I shall just come back again!" meaning that when in the field she would be unable to work, and obliged to return to the hospital. "For this reply," Mr. O—— said, "I gave her a good lashing; it was her business to have gone into the field without answering me, and then we should have soon seen whether she could work or not; I gave it to Chloe too for some such impudence." I give you the words of the conversation, which was prolonged to a great length, the overseer complaining of the sham sicknesses of the slaves, and detailing the most disgusting struggle which is going on the whole time, on the one hand to inflict, and on the other to evade oppression and injustice. With this sauce I ate my dinner, and truly it tasted bitter.

Toward sunset I went on the river to take my rowing lesson. A darling little canoe, which carries two oars and a steersman, and rejoices in the appropriate title of the "Dolphin," is my especial vessel; and with Jack's help and instructions, I contrived this evening to row upward of half a mile, coasting the reed-crowned edge of the island to another very large rice mill, the enormous wheel of which is turned by the tide. A small bank of mud and sand, covered with reedy coarse grass, divides the river into two arms on this side of the island; the deep channel is on the outside of this bank, and as we rowed home this evening, the tide having fallen, we scraped sand almost the whole way. Mr. ——'s domain, it seems to me, will presently fill up this shallow stream, and join itself to the above-mentioned mud-bank. The whole course of this most noble river is full of shoals, banks, mud, and sand-bars, and the navigation, which is difficult to those who know it well, is utterly baffling to the inexperienced. The fact is, that the two elements are so fused hereabouts that there are hardly such things as earth or water proper; that which styles itself the former is a fat, muddy, slimy sponge, that, floating half under the turbid river, looks yet saturated with the thick waves which every now and then reclaim their late dominion, and cover it almost entirely; the water, again, cloudy and yellow, like pea-soup, seems but a solution of such islands, rolling turbid and thick with alluvium, which it both gathers and deposits as it sweeps along with a swollen, smooth rapidity, that almost deceives the eye. Amphibious creatures, alligators, serpents, and wild-fowl haunt these yet but half-formed regions, where land and water are of the consistency of hasty-pudding—the one seeming too unstable to walk on, the other almost too thick to float in. But then the sky —if no human chisel ever yet cut breath, neither did any human pen ever write light; if it did, mine should spread out before you the unspeakable glories of these Southern heavens, the saffron brightness of morning, the blue intense brilliancy of noon, the golden splendor and the rosy softness of sunset. Italy and Claude Lorraine may go hang themselves together! Heaven itself does not seem brighter or more beautiful to the imagination than these surpassing pageants of fiery rays, and piled-up beds of orange, golden clouds, with edges too bright to look on, scattered wreaths of faintest rosy bloom, amber streaks and pale green lakes between, and amid sky all mingled blue and rose tints, a spectacle to make one fall over the side of the boat, with one's head broken off with looking adoringly upward, but which, on paper, means nothing.

At six o'clock our little canoe grazed the steps at the

landing. These were covered with young women, and boys, and girls, drawing water for their various household purposes. A very small cedar pail—a piggin as they termed it—serves to scoop up the river water; and having, by this means, filled a large bucket, they transfer this to their heads, and, thus laden, march home with the purifying element—what to do with it I can not imagine, for evidence of its ever having been introduced into their dwellings I saw none. As I ascended the stairs, they surrounded me with shrieks and yells of joy, uttering exclamations of delight and amazement at my rowing. Considering that they dig, delve, carry burdens, and perform many more athletic exercises than pulling a light oar, I was rather amused at this; but it was the singular fact of seeing a white woman stretch her sinews in any toilsome exercise which astounded them, accustomed as they are to see both men and women of the privileged skin eschew the slightest shadow of labor as a thing not only painful, but degrading. They will learn another lesson from me, however, whose idea of heaven was pronounced by a friend of mine, to whom I once communicated it, to be "devilish hard work!" It was only just six o'clock, and these women had all done their tasks. I exhorted them to go home and wash their children, and clean their houses and themselves, which they professed themselves ready to do, but said they had no soap. Then began a chorus of mingled requests for soap, for summer clothing, and a variety of things, which, if "Missis only give we, we be so clean forever!"

This request for summer clothing, by-the-by, I think a very reasonable one. The allowance of clothes made yearly to each slave by the present regulations of the estate is a certain number of yards of flannel, and as much more of what they call plains—an extremely stout, thick, heavy woolen cloth, of a dark gray or blue color, which resembles the species of carpet we call drugget. This, and two pair of shoes, is the regular ration of clothing; but these plains would be intolerable to any but negroes, even in winter, in this climate, and are intolerable to them in the summer. A far better arrangement, in my opinion, would be to increase their allowance of flannel and under clothing, and to give them dark chintzes instead of these thick carpets, which are very often the only covering they wear at all. I did not impart all this to my petitioners, but, disengaging myself from them, for they held my hands and clothes, I conjured them to offer us some encouragement to better their condition by bettering it as much as they could themselves—enforced the virtue of washing themselves and all belonging to them, and at length made good my retreat. As there is no particular reason why such a letter as this should ever come to an end, I had better spare you for the present. You shall have a faithful journal, I promise you, henceforward, as hitherto, from yours ever.

DEAR E——,—We had a species of fish this morning for our breakfast which deserves more glory than I can bestow upon it. Had I been the ingenious man who wrote a poem upon fish, the white mullet of the Altamaha should have been at least my heroine's cousin. 'Tis the heavenliest creature that goes upon fins. I took a long walk this morning to Settlement No. 3, the third village on the island. My way lay along the side of the canal, beyond which, and only divided from it by a raised narrow causeway, rolled the brimming river, with its girdle of glittering evergreens, while on my other hand a deep trench marked the line of the rice fields. It really seemed as if the increase of merely a shower of rain might join all these waters together, and lay the island under its original covering again. I visited the people and houses here. I found nothing in any respect different from what I have described to you at Settlement No. 1. During the course of my walk, I startled from its repose in one of the rice fields a huge blue heron. You must have seen, as I often have, these creatures stuffed in museums; but 'tis another matter, and far more curious, to see them stalking on their stilts of legs over a rice field, and then, on your near approach, see them spread their wide heavy wings, and throw themselves upon the air, with their long shanks flying after them in a most grotesque and laughable manner. They fly as if they did not know how to do it very well; but standing still, their height (between four and five feet) and peculiar color, a dusky, grayish blue, with black about the head, render their appearance very beautiful and striking.

In the afternoon I and Jack rowed ourselves over to Darien. It is Saturday—the day of the week on which the slaves from the island are permitted to come over to the town to purchase such things as they may require and can afford, and to dispose, to the best advantage, of their poultry, moss, and eggs. I met many of them paddling themselves singly in their slight canoes, scooped out of the trunk of a tree, and parties of three and four rowing boats of their own building, laden with their purchases, singing, laughing, talking, and apparently enjoying their holiday to the utmost. They all hailed me with shouts of delight as I pulled past them, and many were the injunctions bawled after Jack to " mind and take good care of missis!" We returned home through the glory of a sunset all amber-colored and rosy, and found that one of the slaves, a young lad for whom Mr. —— has a particular regard, was dangerously ill. Dr. H—— was sent for; and there is every probability that he, Mr. ——, and Mr. O—— will· be up all night with the poor fellow. I shall write

more to-morrow. To-day being Sunday, dear E——, a
large boat full of Mr. ——'s people from Hampton came
up, to go to church at Darien, and to pay their respects
to their master, and see their new "missis." The same
scene was acted over again that occurred on our first arrival. A crowd clustered round the house door, to whom
I and my babies were produced, and with every individual of whom we had to shake hands some half a dozen
times. They brought us up presents of eggs (their only
wealth), beseeching us to take them; and one young lad,
the son of head man Frank, had a beautiful pair of chick-
ens, which he offered most earnestly to S——. We took
one of them, not to mortify the poor fellow, and a green
ribbon being tied round its leg, it became a sacred fowl,
"little missis's chicken." By-the-by, this young man had
so light a complexion, and such regular straight features,
that, had I seen him any where else, I should have taken
him for a southern European, or, perhaps, in favor of his
tatters, a gipsy; but certainly it never would have occurred to me that he was the son of negro parents. I observed this to Mr. ——, who merely replied, "He is the
son of head man Frank and his wife Betty, and they are
both black enough, as you see." The expressions of devotion and delight of these poor people are the most fervent you can imagine. One of them, speaking to me of
Mr. ——, and saying that they had heard that he had not
been well, added, "Oh! we hear so, missis, and we not
know what to do. Oh! missis, massa sick, all him people
broken!"

Dr. H—— came again to-day to see the poor sick boy,
who is doing much better, and bidding fair to recover.
He entertained me with an account of the Darien society,
its aristocracies and democracies, its little grandeurs and
smaller pettinesses, its circles higher and lower, its social
jealousies, fine invisible lines of demarkation, impercepti-

ble shades of different respectability, and delicate divisions of genteel, genteeler, genteelest. "For me," added the worthy doctor, "I can not well enter into the spirit of these nice distinctions; it suits neither my taste nor my interest, and my house is, perhaps, the only one in Darien where you would find all these opposite and contending elements combined." The doctor is connected with the aristocracy of the place, and, like a wise man, remembers, notwithstanding, that those who are not are quite as liable to be ill, and call in medical assistance, as those who are. He is a shrewd, intelligent man, with an excellent knowledge of his profession, much kindness of heart, and apparent cheerful good temper. I have already severely tried the latter by the unequivocal expression of my opinions on the subject of slavery, and, though I perceived that it required all his self-command to listen with any thing like patience to my highly incendiary and inflammatory doctrines, he yet did so, and though he was, I have no doubt, perfectly horror-stricken at the discovery, lost nothing of his courtesy or good-humor. By-the-by, I must tell you that, at an early period of the conversation, upon my saying, "I put all other considerations out of the question, and first propose to you the injustice of the system alone," "Oh," replied my friend the doctor, "if you put it upon that ground, you *stump* the question at once; I have nothing to say to that whatever, but," and then followed the usual train of pleadings—happiness, tenderness, care, indulgence, etc., etc., etc.—all the substitutes that may or may not be put in the place of *justice*, and which these slaveholders attempt to persuade others, and perhaps themselves, effectually supply its want. After church hours the people came back from Darien. They are only permitted to go to Darien to church once a month. On the intermediate Sundays they assemble in the house of London, Mr. ——'s head cooper, an excellent and pious man, who, Heaven alone knows how, has obtained some little knowledge of reading, and who reads prayers and the Bible to his fellow-slaves, and addresses them with extemporaneous exhortations. I have the greatest desire to attend one of these religious meetings, but fear to put the people under any, the slightest restraint. However, I shall see by-and-by how they feel about it themselves.

You have heard, of course, many and contradictory statements as to the degree of religious instruction afforded to the negroes of the South, and their opportunities of worship, etc. Until the late abolition movement, the spiritual interests of the slaves were about as little regarded as their physical necessities. The outcry which has been raised with threefold force within the last few years against the whole system has induced its upholders and defenders to adopt, as measures of personal extenuation, some appearance of religious instruction (such as it is), and some pretense at physical indulgences (such as they are), bestowed apparently voluntarily upon their dependents. At Darien a church is appropriated to the especial use of the slaves, who are almost all of them Baptists here; and a gentleman officiates in it (of course white), who, I understand, is very zealous in the cause of their spiritual well-being. He, like most Southern men, clergy or others, jump the present life in their charities to the slaves, and go on to furnish them with all requisite conveniences for the next. There were a short time ago two free black preachers in this neighborhood, but they have lately been ejected from the place. I could not clearly learn, but one may possibly imagine, upon what grounds.

I do not think that a residence on a slave plantation is likely to be peculiarly advantageous to a child like my eldest. I was observing her to-day among her swarthy worshipers, for they follow her as such, and saw, with dis-

C 2

may, the universal eagerness with which they sprang to obey her little gestures of command. She said something about a swing, and in less than five minutes head man Frank had erected it for her, and a dozen young slaves were ready to swing little "missis." ——, think of learning to rule despotically your fellow-creatures before the first lesson of self-government has been well spelt over! It makes me tremble; but I shall find a remedy, or remove myself and the child from this misery and ruin.

You can not conceive any thing more grotesque than the Sunday trim of the poor people, their ideality, as Mr. Combe would say, being, I should think, twice as big as any rational bump in their head. Their Sabbath toilet really presents the most ludicrous combination of incongruities that you can conceive—frills, flounces, ribbons; combs stuck in their woolly heads, as if they held up any portion of the stiff and ungovernable hair; filthy finery, every color in the rainbow, and the deepest possible shades blended in fierce companionship round one dusky visage; head-handkerchiefs, that put one's very eyes out from a mile off; chintzes with sprawling patterns, that might be seen if the clouds were printed with them; beads, bugles, flaring sashes, and, above all, little fanciful aprons, which finish these incongruous toilets with a sort of airy grace, which I assure you is perfectly indescribable. One young man, the eldest son and heir of our washerwoman Hannah, came to pay his respects to me in a magnificent black satin waistcoat, shirt gills which absolutely ingulfed his black visage, and neither shoes nor stockings on his feet.

Among our visitors from St. Simon's to-day was Hannah's mother (it seems to me that there is not a girl of sixteen on the plantations but has children, nor a woman of thirty but has grandchildren). Old House Molly, as she is called, from the circumstance of her having been one of the slaves employed in domestic offices during Major ——'s residence on the island, is one of the oldest and most respected slaves on the estate, and was introduced to me by Mr. —— with especial marks of attention and regard; she absolutely embraced him, and seemed unable sufficiently to express her ecstasy at seeing him again. Her dress, like that of her daughter, and all the servants who have at any time been employed about the family, bore witness to a far more improved taste than the half savage adornment of the other poor blacks, and upon my observing to her how agreeable her neat and cleanly appearance was to me, she replied that her old master (Major ——) was extremely particular in this respect, and that in his time all the house servants were obliged to be very nice and careful about their persons.

She named to me all her children, an immense tribe; and, by-the-by, E——, it has occurred to me that whereas the increase of this ill-fated race is frequently adduced as a proof of their good treatment and well being, it really and truly is no such thing, and springs from quite other causes than the peace and plenty which a rapidly increasing population are supposed to indicate. If you will reflect for a moment upon the overgrown families of the half-starved Irish peasantry and English manufacturers, you will agree with me that these prolific shoots by no means necessarily spring from a rich or healthy soil. Peace and plenty are certainly causes of human increase, and so is recklessness; and this, I take it, is the impulse in the instance of the English manufacturer, the Irish peasant, and the negro slave. Indeed here it is more than recklessness, for there are certain indirect premiums held out to obey the early commandment of replenishing the earth which do not fail to have their full effect. In the first place, none of the cares—those noble cares, that holy thoughtfulness which lifts the human above the brute parent, are ever incurred here by either father or mother.

The relation indeed resembles, as far as circumstances can possibly make it do so, the short-lived connection between the animal and its young. The father, having neither authority, power, responsibility, or charge in his children, is of course, as among brutes, the least attached to his offspring; the mother, by the natural law which renders the infant dependent on her for its first year's nourishment, is more so; but as neither of them is bound to educate or to support their children, all the unspeakable tenderness and solemnity, all the rational, and all the spiritual grace and glory of the connection, is lost, and it becomes mere breeding, bearing, suckling, and there an end. But it is not only the absence of the conditions which God has affixed to the relation which tends to encourage the reckless increase of the race; they enjoy, by means of numerous children, certain positive advantages. In the first place, every woman who is pregnant, as soon as she chooses to make the fact known to the overseer, is relieved of a certain portion of her work in the field, which lightening of labor continues, of course, as long as she is so burdened. On the birth of a child certain additions of clothing and an additional weekly ration are bestowed on the family; and these matters, small as they may seem, act as powerful inducements to creatures who have none of the restraining influences actuating them which belong to the parental relation among all other people, whether civilized or savage. Moreover, they have all of them a most distinct and perfect knowledge of their value to their owners as property; and a woman thinks, and not much amiss, that the more frequently she adds to the number of her master's live-stock by bringing new slaves into the world, the more claims she will have upon his consideration and good-will. This was perfectly evident to me from the meritorious air with which the women always made haste to inform me of the number of children they had borne, and the frequent occasions on which the older slaves would direct my attention to their children, exclaiming, " Look, missis! little niggers for you and massa; plenty little niggers for you and little missis !" A very agreeable apostrophe to me indeed, as you will believe.

I have let this letter lie for a day or two, dear E——, from press of more immediate avocations. I have nothing very particular to add to it. On Monday evening I rowed over to Darien with Mr. —— to fetch over the doctor, who was coming to visit some of our people. As I sat waiting in the boat for the return of the gentlemen, the sun went down, or rather seemed to dissolve bodily into the glowing clouds, which appeared but a fusion of the great orb of light; the stars twinkled out in the rose-colored sky, and the evening air, as it fanned the earth to sleep, was as soft as a summer's evening breeze in the north. A sort of dreamy stillness seemed creeping over the world and into my spirit as the canoe just tilted against the steps that led to the wharf, raised by the scarce perceptible heaving of the water. A melancholy, monotonous boat-horn sounded from a distance up the stream, and presently, floating slowly down with the current, huge, shapeless, black, relieved against the sky, came one of those rough barges piled with cotton, called, hereabouts, Ocone boxes. The vessel itself is really nothing but a monstrous square box, made of rough planks, put together in the roughest manner possible to attain the necessary object of keeping the cotton dry. Upon this great tray are piled the swollen, apoplectic-looking cotton-bags, to the height of ten, twelve, and fourteen feet. This huge water-wagon floats lazily down the river, from the upper country to Darien. They are flat-bottomed, and, of course, draw little water. The stream from whence they are named is an up-country river, which, by its junction with the Ocmulgee, forms the Altamaha. Here at least,

you perceive, the Indian names remain, and long may they
do so, for they seem to me to become the very character
of the streams and mountains they indicate, and are indeed significant to the learned in savage tongues, which
is more than can be said of such titles as Jones's Creek,
Onion Creek, etc. These Ocone boxes are broken up at
Darien, where the cotton is shipped either for the Savannah, Charleston, or Liverpool markets, and the timber of
which they are constructed sold.

We rowed the doctor over to see some of his patients
on the island, and before his departure a most animated
discussion took place upon the subject of the President of
the United States, his talents, qualifications, opinions—
above all, his views with regard to the slave system. Mr.
——, who you know is no abolitionist, and is a very de-
voted Van Buren man, maintained with great warmth the
President's straightforwardness, and his evident and expressed intention of protecting the rights of the South.
The doctor, on the other hand, quoted a certain speech of
the President's upon the question of abolishing slavery in
the District of Columbia, which his fears interpreted into
a mere evasion of the matter, and an indication that at
some future period he (Mr. Van Buren) might take a different view of the subject. I confess, for my own part,
that if the doctor quoted the speech right, and if the President is not an honest man, and if I were a Southern slaveholder, I should not feel altogether secure of Mr. Van Buren's present opinions or future conduct upon this subject.
These three *ifs*, however, are material points of consideration. Our friend the doctor inclined vehemently to Mr.
Clay as one on whom the slaveholders could depend.
Georgia, however, as a state, is perhaps the most democratic in the Union ; though here, as well as in other places
that you and I know of, a certain class, calling themselves
the first, and honestly believing themselves the best, set

their faces against the modern fashioned republicanism, professing, and, I have no doubt, with great sincerity, that their ideas of democracy are altogether of a different kind.

I went again to-day to the Infirmary, and was happy to perceive that there really was an evident desire to conform to my instructions, and keep the place in a better condition than formerly. Among the sick I found a poor woman suffering dreadfully from the earache. She had done nothing to alleviate her pain but apply some leaves, of what tree or plant I could not ascertain, and tie up her head in a variety of dirty cloths, till it was as large as her whole body. I removed all these, and found one side of her face and neck very much swollen, but so begrimed with filth that it was really no very agreeable task to examine it. The first process, of course, was washing, which, however, appeared to her so very unusual an operation, that I had to perform it for her myself. Sweet oil and laudanum, and raw cotton, being then applied to her ear and neck, she professed herself much relieved, but I believe in my heart that the warm water sponging had done her more good than any thing else. I was sorry not to ascertain what leaves she had applied to her ear. These simple remedies resorted to by savages, and people as ignorant, are generally approved by experience, and sometimes condescendingly adopted by science. I remember once, when Mr. —— was suffering from a severe attack of inflammatory rheumatism, Dr. C—— desired him to bind round his knee the leaves of the tulip-tree—poplar I believe you call it—saying that he had learned that remedy from the negroes in Virginia, and found it a most effectual one. My next agreeable office in the Infirmary this morning was superintending the washing of two little babies, whose mothers were nursing them with quite as much ignorance as zeal. Having ordered a large tub of water, I desired Rose to undress the little creatures and give them a warm bath; the mothers looked on in unutterable dismay; and one of them, just as her child was going to be put into the tub, threw into it all the clothes she had just taken off it, as she said, to break the unusual shock of the warm water. I immediately rescued them; not but what they were quite as much in want of washing as the baby, but it appeared, upon inquiry, that the woman had none others to dress the child in when it should have taken its bath; they were immediately wrung and hung by the fire to dry; and the poor little patients, having undergone this novel operation, were taken out and given to their mothers. Any thing, however, much more helpless and inefficient than these poor ignorant creatures you can not conceive; they actually seemed incapable of drying or dressing their own babies, and I had to finish their toilet myself. As it is only a very few years since the most absurd and disgusting customs have become exploded among ourselves, you will not, of course, wonder that these poor people pin up the lower part of their infants, bodies, legs, and all, in red flannel as soon as they are born, and keep them in the self-same envelope till it literally falls off.

In the next room I found a woman lying on the floor in a fit of epilepsy, barking most violently. She seemed to excite no particular attention or compassion; the women said she was subject to these fits, and took little or no notice of her, as she lay barking like some enraged animal on the ground. Again I stood in profound ignorance, sickening with the sight of suffering which I knew not how to alleviate, and which seemed to excite no commiseration merely from the sad fact of its frequent occurrence. Returning to the house, I passed up the " street." It was between eleven o'clock and noon, and the people were taking their first meal in the day. By-the-by, E——, how do you think Berkshire county farmers would relish laboring hard all day upon *two meals* of Indian corn or

hominy? Such is the regulation on this plantation, however, and I beg you to bear in mind that the negroes on
Mr.——'s estate are generally considered well off. They
go to .the fields at daybreak, carrying with them their allowance of food for the day, which toward noon, *and not
till then*, they eat, cooking it over a fire, which they kindle as best they can, where they are working. Their second meal in the day is at night, after their labor is over,
having worked, at the *very least*, six hours without intermission of rest or refreshment since their noonday meal
(properly so called, for 'tis meal, and nothing else). Those
that I passed to-day, sitting on their door-steps, or on the
ground round them eating, were the people employed at
the mill and threshing-floor. As these are near to the
settlement, they had time to get their food from the cook-
shop. Chairs, tables, plates, knives, forks, they had none;
they sat, as I before said, on the earth or door-steps, and
ate either out of their little cedar tubs or an iron pot,
some few with broken iron spoons, more with pieces of
wood, and all the children with their fingers. A more
complete sample of savage feeding I never beheld. At
one of the doors I saw three young girls standing, who
might be between sixteen and seventeen years old; they
had evidently done eating, and were rudely playing and
romping with each other, laughing and shouting like wild
things. I went into the house, and such another spectacle of filthy disorder I never beheld. I then addressed
the girls most solemnly, showing them that they were
wasting in idle riot the time in which they might be rendering their abode decent, and told them that it was a
shame for any woman to live in so dirty a place and so
beastly a condition. They said they had seen buckree
(white) women's houses just as dirty, and they could not
be expected to be cleaner than white women. I then
told them that the only difference between themselves and

buckree women was, that the latter were generally better informed, and, for that reason alone, it was more disgraceful to them to be disorderly and dirty. They seemed to listen to me atteptively, and one of them exclaimed, with great satisfaction, that they saw I made no difference between them and white girls, and that they never had been so treated before. I do not know any thing which strikes me as a more melancholy illustration of the degradation of these people than the animal nature of their recreations in their short seasons of respite from labor. You see them, boys and girls, from the youngest age to seventeen and eighteen, rolling, tumbling, kicking, and wallowing in the dust, regardless alike of decency, and incapable of any more rational amusement; or lolling, with half-closed eyes, like so many cats and dogs, against a wall, or upon a bank in the sun, dozing away their short leisure hour, until called to resume their labors in the field or the mill. After this description of the meals of our laborers, you will, perhaps, be curious to know how it fares with our house servants in this respect. Precisely in the same manner, as far as regards allowance, with the exception of what is left from our table, but, if possible, with even less comfort, in one respect, inasmuch as no time whatever is set apart for their meals, which they snatch at any hour, and in any way that they can—generally, however, standing, or squatting on their hams round the kitchen fire. They have no sleeping-rooms in the house, but when their work is over, retire, like the rest, to their hovels, the discomfort of which has to them all the addition of comparison with our mode of living. Now, in all establishments whatever, of course some disparity exists between the comforts of the drawing-room and best bedrooms, and the servants' hall and attics, but here it is no longer a matter of degree. The young woman who performs the office of lady's-maid, and the lads who wait upon us at table, have neither table to feed at nor chair to sit down upon themselves. The boys sleep at night on the hearth by the kitchen fire, and the women upon a rough board bedstead, strewed with a little tree moss. All this shows how very torpid the sense of justice is apt to lie in the breasts of those who have it not awakened by the peremptory demands of others.

In the North we could not hope to keep the worst and poorest servant for a single day in the wretched discomfort in which our negro servants are forced habitually to live. I received a visit this morning from some of the Darien people. Among them was a most interesting young person, from whose acquaintance, if I have any opportunity of cultivating it, I promise myself much pleasure. The ladies that I have seen since I crossed the Southern line have all seemed to me extremely sickly in their appearance—delicate in the refined term, but unfortunately sickly in the truer one. They are languid in their deportment and speech, and seem to give themselves up, without an effort to counteract it, to the enervating effect of their warm climate. It is undoubtedly a most relaxing and unhealthy one, and therefore requires the more imperatively to be met by energetic and invigorating habits both of body and mind. Of these, however, the Southern ladies appear to have, at present, no very positive idea. Doctor —— told us to-day of a comical application which his negro man had made to him for the coat he was then wearing. I forget whether the fellow wanted the loan, or the absolute gift of it, but his argument was (it might have been an Irishman's) that he knew his master intended to give it to him by-and-by, and that he thought he might as well let him have it at once as keep him waiting any longer for it. This story the doctor related with great glee, and it furnishes a very good sample of what the Southerners are fond of exhibiting,

the degree of license to which they capriciously permit
their favorite slaves occasionally to carry their familiarity.
They seem to consider it as an undeniable proof of the
general kindness with which their dependents are treated.
It is as good a proof of it as the maudlin tenderness of a
fine lady to her lapdog is of her humane treatment of animals in general. Servants whose claims to respect are
properly understood by themselves and their employers,
are not made pets, playthings, jesters, or companions of,
and it is only the degradation of the many that admits of
this favoritism to the few—a system of favoritism which,
as it is perfectly consistent with the profoundest contempt
and injustice, degrades the object of it quite as much,
though it oppresses him less, than the cruelty practiced
upon his fellows. I had several of these favorite slaves
presented to me, and one or two little negro children,
who their owners assured me were quite pets. The only
real service which this arbitrary good-will did to the objects of it was quite involuntary and unconscious on the
part of their kind masters—I mean the inevitable improvement in intelligence which resulted to them from being
more constantly admitted to the intercourse of the favored white race.

I must not forget to tell you of a magnificent bald-
headed eagle which Mr. —— called me to look at early
this morning. I had never before seen alive one of these
national types of yours, and stood entranced as the noble
creature swept, like a black cloud, over the river, his bald
white head bent forward and shining in the sun, and his
fierce eyes and beak directed toward one of the beautiful
wild ducks on the water, which he had evidently marked
for his prey. The poor little duck, who was not ambitious
of such a glorification, dived, and the eagle hovered above
the spot. After a short interval, its victim rose to the
surface several yards nearer shore. The great king of

birds stooped nearer, and again the watery shield was in-
terposed. This went on until the poor water-fowl, driven
by excess of fear into unwonted boldness, rose, after repeatedly diving, within a short distance of where we
stood. The eagle, who, I presume, had read how we were
to have dominion over the fowls of the air (bald-headed
eagles included), hovered sulkily a while over the river,
and then, sailing slowly toward the woods on the opposite
shore, alighted and furled his great wings on a huge cypress limb, that stretched itself out against the blue sky,
like the arm of a giant, for the giant bird to perch upon.

I am amusing myself by attempting to beautify, in some
sort, this residence of ours. Immediately at the back of
it runs a ditch, about three feet wide, which empties and
fills twice a day with the tide. This lies like a moat on
two sides of the house. The opposite bank is a steep
dike, with a footpath along the top. One or two willows
droop over this very interesting ditch, and I thought I
would add to their company some magnolias and myrtles,
so as to make a little evergreen plantation round the house.
I went to the swamp reserves I have before mentioned to
you, and chose some beautiful bushes—among others, a
very fine young pine, at which our overseer and all the negroes expressed much contemptuous surprise; for, though
the tree is beautiful, it is also common, and with them, as
with wiser folk, 'tis "nothing pleases but rare accidents."
In spite of their disparaging remarks, however, I persisted
in having my pine-tree planted, and I assure you it formed
a very pleasing variety among the broad, smooth-leaved
evergreens about it. While forming my plantation, I had
a brand thrown into a bed of tall yellow sedges which
screen the brimming waters of the noble river from our
parlor window, and which I therefore wished removed.
The small sample of a Southern conflagration which en-
sued was very picturesque, the flames devouring the light

growth, absolutely licking it off the ground, while the curling smoke drew off in misty wreaths across the river. The heat was intense, and I thought how exceedingly and unpleasantly warm one must feel in the midst of such a forest burning as Cooper describes. Having worked my appointed task in the garden, I rowed over to Darien and back, the rosy sunset changing mean time to starry evening, as beautiful as the first the sky ever was arrayed in.

I saw an advertisement this morning in the paper which occasioned me much thought. Mr. J—— C—— and a Mr. N——, two planters of this neighborhood, have contracted to dig a canal, called the Brunswick Canal, and, not having hands enough for the work, advertise at the same time for negroes on hire and for Irish laborers. Now the Irishmen are to have twenty dollars a month wages, and to be "found" (to use the technical phrase), which finding means abundant food, and the best accommodations which can be procured for them. The negroes are hired from their masters, who will be paid, of course, as high a price as they can obtain for them—probably a very high one, as the demand for them is urgent—they, in the mean time, receiving no wages, and nothing more than the miserable negro fare of rice and corn grits. Of course the Irishmen and these slaves are not allowed to work together, but are kept at separate stations on the canal. This is every way politic, for the low Irish seem to have the same sort of hatred of negroes which sects, differing but little in their tenets, have for each other. The fact is, that a condition in their own country nearly similar has made the poor Irish almost as degraded a class of beings as the negroes are here, and their insolence toward them, and hatred of them, are precisely in proportion to the resemblance between them. This hiring out of negroes is a horrid aggravation of the miseries of their condition; for if, on the plantations, and under the masters to whom they belong, their labor is severe and their food inadequate, think what it must be when they are hired out for a stipulated sum to a temporary employer, who has not even the interest which it is pretended an owner may feel in the welfare of his slaves, but whose chief aim it must necessarily be to get as much out of them, and expend as little on them, as possible. Ponder this new form of iniquity, and believe me ever your most sincerely attached.

———————

DEAREST E——,—After finishing my last letter to you, I went out into the clear starlight to breathe the delicious mildness of the air, and was surprised to hear rising from one of the houses of the settlement a hymn sung apparently by a number of voices. The next morning I inquired the meaning of this, and was informed that those negroes on the plantation who were members of the Church were holding a prayer-meeting. There is an immensely strong devotional feeling among these poor people. The worst of it is, that it is zeal without understanding, and profits them but little; yet light is light, even that poor portion that may stream through a keyhole, and I welcome this most ignorant profession of religion in Mr. ——'s dependents as the herald of better and brighter things for them. Some of the planters are entirely inimical to any such proceedings, and neither allow their negroes to attend worship, or to congregate together for religious purposes, and truly I think they are wise in their own generation. On other plantations, again, the same rigid discipline is not observed; and some planters and overseers go even farther than toleration, and encourage these devotional exercises and professions of religion, having actually discovered that a man may become more faithful and trustworthy, even as a slave, who acknowledges the higher influences of Christianity, no matter in how small a degree. Slaveholding clergymen, and certain piously inclined planters, undertake, accordingly, to enlighten these poor creatures upon these matters, with a safe understanding, however, of what truth is to be given to them, and what is not; how much they may learn to become better slaves, and how much they may not learn, lest they cease to be slaves at all. The process is a very ticklish one, and but for the Northern public opinion, which is now pressing the slaveholders close, I dare say would not be attempted at all. As it is, they are putting their own throats and their own souls in jeopardy by this very endeavor to serve God and Mammon. The light that they are letting in between their fingers will presently strike them blind, and the mighty flood of truth which they are straining through a sieve to the thirsty lips of their slaves sweep them away like straws from their cautious moorings, and overwhelm them in its great deeps, to the waters of which man may in nowise say, thus far shall ye come and no farther. The community I now speak of, the white population of Darien, should be a religious one, to judge by the number of churches it maintains. However, we know the old proverb, and, at that rate, it may not be so godly after all. Mr. —— and his brother have been called upon at various times to subscribe to them all; and I saw this morning a most fervent appeal, extremely ill spelled, from a gentleman living in the neighborhood of the town, and whose slaves are notoriously ill treated, reminding Mr. —— of the precious souls of his human cattle, and requesting a farther donation for the Baptist Church, of which most of the people here are members. Now this man is known to be a hard master; his negro houses are sheds not fit to stable beasts in; his slaves are ragged, half naked, and miserable; yet he is urgent for their religious comforts, and writes to Mr. —— about "their souls—their precious souls." He was over here a few days ago, and pressed me very much to attend his church. I told him I would not go to a church where the people who worked for us were parted off from us as if they had the pest, and we should catch it of them. I asked him, for I was curious to know, how they managed to administer the sacrament to a mixed congregation? He replied, Oh, very easily; that the white portion of the assembly received it first, and the blacks afterward. "A new commandment I give unto you, that ye love one another, even as I have loved you." Oh, what a shocking mockery! However, they show their faith, at all events, in the declaration that God is no respecter of persons, since they do not pretend to exclude from His table those whom they most certainly would not admit to their own.

I have, as usual, allowed this letter to lie by, dear E——, not in the hope of the occurrence of any event—for that is hopeless—but until my daily avocations allowed me leisure to resume it, and afforded me, at the same time, matter wherewith to do so. I really never was so busy in all my life as I am here. I sit at the receipt of custom (involuntarily enough) from morning till night—no time, no place, affords me a respite from my innumerable petitioners; and whether I be asleep or awake, reading, eating, or walking—in the kitchen, my bedroom, or the parlor, they flock in with urgent entreaties and pitiful stories, and my conscience forbids my ever postponing their business for any other matter; for, with shame and grief of heart I say it, by their unpaid labor I live—their nakedness clothes me, and their heavy toil maintains me in luxurious idleness. Surely the least I can do is to hear these, my most injured benefactors; and, indeed, so intense in me is the sense of the injury they receive from me and mine, that I should scarce dare refuse them the very clothes from my back, or food from

D

my plate, if they asked me for it. In taking my daily walk round the banks yesterday, I found that I was walking over violet roots. The season is too little advanced for them to be in bloom, and I could not find out whether they were the fragrant violet or not.

Mr. —— has been much gratified to-day by the arrival of Mr. K——, who, with his father, for nineteen years was the sole manager of these estates, and discharged his laborious task with great ability and fidelity toward his employers. How far he understood his duties to the slaves, or whether, indeed, an overseer can, in the nature of things, acknowledge any duty to them, is another question. He is a remarkable man, and is much respected for his integrity and honorable dealing by every body here. His activity and energy are wonderful; and the mere fact of his having charge of for nineteen years, and personally governing, without any assistance whatever, seven hundred people scattered over three large tracts of land, at a considerable distance from each other, certainly bespeaks efficiency and energy of a very uncommon order. The character I had heard of him from Mr. —— had excited a great deal of interest in me, and I was very glad of this opportunity of seeing a man who for so many years had been sovereign over the poor people here. I met him walking on the banks with Mr. —— as I returned from my own ramble, during which nothing occurred or appeared to interest me, except, by-the-by, my unexpectedly coming quite close to one of those magnificent scarlet birds which abound here, and which dart across your path like a winged flame. Nothing can surpass the beauty of their plumage, and their voice is excellently melodious—they are lovely.

My companions, when I do not request the attendance of my friend Jack, are a couple of little terriers, who are endowed to perfection with the ugliness and the intelli-

gence of their race; they are of infinite service on the
plantation, as, owing to the immense quantity of grain,
and chaff, and such matters, rats and mice abound in the
mills and store-houses. I crossed the threshing-floor to-
day—a very large square, perfectly level, raised by artificial means about half a foot from the ground, and covered equally all over, so as to lie quite smooth, with some
preparation of tar. It lies immediately between the house
and the steam mill, and on it much of the negroes' work
is done—the first threshing is given to the rice, and other
labors are carried on. As I walked across it to-day, passing through the busy groups, chiefly of women, that covered it, I came opposite to one of the drivers, who held in
his hand his whip, the odious insignia of his office. I took
it from him; it was a short stick of moderate size, with a
thick square leather thong attached to it. As I held it in
my hand, I did not utter a word; but I conclude, as is oft-
en the case, my face spoke what my tongue did not, for
the driver said, "Oh, missis, me use it for measure; me
seldom strike nigger with it." For one moment I thought
I must carry the hateful implement into the house with
me. An instant's reflection, however, served to show me
how useless such a proceeding would be. The people are
not mine, nor their drivers, nor their whips. I should but
have impeded, for a few hours, the man's customary office,
and a new scourge would have been easily provided, and
I should have done nothing, perhaps worse than nothing.

After dinner I had a most interesting conversation with
Mr. K——. Among other subjects, he gave me a lively
and curious description of the Yeomanry of Georgia, more
properly termed pine-landers. Have you visions now of
well-to-do farmers with comfortable homesteads, decent
habits, industrious, intelligent, cheerful, and thrifty? Such,
however, is not the Yeomanry of Georgia. Labor being

here the especial portion of slaves, it is thenceforth degraded, and considered unworthy of all but slaves. No white man, therefore, of any class puts hand to work of any kind soever. This is an exceedingly dignified way of proving their gentility for the lazy planters who prefer an idle life of semistarvation and barbarism to the degradation of doing any thing themselves; but the effect on the poorer whites of the country is terrible. I speak now of the scattered white population, who, too poor to possess land or slaves, and having no means of living in the towns, squat (most appropriately is it so termed) either on other men's land or government districts—always here swamp or pine barren—and claim masterdom over the place they invade till ejected by the rightful proprietors. These wretched creatures will not, for they are whites (and labor belongs to blacks and slaves alone here), labor for their own subsistence. They are hardly protected from the weather by the rude shelters they frame for themselves in the midst of these dreary woods. Their food is chiefly supplied by shooting the wild-fowl and venison, and stealing from the cultivated patches of the plantations nearest at hand. Their clothes hang about them in filthy tatters, and the combined squalor and fierceness of their appearance is really frightful.

This population is the direct growth of slavery. The planters are loud in their execrations of these miserable vagabonds; yet they do not see that so long as labor is considered the disgraceful portion of slaves, these free men will hold it nobler to starve or steal than till the earth, with none but the despised blacks for fellow-laborers. The blacks themselves—such is the infinite power of custom—acquiesce in this notion, and, as I have told you, consider it the lowest degradation in a white to use any exertion. I wonder, considering the burdens they have seen me lift, the digging, the planting, the rowing, and the walking I do, that they do not utterly contemn me, and, indeed, they seem lost in amazement at it.

Talking of these pine-landers—gipsies, without any of the romantic associations that belong to the latter people —led us to the origin of such a population, slavery; and you may be sure I listened with infinite interest to the opinions of a man of uncommon shrewdness and sagacity, who was born in the very bosom of it, and has passed his whole life among slaves. If any one is competent to judge of its effects, such a man is the one; and this was his verdict: "I hate slavery with all my heart; I consider it an absolute curse wherever it exists. It will keep those states where it does exist fifty years behind the others in improvement and prosperity." Farther on in the conversation he made this most remarkable observation: "As for its being an irremediable evil—a thing not to be helped or got rid of—that's all nonsense; for, as soon as people become convinced that it is their interest to get rid of it, they will soon find the means to do so, depend upon it." And undoubtedly this is true. This is not an age, nor yours a country, where a large mass of people will long endure what they perceive to be injurious to their fortunes and advancement. Blind as people often are to their highest and truest interests, your country folk have generally shown remarkable acuteness in finding out where their worldly progress suffered let or hinderance, and have removed it with laudable alacrity. Now the fact is not at all as we at the North are sometimes told, that the Southern slaveholders deprecate the evils of slavery quite as much as we do; that they see all its miseries; that, moreover, they are most anxious to get rid of the whole thing, but want the means to do so, and submit most unwillingly to a necessity from which they can not extricate themselves. All this I thought might be true before I went to the South, and often has the charitable supposition checked the condemnation which was indignantly rising to my lips against these murderers of their brethren's peace. A little reflection, however, even without personal observation, might have convinced me that this could not be the case. If the majority of Southerners were satisfied that slavery was contrary to their worldly fortunes, slavery would be at an end from that very moment; but the fact is—and I have it not only from observation of my own, but from the distinct statement of some of the most intelligent Southern men that I have conversed with—the only obstacle to immediate abolition throughout the South is the immense value of the human property, and, to use the words of a very distinguished Carolinian, who thus ended a long discussion we had on the subject, "I'll tell you why abolition is impossible: because every healthy negro can fetch a thousand dollars in the Charleston market at this moment." And this opinion, you see, tallies perfectly with the testimony of Mr. K——.

He went on to speak of several of the slaves on this estate as persons quite remarkable for their fidelity and intelligence, instancing old Molly, Ned the engineer, who has the superintendence of the steam-engine in the rice mill, and head man Frank, of whom, indeed, he wound up the eulogium by saying he had quite the principles of a white man, which I thought most equivocal praise, but he did not intend it as such. As I was complaining to Mr. —— of the terribly neglected condition of the dikes, which are in some parts so overgrown with gigantic briers that 'tis really impossible to walk over them, and the trench on one hand, and river on the other, afford one extremely disagreeable alternatives, Mr. K—— cautioned me to be particularly on my guard not to step on the thorns of the orange-tree. These, indeed, are formidable spikes, and, he assured me, were peculiarly poisonous to the flesh. Some of the most painful and tedious wounds he had ever seen, he said, were incurred by the negroes running these large green thorns into their feet.

This led him to speak of the glory and beauty of the orange-trees on the island before a certain uncommonly severe winter, a few years ago, destroyed them all. For five miles round the banks grew a double row of noble orange-trees, as large as our orchard apple-trees, covered with golden fruit and silver flowers. It must have been a most magnificent spectacle, and Captain F——, too, told me, in speaking of it, that he had brought Basil Hall here in the season of the trees blossoming, and he had said it was as well worth crossing the Atlantic to see that as to see the Niagara. Of all these noble trees nothing now remains but the roots, which bear witness to their size, and some young sprouts shooting up, affording some hope that, in the course of years, the island may wear its bridal garland again. One huge stump close to the door is all that remains of an enormous tree that overtopped the house, from the upper windows of which oranges have been gathered from off its branches, and which, one year, bore the incredible number of 8542 oranges. Mr. K—— assured me of this as a positive fact, of which he had at the time made the entry in his journal, considering such a crop from a single tree well worthy of record. Mr. —— was called out this evening to listen to a complaint of overwork from a gang of pregnant women. I did not stay to listen to the details of their petition, for I am unable to command myself on such occasions, and Mr. —— seemed positively degraded in my eyes as he stood enforcing upon these women the necessity of their fulfilling their appointed tasks. How honorable he would have appeared to me begrimed with the sweat and soil of the coarsest manual labor, to what he then seemed, setting forth to these wretched, ignorant women, as a duty, their unpaid exacted labor! I turned away in bitter disgust. I hope this sojourn among Mr. ——'s slaves may not lessen my respect for him, but I fear it; for the details of slaveholding are so unmanly, letting alone every other consideration, that I know not how any one with the spirit of a man can condescend to them.

I have been out again on the river, rowing. I find nothing new. Swamps crowned with perfect evergreens are the only land (that's Irish!) about here, and, of course, turn which way I will, the natural features of river and shore are the same. I do not weary of these most exquisite watery woods, but you will of my mention of them, I fear. Adieu.

DEAREST E——,—Since I last wrote to you I have been actually engaged in receiving and returning visits; for even to this *ultima thule* of all civilization do these polite usages extend. I have been called upon by several families residing in and about Darien, and rowed over in due form to acknowledge the honor. How shall I describe Darien to you? The abomination of desolation is but a poor type of its forlorn appearance, as, half buried in sand, its straggling, tumble-down wooden houses peer over the muddy bank of the thick slimy river. The whole town lies in a bed of sand: side-walks, or mid-walks, there be none distinct from each other; at every step I took my feet were ankle deep in the soil, and I had cause to rejoice that I was booted for the occasion. Our worthy doctor, whose lady I was going to visit, did nothing but regret that I had not allowed him to provide me a carriage, though the distance between his house and the landing is not a quarter of a mile. The magnitude of the exertion seemed to fill him with amazement, and he over and over again repeated how impossible it would be to prevail on any of the ladies there to take such a walk. The houses

seemed scattered about here and there, apparently without
any design, and looked, for the most part, either unfinished
or ruinous. One feature of the scene alone recalled the
villages of New England—the magnificent oaks, which
seemed to add to the meanness and insignificance of the
human dwellings they overshadowed by their enormous
size and grotesque forms. They reminded me of the elms
of New Haven and Stockbridge. They are quite as large,
and more picturesque, from their sombre foliage and the
infinite variety of their forms—a beauty wanting in the
New England elm, which invariably rises and spreads in
a way which, though the most graceful in the world, at
length palls on the capricious human eye, which seeks,
above all other beauties, variety. Our doctor's wife is a
New England woman; how can she live here? She had
the fair eyes and hair, and fresh complexion of your part
of the country, and its dearly beloved snuffle, which seemed
actually dearly beloved when I heard it down here. She
gave me some violets and narcissus, already blossoming
profusely—in January—and expressed, like her husband,
a thousand regrets at my having walked so far.

A transaction of the most amusing nature occurred to-
day with regard to the resources of the Darien Bank, and
the mode of carrying on business in that liberal and enlightened institution, the funds of which I should think
quite incalculable—impalpable, certainly, they appeared
by our experience this morning.

The river, as we came home, was covered with Ocone
boxes. It is well for them they are so shallow-bottomed,
for we rasped sand all the way home through the cut and
in the shallows of the river.

I have been over the rice mill, under the guidance of
the overseer and head man Frank, and have been made
acquainted with the whole process of threshing the rice,
which is extremely curious; and here I may again men-

tion another statement of Miss Martineau's, which I am told is, and I should suppose, from what I see here, must be a mistake. She states that the chaff of the husks of the rice is used as a manure for the fields, whereas the people have to-day assured me that it is of so hard, stony, and untractable a nature as to be literally good for nothing. Here I know it is thrown away by cart-loads into the river, where its only use appears to be to act like ground-bait, and attract a vast quantity of small fish to its vicinity. The number of hands employed in this threshing mill is very considerable, and the whole establishment, comprising the fires, and boilers, and machinery of a powerful steam-engine, are all under negro superintendence and direction. After this survey I occupied myself with my infant plantation of evergreens round the dike, in the midst of which interesting pursuit I was interrupted by a visit from Mr. B———, a neighboring planter, who came to transact some business with Mr. —— about rice which he had sent to our mill to have threshed, and the price to be paid for such threshing. The negroes have presented a petition to-day that they may be allowed to have a ball in honor of our arrival, which demand has been acceded to, and furious preparations are being set on foot.

On visiting the Infirmary to-day, I was extremely pleased with the increased cleanliness and order observable in all the rooms. Two little filthy children, however, seemed to be still under the *ancien régime* of non-ablution; but upon my saying to the old nurse Molly, in whose ward they were, " Why, Molly, I don't believe you have bathed those children to-day," she answered, with infinite dignity, " Missis no b'lieve me wash um pickaninny ! and yet she 'tress me wid all um niggar when 'em sick." The injured innocence and lofty conscious integrity of this speech silenced and abashed me; and yet I can't help it, but I don't believe to this present hour that those children had had any experience of water, at least not washing water, since they first came into the world.

I rowed over to Darien again, to make some purchases, yesterday, and, inquiring the price of various articles, could not but wonder to find them at least three times as dear as in your Northern villages The profits of these Southern shopkeepers (who for the most part are thoroughbred Yankees, with the true Yankee propensity to trade, no matter on how dirty a counter, or in what manner of wares) are enormous. The prices they ask for every thing, from colored calicoes for negro dresses to piano-fortes (one of which, for curiosity sake, I inquired the value of), are fabulous, and such as none but the laziest and most reckless people in the world would consent to afford. On our return we found the water in the cut so extremely low that we were obliged to push the boat through it, and did not accomplish it without difficulty. The banks of this canal, when they are thus laid bare, present a singular appearance enough — two walls of solid mud, through which matted, twisted, twined, and tangled, like the natural veins of wood, runs an everlasting net of indestructible roots, the thousand toes of huge cypress feet. The trees have been cut down long ago from the soil, but these fangs remain in the earth without decaying for an incredible space of time. This long endurance of immersion is one of the valuable properties of these cypress roots; but, though excellent binding stuff for the sides of a canal, they must be pernicious growth in any land used for cultivation that requires deep tillage. On entering the Altamaha, we found the tide so low that we were much obstructed by the sand-banks, which, but for their constant shifting, would presently take entire possession of this noble stream, and render it utterly impassable from shore to shore, as it already is in several parts of the channel at certain seasons of the tide. On landing,

I was seized hold of by a hideous old negress, named Sinda, who had come to pay me a visit, and of whom Mr. —— told me a strange anecdote. She passed at one time for a prophetess among her fellow-slaves on the plantation, and had acquired such an ascendency over them that, having given out, after the fashion of Mr. Miller, that the world was to come to an end at a certain time, and that not a very remote one, the belief in her assertion took such possession of the people on the estate that they refused to work, and the rice and cotton fields were threatened with an indefinite fallow in consequence of this strike on the part of the cultivators. Mr. K——, who was then overseer of the property, perceived the impossibility of arguing, remonstrating, or even flogging this solemn panic out of the minds of the slaves. The great final emancipation which they believed at hand had stripped even the lash of its prevailing authority, and the terrors of an overseer for once were as nothing, in the terrible expectation of the advent of the universal Judge of men. They were utterly impracticable; so, like a very shrewd man as he was, he acquiesced in their determination not to work; but he expressed to them his belief that Sinda was mistaken, and he warned her that if, at the appointed time, it proved so, she would be severely punished. I do not know whether he confided to the slaves what he thought likely to be the result if she was in the right; but poor Sinda was in the wrong. Her day of judgment came indeed, and a severe one it proved, for Mr. K—— had her tremendously flogged, and her end of things ended much like Mr. Miller's; but whereas he escaped unhanged in spite of his atrocious practices upon the fanaticism and credulity of his country people, the spirit of false prophecy was mercilessly scourged out of her, and the faith of her people of course reverted from her to the omnipotent lash again. Think what a dream that must have been while it lasted for those infinitely oppressed people—freedom without entering it by the grim gate of death, brought down to them at once by the second coming of Christ, whose first advent has left them yet so far from it! Farewell; it makes me giddy to think of having been a slave while that delusion lasted and after it vanished.

DEAREST E——,—I received early this morning a visit from a young negro called Morris, who came to request permission to be baptized. The master's leave is necessary for this ceremony of acceptance into the bosom of the Christian Church; so all that can be said is, that it is to be hoped the rite itself may *not* be indispensable for salvation, as, if Mr. —— had thought proper to refuse Morris's petition, he must infallibly have been lost, in spite of his own best wishes to the contrary. I could not, in discoursing with him, perceive that he had any very distinct ideas of the advantages he expected to derive from the ceremony; but perhaps they appeared all the greater for being a little vague. I have seldom seen a more pleasing appearance than that of this young man; his figure was tall and straight, and his face, which was of a perfect oval, rejoiced in the grace, very unusual among his people, of a fine high forehead, and the much more frequent one of a remarkably gentle and sweet expression. He was, however, jet black, and certainly did not owe these personal advantages to any mixture in his blood. There is a certain African tribe from which the West Indian slave - market is chiefly recruited, who have these same characteristic features, and do not at all present the ignoble and ugly negro type, so much more commonly seen here. They are a tall, powerful people, with remarkably fine figures, regular features, and a singularly warlike and fierce disposition, in which respect they also differ

from the race of negroes existing on the American plantations. I do not think Morris, however, could have belonged to this tribe, though perhaps Othello did, which
would at once settle the difficulties of those commentators
who, abiding by Iago's very disagreeable suggestions as
to his purely African appearance, are painfully compelled
to forego the mitigation of supposing him a Moor and
not a negro. Did I ever tell you of my dining in Boston,
at the H——'s, on my first visit to that city, and sitting
by Mr. John Quincy Adams, who, talking to me about
Desdemona, assured me, with a most serious expression
of sincere disgust, that he considered all her misfortunes
as a very just judgment upon her for having married a
"nigger?" I think, if some ingenious American actor of
the present day, bent upon realizing Shakspeare's finest
conceptions, with all the advantages of modern enlightenment, could contrive to slip in that opprobrious title, with
a true South Carolinian anti-Abolitionist expression, it
might really be made quite a point for Iago, as, for instance, in his first soliloquy—"I hate the nigger," given
in proper Charleston or Savannah fashion, I am sure would
tell far better than "I hate the Moor." Only think, E——,
what a very·new order of interest the whole tragedy
might receive, acted throughout from this stand-point, as
the Germans call it in this country, and called "Amalgamation, or the Black Bridal."

On their return from their walk this afternoon the children brought home some pieces of sugar-cane, of which a
small quantity grows on the island. When I am most
inclined to deplore the condition of the poor slaves on
these cotton and rice plantations, the far more intolerable
existence and harder labor of those employed on the sugar estates occurs to me, sometimes producing the effect
of a lower circle in Dante's "Hell of Horrors," opening
beneath the one where he seems to have reached the

climax of infernal punishment. You may have seen this
vegetable, and must at any rate, I should think, be familiar with it by description. It is a long green reed,
like the stalk of the maize, or Indian corn, only it shoots
up to a much more considerable height, and has a consistent pith, which, together with the rind itself, is extremely
sweet. The principal peculiarity of this growth, as per
haps you know, is that they are laid horizontally in the
earth when they are planted for propagation, and from
each of the notches or joints of the recumbent cane a
young shoot is produced at the germinating season.

A very curious and interesting circumstance to me just
now in the neighborhood is the projection of a canal, to
be called the Brunswick Canal, which, by cutting through
the lower part of the main land, toward the southern extremity of Great St. Simon's Island, is contemplated as a
probable and powerful means of improving the prosperity of the town of Brunswick, by bringing it into immediate communication with the Atlantic. The scheme,
which I think I have mentioned to you before, is, I believe, chiefly patronized by your States' folk—Yankee
enterprise and funds being very essential elements, it appears to me, in all Southern projects and achievements.
This speculation, however, from all I hear of the difficulties of the undertaking, from the nature of the soil, and
the impossibility almost of obtaining efficient labor, is not
very likely to arrive at any very satisfactory result; and,
indeed, I find it hard to conceive how this part of Georgia
can possibly produce a town which can be worth the digging of a canal, even to Yankee speculators. There is
one feature of the undertaking, however, which more than
all the others excites my admiration, namely, that Irish
laborers have been advertised for to work upon the canal,
and the terms offered them are twenty dollars a month
per man and their board. Now these men will have for

fellow-laborers negroes who not only will receive nothing
at all for their work, but who will be hired by the con-
tractors and directors of the works from their masters, to
whom they will hand over the price of their slaves' labor;
while it will be the interest of the person hiring them not
only to get as much work as possible out of them, but
also to provide them as economically with food, combin-
ing the two praiseworthy endeavors exactly in such judicious proportions as not to let them neutralize each other.
You will observe that this case of a master hiring out his
slaves to another employer, from whom he receives their
rightful wages, is a form of slavery which, though extremely common, is very seldom adverted to in those ar-
guments for the system which are chiefly founded upon
the master's presumed regard for his human property.
People who have ever let a favorite house to the temporary occupation of strangers can form a tolerable idea of
the difference between one's own regard and care of one's
goods and chattels and that of the most conscientious
tenant; and whereas I have not yet observed that ownership is a very effectual protection to the slaves against
ill usage and neglect, I am quite prepared to admit that
it is a vastly better one than the temporary interest
which a lessee can feel in the live-stock he hires, out of
whom it is his manifest interest to get as much, and into
whom to put as little, as possible. Yet thousands of
slaves throughout the Southern states are thus handed
over by the masters who own them to masters who do
not; and it does not require much demonstration to prove
that their estate is not always the more gracious. Now
you must not suppose that these same Irish free laborers
and negro slaves will be permitted to work together at
this Brunswick Canal. They say that this would be utterly impossible; for why? there would be tumults, and
risings, and broken heads, and bloody bones, and all the

natural results of Irish intercommunion with their fellow-creatures, no doubt—perhaps even a little more riot and violence than merely comports with their usual habits of Milesian good fellowship; for, say the masters, the Irish hate the negroes more even than the Americans do, and there would be no bound to their murderous animosity if they were brought in contact with them on the same portion of the works of the Brunswick Canal. Doubtless there is some truth in this; the Irish laborers who might come hither would be apt enough, according to a universal moral law, to visit upon others the injuries they had received from others. They have been oppressed enough themselves to be oppressive whenever they have a chance; and the despised and degraded condition of the blacks, presenting to them a very ugly resemblance of their own home, circumstances naturally excite in them the exercise of the disgust and contempt of which they themselves are very habitually the objects; and that such circular distribution of wrongs may not only be pleasant, but have something like the air of retributive right to very ignorant folks, is not much to be wondered at. Certain is the fact, however, that the worst of all tyrants is the one who has been a slave; and, for that matter (and I wonder if the Southern slaveholders hear it with the same ear that I do, and ponder it with the same mind?), the command of one slave to another is altogether the most uncompromising utterance of insolent truculent despotism that it ever fell to my lot to witness or listen to. "You nigger—I say, you black nigger—you no hear me call you—what for you no run quick?" All this, dear E——, is certainly reasonably in favor of division of labor on the Brunswick Canal; but the Irish are not only quarrelers, and rioters, and fighters, and drinkers, and despisers of niggers—they are a passionate, impulsive, warm-hearted, generous people, much given to

powerful indignations, which break out suddenly when
not compelled to smoulder sullenly—pestilent sympa-
thizers too, and with a sufficient dose of American atmospheric air in their lungs, properly mixed with a right proportion of ardent spirits, there is no saying but what they
might actually take to sympathy with the slaves, and I
leave you to judge of the possible consequences. You
perceive, I am sure, that they can by no means be allowed
to work together on the Brunswick Canal.

I have been taking my daily walk round the island, and
visited the sugar mill and the threshing mill again.

Mr. —— has received another letter from Parson S——
upon the subject of more church building in Darien. It
seems that there has been a very general panic in this part
of the slave states lately, occasioned by some injudicious
missionary preaching, which was pronounced to be of a
decidedly abolitionist tendency. The offensive preachers,
after sowing God only knows what seed in this tremendous soil, where one grain of knowledge may spring up a
gigantic upas-tree to the prosperity of its most unfortunate possessors, were summarily and ignominiously ex-
pulsed; and now some shortsighted, uncomfortable Christians in these parts, among others this said Parson S——,
are possessed with the notion that something had better
be done to supply the want created by the cessation of
these dangerous exhortations, to which the negroes have
listened, it seems, with complacency   Parson S—— seems
to think that, having driven out two preachers, it might
be well to build one church, where, at any rate, the negroes
might be exhorted in a safe and salutary manner, "qui ne
leur donnerait point d'idées," as the French would say.
Upon my word, E——, I used to pity the slaves, and I do
pity them with all my soul; but, oh dear! oh dear! their
case is a bed of roses to that of their owners, and I would
go to the slave-block in Charleston to-morrow cheerfully

to be purchased if my only option was to go thither as a purchaser. I was looking over this morning, with a most indescribable mixture of feelings, a pamphlet published in the South upon the subject of the religious instruction of the slaves, and the difficulty of the task undertaken by these reconcilers of God and Mammon really seems to me nothing short of piteous. " We must give our involuntary servants" (they seldom call them slaves, for it is an ugly word in an American mouth, you know) " Christian enlightenment," say they; and where shall they begin? " Whatsoever ye would that men should do unto you, do ye also unto them ?" No; but "Servants, obey your masters ;" and there, I think, they naturally come to a full stop. This pamphlet forcibly suggested to me the necessity for a slave Church Catechism, and also, indeed, if it were possible, a slave Bible. If these heaven-blinded negro enlighteners persist in their pernicious plan of making Christians of their cattle, something of the sort must be done, or they will infallibly cut their own throats with this two-edged sword of truth, to which they should in no wise have laid their hand, and would not, doubtless, but that it is now thrust at them so threateningly that they have no choice. Again and again, how much I do pity them!

I have been walking to another cluster of negro huts, known as Number Two, and here we took a boat and rowed across the broad brimming Altamaha to a place called Woodville, on a part of the estate named Hammersmith, though why that very thriving suburb of the great city of London should have been selected as the name of the lonely plank house in the midst of the pine woods which here enjoys that title I can not conceive, unless it was suggested by the contrast. This settlement is on the main land, and consists apparently merely of this house (to which the overseer retires when the poisonous malaria of the rice plantations compels him to withdraw from

it), and a few deplorably miserable hovels, which appeared
to me to be chiefly occupied by the most decrepid and infirm samples of humanity it was ever my melancholy lot
to behold.

The air of this pine barren is salubrious compared with
that of the rice islands, and here some of the oldest slaves
who will not die yet, and can not work any more, are sent,
to go, as it were, out of the way. Remote recollections
of former dealings with civilized human beings in the
shape of masters and overseers seemed to me to be the
only idea not purely idiotic in the minds of the poor old
tottering creatures that gathered to stare with dim and
blear eyes at me and my children.

There were two very aged women, who had seen different, and, to their faded recollections, better times, who
spoke to me of Mr. ——'s grandfather, and of the early
days of the plantation, when they were young and strong,
and worked as their children and grandchildren were now
working, neither for love nor yet for money. One of these
old crones, a hideous, withered, wrinkled piece of woman-
hood, said that she had worked as long as her strength
had lasted, and that then she had still been worth her
keep, for, said she, "Missus, tho' we no able to work, we
make little niggers for massa." Her joy at seeing her
present owner was unbounded, and she kept clapping her
horny hands together and exclaiming, "While there is life
there is hope; we seen massa before we die." These demonstrations of regard were followed up by piteous complaints of hunger and rheumatism, and their usual requests
for pittances of food and clothing, to which we responded
by promises of additions in both kinds; and I was extri-
cating myself as well as I could from my petitioners, with
the assurance that I would come by-and-by and visit them
again, when I felt my dress suddenly feebly jerked, and a
shrill cracked voice on the other side of me exclaimed,

"Missus, no go yet—no go away yet; you no see me, missus, when you come by-and-by; but," added the voice, in a sort of wail, which seemed to me as if the thought was full of misery, " you see many, many of my offspring." These melancholy words, particularly the rather unusual one at the end of the address, struck me very much. They were uttered by a creature which *was* a woman, but looked like a crooked, ill-built figure set up in a field to scare crows, with a face infinitely more like a mere animal's than any human countenance I ever beheld, and with that peculiar, wild, restless look of indefinite and, at the same time, intense sadness that is so remarkable in the countenance of some monkeys. It was almost with an effort that I commanded myself so as not to withdraw my dress from the yellow, crumpled, filthy claws that griped it, and it was not at last without the authoritative voice of the overseer that the poor creature released her hold of me.

We returned home certainly in the very strangest vehicle that ever civilized gentlewoman traveled in—a huge sort of cart, made only of some loose boards, on which I lay, supporting myself against one of the four posts which indicated the sides of my carriage; six horned creatures, cows or bulls, drew this singular equipage, and a yelping, howling, screaming, leaping company of half-naked negroes ran all round them, goading them with sharp sticks, frantically seizing hold of their tails, and inciting them by every conceivable and inconceivable encouragement to quick motion: thus, like one of the ancient Merovingian monarchs, I was dragged through the deep sand from the settlement back to the river, where we re-embarked for the island.

As we crossed the broad flood, whose turbid waters always look swollen as if by a series of freshets, a flight of birds sprang from the low swamp we were approaching, and literally, as it rose in the air, cast a shadow like that of a cloud, which might be said, with but little exaggeration, to darken the sun for a few seconds. How well I remember my poor Aunt Whitelock describing such phenomena as of frequent occurrence in America, and the scornful incredulity with which we heard, without accepting, these legends of her Western experience! How little I then thought that I should have to cry peccavi to her memory from the bottom of such ruts, and under the shadow of such flights of winged creatures as she used to describe from the muddy ways of Pennsylvania and the muddy waters of Georgia.

The vegetation is already in an active state of demonstration, sprouting into lovely pale green and vivid red-brown buds and leaflets, though 'tis yet early in January.

After our return home we had a visit from Mr. C——, one of our neighbors, an intelligent and humane man, to whose account of the qualities and characteristics of the slaves, as he had observed and experienced them, I listened with great interest. The Brunswick Canal was again the subject of conversation, and again the impossibility of allowing the negroes and Irish to work in proximity was stated, and admitted as an indisputable fact. It strikes me with amazement to hear the hopeless doom of incapacity for progress pronounced upon these wretched slaves, when in my own country the very same order of language is perpetually applied to these very Irish, here spoken of as a sort of race of demigods by negro comparison. And it is most true that in Ireland nothing can be more savage, brutish, filthy, idle, and incorrigibly and hopelessly helpless and incapable than the Irish appear; and yet, transplanted to your Northern states, freed from the evil influences which surround them at home, they and their children become industrious, thrifty, willing to learn, able to improve, and forming, in the course of two generations, a most valuable accession to your laboring population.

How is it that it never occurs to these emphatical denouncers of the whole negro race that the Irish at home are esteemed much as they esteem their slaves, and that the sentence pronounced against their whole country by one of the greatest men of our age, an Irishman, was precisely that nothing could save, redeem, or regenerate Ireland unless, as a preparatory measure, the island were submerged and all its inhabitants drowned off?

I have had several women at the house to-day asking for advice and help for their sick children: they all came from No. 2, as they call it, that is, the settlement or cluster of negro huts nearest to the main one, where we may be said to reside. In the afternoon I went thither, and found a great many of the little children ailing: there had been an unusual mortality among them at this particular settlement this winter. In one miserable hut I heard that the baby was just dead; it was one of thirteen, many of whom had been, like itself, mercifully removed from the life of degradation and misery to which their birth appointed them; and whether it was the frequent repetition of similar losses, or an instinctive consciousness that death was indeed better than life for such children as theirs, I know not, but the father and mother, and old Rose, the nurse, who was their little baby's grandmother, all seemed apathetic, and apparently indifferent to the event. The mother merely repeated over and over again, "I've lost a many; they all goes so;" and the father, without word or comment, went out to his enforced labor.

As I left the cabin, rejoicing for them at the deliverance out of slavery of their poor child, I found myself suddenly surrounded by a swarm of young ragamuffins in every stage of partial nudity, clamoring from out of their filthy remnants of rags for donations of scarlet ribbon for the ball, which was to take place that evening. The melancholy scene I had just witnessed, and the still sadder reflection it had given rise to, had quite driven all thoughts of the approaching festivity from my mind; but the sudden demand for these graceful luxuries by Mr. ——'s half-naked dependents reminded me of the grotesque mask which life wears on one of its mysterious faces; and with as much sympathy for rejoicing as my late sympathy for sorrow had left me capable of, I procured the desired ornaments. I have considerable fellow-feeling for the passion for all shades of red which prevails among these dusky fellow-creatures of mine, a savage propensity for that same color in all its modifications being a tendency of my own.

At our own settlement (No. 1) I found every thing in a high fever of preparation for the ball. A huge boat had just arrived from the cotton plantation at St. Simon's, laden with the youth and beauty of that portion of the estate who had been invited to join the party; and the greetings among the arrivers and welcomers, and the heaven-defying combinations of color in the gala attire of both, surpass all my powers of description. The ball, to which of course we went, took place in one of the rooms of the Infirmary. As the room had, fortunately, but few occupants, they were removed to another apartment, and, without any very tender consideration for their not very remote, though invisible sufferings, the dancing commenced, and was continued. Oh, my dear E——, I have seen Jim Crow — the veritable James: all the contortions, and springs, and flings, and kicks, and capers you have been beguiled into accepting as indicative of him are spurious, faint, feeble, impotent — in a word, pale Northern reproductions of that ineffable black conception. It is impossible for words to describe the things these people did with their bodies, and, above all, with their faces, the whites of their eyes, and the whites of their teeth, and certain outlines which either naturally and by the grace of heaven, or by the practice of some peculiar artistic dexterity, they bring into prominent and most ludicrous display. The languishing elegance of some—the painstaking laboriousness ,of others—above all, the feats of a certain enthusiastic banjo-player, who seemed to me to thump his instrument with every part of his body at once, at last so utterly overcame any attempt at decorous gravity on my part that I was obliged to secede; and, considering what the atmosphere was that we inhaled during the exhibition, it is only wonderful to me that we were not made ill by the double effort not to laugh, and, if possible, not to breathe.

Monday, 20th.

MY DEAREST E——,—A rather longer interval than usual has elapsed since I last wrote to you, but I must beg you to excuse it. I have had more than a usual amount of small daily occupations to fill my time; and, as a mere enumeration of these would not be very interesting to you, I will tell you a story which has just formed an admirable illustration for my observation of all the miseries of which this accursed system of slavery is the cause, even under the best and most humane administration of its laws and usages. Pray note it, my dear friend, for you will find, in the absence of all voluntary or even conscious cruelty on the part of the master, the best possible comment on a state of things which, without the slightest desire to injure and oppress, produces such intolerable results of injury and oppression.

We have, as a sort of under nursemaid and assistant of my dear M——, whose white complexion, as I wrote you, occasioned such indignation to my Southern fellow-travelers, and such extreme perplexity to the poor slaves on our arrival here, a much more orthodox servant for these

E

parts, a young woman named Psyche, but commonly called Sack, not a very graceful abbreviation of the divine
heathen appellation : she can not be much over twenty,
has a very pretty figure, a graceful, gentle deportment,
and a face which, but for its color (she is a dingy mulatto), would be pretty, and is extremely pleasing, from the
perfect sweetness of its expression ; she is always serious,
not to say sad and silent, and has always an air of melancholy and timidity, that has frequently struck me very
much, and would have made me think some special anxiety or sorrow must occasion it, but that God knows the
whole condition of these wretched· people naturally produces such a deportment, and there is no necessity to seek
for special or peculiar causes to account for it.   Just in
proportion as I have found the slaves on this plantation
intelligent·and advanced beyond the general brutish level
of the majority, I have observed this pathetic expression
of countenance in them, a mixture of sadness and fear, the
involuntary exhibition of the two feelings, which I suppose must be the predominant experience of their whole
lives, regret and apprehension, not the less heavy, either
of them, for being, in some degree, vague and indefinite—
a sense of incalculable past loss and injury, and a dread
of incalculable future loss and injury.

I have never questioned Psyche as to her sadness, because, in the first place, as I tell you, it appears to me
most natural, and is observable in all the slaves whose
superior natural or acquired intelligence allows of their
filling situations of trust or service about the house and
family ; and, though I can not and will not refuse to hear
any and every tale of suffering which these unfortunates
bring to me, I am anxious to spare both myself and them
the pain of vain appeals to me for redress and help, which,
alas ! it is too often utterly out of my power to give them.
It is useless, and, indeed, worse than useless, that they

should see my impotent indignation and unavailing pity, and hear expressions of compassion for them, and horror at their condition, which might only prove incentives to a hopeless resistance on their part to a system, under the hideous weight of whose oppression any individual or partial revolt must be annihilated and ground into the dust. Therefore, as I tell you, I asked Psyche no questions; but, to my great astonishment, the other day M—— asked me if I knew to whom Psyche belonged, as the poor woman had inquired of her with much hesitation and anguish if she could tell her who owned her and her children. She has two nice little children under six years old, whom she keeps as clean and tidy, and who are sad and as silent as herself. My astonishment at this question was, as you will readily believe, not small, and I forthwith sought out Psyche for an explanation. She was thrown into extreme perturbation at finding that her question had been referred to me, and it was some time before I could sufficiently reassure her to be able to comprehend, in the midst of her reiterated entreaties for pardon, and hopes that she had not offended me, that she did not know herself who owned her. She was, at one time, the property of Mr. K——, the former overseer, of whom I have already spoken to you, and who has just been paying Mr. —— a visit. He, like several of his predecessors in the management, has contrived to make a fortune upon it (though it yearly decreases in value to the owners, but this is the inevitable course of things in the Southern states), and has purchased a plantation of his own in Alabama, I believe, or one of the Southwestern states. Whether she still belonged to Mr. K—— or not she did not know, and entreated me, if she did, to endeavor to persuade Mr. —— to buy her. Now you must know that this poor woman is the wife of one of Mr. B——'s slaves, a fine, intelligent, active, excellent young man, whose whole family are

among some of the very best specimens of character and
capacity on the estate. I was so astonished at the (to
me) extraordinary state of things revealed by poor Sack's
petition, that I could only tell her that I had supposed all
the negroes on the plantation were Mr. ——'s property,
but that I would certainly inquire, and find out for her, if
I could, to whom she belonged, and if I could, endeavor
to get Mr. —— to purchase her, if she really was not his.

Now, E——, just conceive for one moment the state of
mind of this woman, believing herself to belong to a man
Who in a few days was going down to one of those abhorred and dreaded Southwestern states, and who would
then compel her, with her poor little children, to leave her
husband and the only home she had ever known, and all
the ties of affection, relationship, and association of her
former life, to follow him thither, in all human probability
never again to behold any living creature that she had
seen before; and this was so completely a matter of
course that it was not even thought necessary to apprise
her positively of the fact, and the only thing that inter-
posed between her and this most miserable fate was the
faint hope that Mr. —— *might have* purchased her and
her children. But if he had, if this great deliverance had
been vouchsafed to her, the knowledge of it was not
thought necessary; and with this deadly dread at her
heart she was' living day after day, waiting upon me and
seeing me, with my husband beside me, and my children
in my arms in blessed security, safe from all separation
but the one reserved in God's great providence for all His
creatures. Do you think I wondered any more at the
wo-begone expression of her countenance, or do you think
it was easy for me to restrain within prudent and proper
limits the expression of my feelings at such a state of
things ? And she had gone on from day to day enduring
this agony, till I suppose its own intolerable pressure and

M——'s sweet countenance and gentle sympathizing voice and manner had constrained her to lay down this great burden of sorrow at our feet. I did not see Mr. —— until the evening; but, in the mean time, meeting Mr. O——, the overseer, with whom, as I believe I have already told you, we are living here, I asked him about Psyche, and who was her proprietor, when, to my infinite surprise, he told me that *he* had bought her and her children from Mr. K——, who had offered them to him, saying that they would be rather troublesome to him than otherwise down where he was going; "and so," said Mr. O——, "as I had no objection to investing a little money that way, I bought them." With a heart much lightened, I flew to tell poor Psyche the news, so that, at any rate, she might be relieved from the dread of any immediate separation from her husband. You can imagine better than I can tell you what her sensations were; but she still renewed her prayer that I would, if possible, induce Mr. —— to purchase her, and I promised to do so.

Early the next morning, while I was still dressing, I was suddenly startled by hearing voices in loud tones in Mr. ——'s dressing-room, which adjoins my bedroom, and the noise increasing until there was an absolute cry of despair uttered by some man. I could restrain myself no longer, but opened the door of communication and saw Joe, the young man, poor Psyche's husband, raving almost in a state of frenzy, and in a voice broken with sobs and almost inarticulate with passion, reiterating his determination never to leave this plantation, never to go to Alabama, never to leave his old father and mother, his poor wife and children, and dashing his hat, which he was wringing like a cloth in his hands, upon the ground, he declared he would kill himself if he was compelled to follow Mr. K——. I glanced from the poor wretch to Mr ——, who was standing, leaning against a table with his arms folded, occasionally uttering a few words of counsel to his slave to be quiet and not fret, and not make a fuss about what there was no help for. I retreated immediately from the horrid scene, breathless with surprise and dismay, and stood for some time in my own room, with my heart and temples throbbing to such a degree that I could hardly support myself. As soon as I recovered myself I again sought Mr. O——, and inquired of him if he knew the cause of poor Joe's distress. He then told me that Mr. ——, who is highly pleased with Mr. K——'s past administration of his property, wished, on his departure for his newly-acquired slave plantation, to give him some token of his satisfaction, and *had made him a present* of the man Joe, who had just received the intelligence that he was to go down to Alabama with his new owner the next day, leaving father, mother, wife, and children behind. You will not wonder that the man required a little judicious soothing under such circumstances, and you will also, I hope, admire the humanity of the sale of his wife and children by the owner who was going to take him to Alabama, because *they* would be encumbrances rather than otherwise down there. If Mr. K—— did not do this after he knew that the man was his, then Mr. —— gave him to be carried down to the South after his wife and children were sold to remain in Georgia. I do not know which was the real transaction, for I have not had the heart to ask; but you will easily imagine which of the two cases I prefer believing.

When I saw Mr. —— after this most wretched story became known to me in all its details, I appealed to him, for his own soul's sake, not to commit so great a cruelty. Poor Joe's agony while remonstrating with his master was hardly greater than mine while arguing with him upon this bitter piece of inhumanity—how I cried, and how I adjured, and how all my sense of justice, and of

mercy, and of pity for the poor wretch, and of wretchedness at finding myself implicated in such a state of things,
broke in torrents of words from my lips and tears from
my eyes! God knows such a sorrow at seeing any one I
belonged to commit such an act was indeed a new and
terrible experience to me, and it seemed to me that I was
imploring Mr. —— to save himself more than to spare
these wretches. He gave me no answer whatever, and I
have since thought that the intemperate vehemence of my
entreaties and expostulations perhaps deserved that he
should leave me as he did without one single word of reply; and miserable enough I remained. Toward evening,
as I was sitting alone, my children having gone to bed,
Mr. O—— came into the room. I had but one subject in
my mind; I had not been able to eat for it. I could hardly sit still for the nervous distress which every thought
of these poor people filled me with. As he sat down looking over some accounts, I said to him, " Have you seen
Joe this afternoon, Mr. O——?" (I give you our conversation as it took place.) " Yes, ma'am; he is a great
deal happier than he was this morning." " Why, how is
that?" asked I, eagerly. " Oh, he is not going to Alabama. Mr. K—— heard that he had kicked up a fuss
about it (being in despair at being torn from one's wife
and children is called *kicking up a fuss;* this is a sample
of overseer appreciation of human feelings), and said that
if the fellow wasn't willing to go with him, he did not
wish to be bothered with any niggers down there who
were to be troublesome, so he might stay behind." "And
does Psyche know this?" "Yes, ma'am, I suppose so."
I drew a long breath; and whereas my needle had stum-
bled through the stuff I was sewing for an hour before, as
if my fingers could not guide it, the regularity and rapidity of its evolutions were now quite edifying. The man
was for the present safe, and I remained silently ponder-

ing his deliverance and the whole proceeding, and the
conduct of every one engaged in it, and, above all, Mr.
——'s share in the transaction, and I think, for the first
time, almost a sense of horrible personal responsibility and
implication took hold of my mind, and I felt the weight
of an unimagined guilt upon my conscience; and yet, God
knows, this feeling of self-condemnation is very gratuitous
on my part, since when I married Mr. —— I knew nothing of these dreadful possessions of his, and even if I had
I should have been much puzzled to have formed any idea
of the state of things in which I now find myself plunged,
together with those whose well-doing is as vital to me almost as my own.

With these agreeable reflections I went to bed. Mr.
—— said not a word to me upon the subject of these
poor people all the next day, and in the mean time I became very impatient of this reserve on his part, because I
was dying to prefer my request that he would purchase
Psyche and her children, and so prevent any future separation between her and her husband, as I supposed he
would not again attempt to make a present of Joe, at
least to any one who did not wish to be *bothered* with his
wife and children. In the evening I was again with Mr.
O—— alone in the strange, bare, wooden-walled sort of
shanty which is our sitting-room, and revolving in my
mind the means of rescuing Psyche from her miserable
suspense, a long chain of all my possessions, in the shape
of bracelets, necklaces, brooches, earrings, etc., wound in
glittering procession through my brain, with many hypo-
thetical calculations of the value of each separate orna-
ment, and the very doubtful probability of the amount of
the whole being equal to the price of this poor creature
and her children; and then the great power and privilege
I had foregone of earning money by my own labor occurred to me, and I think, for the first time in my life, my

past profession assumed an aspect that arrested my thoughts most seriously. For the last four years of my life that preceded my marriage I literally coined money, and never until this moment, I think, did I reflect on the great means of good, to myself and others, that I so gladly agreed to give up forever for a maintenance by the unpaid labor of slaves—people toiling not only unpaid, but under the bitter conditions the bare contemplation of which was then wringing my heart. You will not wonder that when, in the midst of such cogitations, I suddenly accosted Mr. O——, it was to this effect: "Mr. O——, I have a particular favor to beg of you. Promise me that you will never sell Psyche and her children without first letting me know of your intention to do so, and giving me the option of buying them." Mr. O—— is a remarkably deliberate man, and squints, so that, when he has taken a little time in directing his eyes to you, you are still unpleasantly unaware of any result in which you are concerned; he laid down a book he was reading, and directed his head and one of his eyes toward me and answered, "Dear me, ma'am, I am very sorry—I have sold them." My work fell down on the ground, and my mouth opened wide, but I could utter no sound, I was so dismayed and surprised; and he deliberately proceeded: "I didn't know, ma'am, you see, at all, that you entertained any idea of making an investment of that nature; for I'm sure, if I had, I would willingly have sold the woman to you; but I sold her and her children this morning to Mr. ——." My dear E——, though —— had resented my unmeasured upbraidings, you see they had not been without some good effect, and though he had, perhaps justly, punished my violent outbreak of indignation about the miserable scene I witnessed by not telling me of his humane purpose, he had bought these poor creatures, and so, I trust, secured them from any such misery in future. I

E 2

jumped up and left Mr. O—— still speaking, and ran to find Mr. ——, to thank him for what he had done, and with that will now bid you good-by. Think, E——, how it fares with slaves on plantations where there is no crazy Englishwoman to weep, and entreat, and implore, and upbraid for them, and no master willing to listen to such appeals.

DEAR E——,—There is one privilege which I enjoy here which I think few Cockneynesses have ever had experience of, that of hearing my own extemporaneous praises chanted bard-fashion by our negroes in rhymes as rude and to measures as simple as ever any illustrious female of the days of King Brian Boroihme listened to. Rowing yesterday evening through a beautiful sunset into a more beautiful moonrise, my two sable boatmen entertained themselves and me with alternate strophe and antistrophe of poetical description of my personal attractions, in which my "wire waist" recurred repeatedly, to my intense amusement. This is a charm for the possession of which M—— (my white nursemaid) is also invariably celebrated; and I suppose that the fine round natural proportions of the uncompressed waists of the sable beauties of these regions appear less symmetrical to eyes accustomed to them than our stay-cased figures, since "nothing pleaseth but rare accidents." Occasionally I am celebrated in these rowing chants as "Massa's darling," and S—— comes in for endless glorification on account of the brilliant beauty of her complexion; the other day, however, our poets made a diversion from the personal to the moral qualities of their small mistress, and after the usual tribute to her roses and lilies came the following rather significant couplet:

> "Little Missis Sally,
> That's a ruling lady."

At which all the white teeth simultaneously lightened from the black visages, while the subject of this equivocal commendation sat with infantine solemnity (the profoundest, I think, that the human countenance is capable of), surveying her sable dependents with imperturbable gravity.

Yesterday morning I amused myself with an exercise of a talent I once possessed, but have so neglected that my performance might almost be called an experiment. I cut out a dress for one of the women. My education in France—where, in some important respects, I think girls are better trained than with us—had sent me home to England, at sixteen, an adept in the female mystery of needle-work. Not only owing to the Saturday's discipline of clothes-mending by all the classes—while l'Abbé Millot's history (of blessed boring memory) was being read aloud, to prevent "vain babblings," and insure wholesome mental occupation the while—was I an expert patcher and mender, darner and piecer (darning and marking were my specialties), but the white cotton embroidery of which every French woman has always a piece under her hand *pour les momens perdus,* which are thus any thing but *perdus,* was as familar to us as to the Irish cottagers of the present day, and cutting out and making my dresses was among the more advanced branches of *the* female accomplishment to which I attained.*   The luxury of a lady's

---

* Some of our great English ladies are, I know, exquisite needle-women; but I do not think, in spite of these exceptional examples, that young English ladies of the higher classes are much skilled in this respect at the present day; and as for the democratic daughters of America, who for many reasons might be supposed likely to be well up in such housewifely lore, they are, for the most part, so ignorant of it that I have heard the most eloquent preacher of the city of New

maid of my own, indulged in ever since the days of my
"coming out," has naturally enough caused my right hand
to forget its cunning, and regret and shame at having lost
any useful lore in my life made me accede, for my own
sake, to the request of one of our multitudinous Dianas
and innumerable Chloes to cut out dresses for each of
them, especially as they (wonderful to relate) declared
themselves able to stitch them if I would do the cutting.
Since I have been on the plantation I have already spent
considerable time in what the French call "confection-
ing" baby bundles, *i. e.*, the rough and very simple tiny
habiliments of coarse cotton and scarlet flannel which form
a baby's layette here, and of which I have run up some
scores; but my present task was far more difficult.
Chloe was an ordinary mortal negress enough, but Diana
might have been the Huntress of the Woods herself, done
into the African type.   Tall, large, straight, well made,
profoundly serious, she stood like a bronze statue, while I,
mounted on a stool (the only way in which I could attain
to the noble shoulders and bust of my lay figure), pinned
and measured, and cut and shaped, under the superintendence of M——, and had the satisfaction of seeing the fine
proportions of my black goddess quite becomingly clothed
in a high, tight-fitting body of the gayest chintz, which
she really contrived to put together quite creditably.

I was so elated with my own part of this performance

York advert to their incapacity in this respect as an impediment to
their assistance of the poor, and ascribe to the fact that the daughters
of his own parishioners did not know how to sew, the impossibility of
their giving the most valuable species of help to the women of the
needier classes, whose condition could hardly be more effectually improved than by acquiring such useful knowledge.   I have known
young American school-girls duly instructed in the nature of the par-
allaxes of the stars, but, as a rule, they do not know how to darn their
stockings.   Les Dames du Sacré Cœur do better for their high-born
and well-bred pupils than this.

that I then and there determined to put into execution a plan I had long formed of endowing the little boat in which I take what the French call my walks on the water with cushions for the back and seat of the benches usually occupied by myself and Mr. ——; so, putting on my large straw hat, and plucking up a paper of pins, scissors, and my brown holland, I walked to the steps, and, jumping into the little canoe, began piecing, and measuring, and cutting the cushions, which were to be stuffed with the tree moss by some of the people who understand making a rough kind of mattress. My inanimate subject, however, proved far more troublesome to fit than my living lay figure, for the little cockle-shell ducked, and dived, and rocked, and tipped, and courtesied, and tilted, as I knelt first on one side and then on the other, fitting her, till I was almost in despair; however, I got a sort of pattern at last, and by dint of some pertinacious efforts—which, in their incompleteness, did not escape some sarcastic remarks from Mr. —— on the capabilities of "women of genius" applied to commonplace objects—the matter was accomplished, and the little Dolphin rejoiced in very tidy back and seat cushions, covered with brown holland, and bound with green serge. My ambition then began to contemplate an awning; but the boat being of the nature of a canoe—though not a real one, inasmuch as it is not made of a single log—does not admit of supports for such an edifice.

I had rather a fright the other day in that same small craft, into which I had taken S——, with the intention of paddling myself a little way down the river and back. I used to row tolerably well, and was very fond of it, and frequently here take an oar, when the men are rowing me in the long-boat, as some sort of equivalent for my riding, of which, of course, I am entirely deprived on this little dikeland of ours; but paddling is a perfectly different pro-

cess, and one that I was very anxious to achieve. My
first strokes answered the purpose of sending the boat off
from shore, and for a few minutes I got on pretty well;
but presently I got tired of shifting the paddle from side
to side, a manœuvre which I accomplished very clumsily
and slowly, and yet, with all my precautions, not without
making the boat tip perilously. The immense breadth
and volume of the river suddenly seized my eyes and imagination as it were, and I began to fancy that if I got
into the middle of the stream I should not be able to
paddle myself back against it—which, indeed, might very
well have proved the case. Then I became nervous, and
paddled all on one side, by which means, of course, I only
turned the boat round. S—— began to fidget about,
getting up from where I had placed her, and terrifying
me with her unsteady motions and the rocking of the
canoe. I was now very much frightened, and saw that
I *must* get back to shore before I became more helpless
than I was beginning to feel; so, laying S—— down in
the bottom of the boat as a preliminary precaution, I
said to her with infinite emphasis, "Now lie still there,
and don't stir, or you'll be drowned," to which, with her
clear gray eyes fixed on me, and no sign whatever of
emotion, she replied deliberately, "I shall lie still here,
and won't stir, for I should not like to be drowned,"
which, for an atom not four years old, was rather philo-
sophical. Then I looked about me, and of course having
drifted, set steadily to work and paddled home, with my
heart in my mouth almost till we grazed the steps, and I
got my precious freight safe on shore again, since which I
have taken no more paddling lessons without my slave
and master, Jack.

We have had a death among the people since I last
wrote to you. A very valuable slave called Shadrach was
seized with a disease which is frequent, and very apt to

be fatal here—peripneumonia; and, in spite of all that could be done to save him, sank rapidly, and died after an acute illness of only three days.. The doctor came repeatedly from Darien, and the last night of the poor fellow's life —— himself watched with him. I suppose the general low diet of the negroes must produce some want of stamina in them; certainly, either from natural constitution or the effect of their habits of existence, or both, it is astonishing how much less power of resistance to disease they seem to possess than we do. If they are ill, the vital energy seems to sink immediately. This rice cultivation, too, although it does not affect them as it would whites—to whom, indeed, residence on the rice plantation after a certain season is impossible—is still, to a certain degree, deleterious even to the negroes. The proportion of sick is always greater here than on the cotton plantation, and the invalids of this place are not unfrequently sent down to St. Simon's to recover their strength, under the more favorable influences of the sea air and dry sandy soil of Hampton Point.

Yesterday afternoon the tepid warmth of the air and glassy stillness of the river seemed to me highly suggestive of fishing, and I determined, not having yet discovered what I could catch with what in these unknown waters, to try a little innocent paste bait—a mystery his initiation into which caused Jack much wonderment. The only hooks I had with me, however, had been bought in Darien —made, I should think, at the North expressly for this market; and so villainously bad were they, that, after trying them and my patience a reasonable time, I gave up the attempt and took a lesson in paddling instead. Among other items Jack told me of his own fishing experience was that he had more than once caught those most excellent creatures, Altamaha shad, by the fish themselves leaping out of the water and *landing*, as Jack expressed it, to

escape from the porpoises, which come in large schools up
the river to a considerable distance, occasioning, evidently,
much emotion in the bosoms of the legitimate inhabitants
of these muddy waters. Coasting the island on our return home, we found a trap, which the last time we exam-
ined it was tenanted by a creature called a mink, now occupied by an otter. The poor beast did not seem pleased
with his predicament; but the trap had been set by one
of the drivers, and, of course, Jack would not have meddled with it except upon my express order, which, in spite
of some pangs of pity for the otter, I did not like to give
him, as, in the extremely few resources of either profit or
pleasure possessed by the slaves, I could not tell at all
what might be the value of an otter to his captor.

Yesterday evening the burial of the poor man Shadrach
took place. I had been applied to for a sufficient quantity
of cotton cloth to make a winding-sheet for him, and just
as the twilight was thickening into darkness I went with
Mr. —— to the cottage of one of the slaves whom I may
have mentioned to you before—a cooper of the name of
London, the head of the religious party of the inhabitants
of the island, a Methodist preacher of no small intelligence
and influence among the people—who was to perform the
burial service. The coffin was laid on trestles in front of
the cooper's cottage, and a large assemblage of the people
had gathered round, many of the men carrying pine-wood
torches, the fitful glare of which glanced over the strange
assembly, where every pair of large white-rimmed eyes
turned upon —— and myself; we two poor creatures, on
this more solemn occasion, as well as on every other when
these people encounter us, being the objects of admiration
and wonderment, on which their gaze is immovably rivet-
ed. Presently the whole congregation uplifted their voices
in a hymn, the first high wailing notes of which—sung all
in unison, in the midst of these unwonted surroundings—

sent a thrill through all my nerves. When the chant ceased, cooper London began a prayer, and all the people knelt down in the sand, as I did also. Mr. —— alone remained standing in the presence of the dead man and of the living God to whom his slaves were now appealing. I can not tell you how profoundly the whole ceremony, if such it could be called, affected me; and there was nothing in the simple and pathetic supplication of the poor black artisan to check or interfere with the solemn influences of the whole scene. It was a sort of conventional Methodist prayer, and probably quite as conventional as all the rest was the closing invocation of God's blessing upon their master, their mistress, and our children; but this fairly overcame my composure, and I began to cry very bitterly; for these same individuals, whose implication in the state of things in the midst of which we are living, seemed to me as legitimate a cause for tears as for prayers. When the prayer was concluded we all rose, and, the coffin being taken up, proceeded to the people's burial-ground, when London read aloud portions of the funeral service from the Prayer-book — I presume the American Episcopal version of our Church service, for what he read appeared to be merely a selection from what was perfectly familiar to me; but whether he himself extracted what he uttered I did not inquire. Indeed, I was too much absorbed in the whole scene, and the many mingled emotions it excited of awe and pity, and an indescribable sensation of wonder at finding myself on this slave soil, surrounded by MY slaves, among whom again I knelt while the words proclaiming to the living and the dead the everlasting covenant of freedom, " I am the resurrection and the life," sounded over the prostrate throng, and mingled with the heavy flowing of the vast river sweeping, not far from where we stood, through the darkness by which we were now encompassed (beyond the immediate circle of our torch-bearers). There was some-thing painful to me in ——'s standing while we all knelt on the earth; for, though in any church in Philadelphia he would have stood during the praying of any minister, here I wished he would have knelt, to have given his slaves some token of his belief that—at least in the sight of that Master to whom we were addressing our worship —all men are equal. The service ended with a short address from London upon the subject of Lazarus, and the confirmation which the story of his resurrection afforded our hopes. The words were simple and rustic, and of course uttered in the peculiar sort of jargon which is the habitual negro speech; but there was nothing in the slight-est degree incongruous or grotesque in the matter or manner, and the exhortations not to steal, or lie, or neglect to work well for massa, with which the glorious hope of immortality was blended in the poor slave preacher's closing address, was a moral adaptation, as wholesome as it was touching, of the great Christian theory to the capacities and consciences of his hearers. When the coffin was lowered the grave was found to be partially filled with water —naturally enough, for the whole island is a mere swamp, off which the Altamaha is only kept from sweeping by the high dikes all round it. This seemed to shock and distress the people, and for the first time during the whole ceremony there were sounds of crying and exclamations of grief heard among them. Their chief expression of sorrow, however, when Mr. —— and myself bade them good-night at the conclusion of the service, was on account of my crying, which appeared to affect them very much, many of them mingling with their "Farewell, good-night, massa and missis," affectionate exclamations of "God bless you, missis; don't cry!" "Lor, missis, don't you cry so!" Mr. —— declined the assistance of any of the torch-bearers home, and bade them all go quietly to their

quarters; and as soon as they had dispersed, and we had
got beyond the fitful and unequal glaring of the torches,
we found the shining of the stars in the deep blue lovely
night sky quite sufficient to light our way along the dikes.
I could not speak to ——, but continued to cry as we
walked silently home; and, whatever his cogitations were,
they did not take the usual form with him of wordy demonstration, and so we returned from one of the most striking religious ceremonies at which I ever assisted. Arrived at the door of the house, we perceived that we had
been followed the whole way by the naked, noiseless feet
of a poor half-witted creature, a female idiot, whose mental incapacity, of course, in no respect unfits her for the
life of toil, little more intellectual than that of any beast
of burden, which is her allotted portion here. Some small
gratification was given to her, and she departed gibbering
and muttering in high glee. Think, E——, of that man
London, who, in spite of all the bitter barriers in his way,
has learned to read, has read his Bible, teaches it to his
unfortunate fellows, and is used by his owner and his owner's agents, for all these causes, as an effectual influence
for good over the slaves of whom he is himself the despised and injured companion. Like them, subject to the
driver's lash; like them, the helpless creature of his master's despotic will, without a right or a hope in this dreary
world. But, though the light he has attained must show
him the terrible aspects of his fate hidden by blessed ignorance from his companions, it reveals to him also other
rights and other hopes — another world, another life —
toward which he leads, according to the grace vouchsafed
to him, his poor fellow-slaves. How can we keep this
man in such a condition? How is such a cruel sin of injustice to be answered? Mr. ——, of course, sees and
feels none of this as I do, and, I should think, must regret
that he ever brought me here, to have my abhorrence of

the theory of slavery deepened, and strengthened every hour of my life, by what I see of its practice.

This morning I went over to Darien upon the very female errands of returning visits and shopping. ` In one respect (assuredly in none other) our life here resembles existence in Venice: we can never leave home for any purpose or in any direction but by boat—not, indeed, by gondola, but the sharp-cut, well-made light craft in which we take our walks on the water is a very agreeable species of conveyance. One of my visits this morning was to a certain Miss ——, whose rather grandiloquent name and very striking style of beauty exceedingly well became the daughter of an ex-governor of Georgia. As for the residence of this princess, it was like all the planters' residences that I have seen, and such as a well-to-do English farmer would certainly not inhabit. Occasional marks of former elegance or splendor survive sometimes in the size of the rooms, sometimes in a little carved woodwork about the mantel-pieces or wainscotings of these mansions; but all things have a Castle Rackrent air of neglect, and dreary, careless untidiness, with which the dirty, barefooted negro servants are in excellent keeping. Occasionally a huge pair of dazzling shirt-gills, out of which a black visage grins as out of some vast white paper cornet, adorns the sable footman of the establishment, but unfortunately without at all necessarily indicating any downward prolongation of the garment; and the perfect tulip-bed of a head-handkerchief with which the female attendants of these "great families" love to bedizen themselves frequently stands them instead of every other most indispensable article of female attire.

As for my shopping, the goods, or rather "bads," at which I used to grumble, in your village emporium at Lenox, are what may be termed "first rate," both in excellence and elegance, compared with the vile products of every sort which we wretched Southerners are expected to accept as the conveniences of life in exchange for current coin of the realm. I regret to say, moreover, that all these infamous articles are Yankee made—expressly for this market, where every species of *thing* (to use the most general term I can think of), from list shoes to piano-fortes, is procured from the North—almost always New England, utterly worthless of its kind, and dearer than the most perfect specimens of the same articles would be any where else. The incredible variety and ludicrous combinations of goods to be met with in one of these Southern shops beats the stock of your village omnium-gatherum hollow : to be sure, one class of articles, and that probably the most in demand here, is not sold over any counter in Massachusetts—cowhides and man-traps, of which a large assortment enters necessarily into the furniture of every Southern shop.

In passing to-day along the deep sand road calling itself the street of Darien, my notice was attracted by an extremely handsome and intelligent-looking poodle, standing by a little wizen-looking knife-grinder, whose features were evidently European, though he was nearly as black as a negro, who, strange to say, was discoursing with him in very tolerable French. The impulse of curiosity led me to accost the man at the grindstone, when his companion immediately made off. The itinerant artisan was from Aix, in Provence : think of wandering thence to Darien in Georgia! I asked him about the negro who was talking to him ; he said he knew nothing of him but that he was a slave belonging to somebody in the town. And upon my expressing surprise at his having left his own beautiful and pleasant country for this dreary distant region, he answered, with a shrug and a smile, " Oui, madame, c'est vrai ; c'est un joli pays, mais dans ce pays-là, quand un homme n'a rien, c'est rien pour toujours." A property which many, no doubt, have come hither, like the little French knife-grinder, to increase, without succeeding in the struggle much better than he appeared to have done.

DEAR E——,—Having made a fresh, and, as I thought, more promising purchase of fishing-tackle, Jack and I betook ourselves to the river, and succeeded in securing some immense catfish, of which, to tell you the truth, I am most horribly afraid when I have caught them. The dexterity necessary for taking them off the hook so as to avoid the spikes on their backs, and the spikes on each side of their gills, the former having to be pressed down, and the two others pressed up, before you can get any purchase on the slimy beast (for it is smooth skinned and without scales, to add to the difficulty)—these conditions, I say, make the catching of catfish questionable sport. Then, too, they hiss, and spit, and swear at one, and are altogether devilish in their aspect and demeanor; nor are they good for food, except, as Jack with much humility said this morning, for colored folks—"Good for colored folks, missis; me 'spect not good enough for white people." That 'spect, meaning *expect*, has sometimes a possible meaning of *suspect*, which would give the sentence in which it occurs a very humorous turn, and I always take the benefit of that interpretation. After exhausting the charms of our occupation, finding that catfish were likely to be our principal haul, I left the river and went my rounds to the hospitals. On my way I encountered two batches of small black fry, Hannah's children and poor Psyche's children, looking really as neat and tidy as children of the bettermost class of artisans among ourselves. These people are so quick and so imitative that it would be the easiest thing in the world to improve their physical condition by appealing to their emulative propensities

Their passion for what is *genteel* might be used most advantageously in the same direction; and, indeed, I think it would be difficult to find people who offered such a fair purchase by so many of their characteristics to the hand of the reformer.

Returning from the hospital, I was accosted by poor old Teresa, the wretched negress who had complained to me so grievously of her back being broken by hard work and childbearing. She was in a dreadful state of excitement, which she partly presently communicated to me, because she said Mr. O—— had ordered her to be flogged for having complained to me as she did. It seems to me that I have come down here to be tortured, for this punishing these wretched creatures for crying out to me for help is really converting me into a source of increased misery to them. It is almost more than I can endure to hear these horrid stories of lashings inflicted because I have been invoked; and though I dare say Mr. ——, thanks to my passionate appeals to him, gives me little credit for prudence or self-command, I have some, and I exercise it, too, when I listen to such tales as these with my teeth set fast and my lips closed. Whatever I may do to the master, I hold my tongue to the slaves, and I wonder how I do it.

In the afternoon I rowed with Mr. —— to another island in the broad waters of the Altamaha, called Tunno's Island, to return the visit of a certain Dr. T——, the proprietor of the island, named after him, as our rice swamp is after Major ——. I here saw growing in the open air the most beautiful gardinias I ever beheld; the branches were as high and as thick as the largest clumps of kalmia that grow in your woods; but whereas the tough, stringy, fibrous branches of these gives them a straggling appearance, these magnificent masses of dark, shiny, glossy green leaves were quite compact, and I can not conceive any thing lovelier or more delightful than they would be starred all over with their thick-leaved, cream-white odoriferous blossoms.

In the course of our visit a discussion arose as to the credibility of any negro assertion, though, indeed, that could hardly be called a discussion that was simply a chorus of assenting opinions. No negro was to be believed on any occasion or any subject. No doubt they are habitual liars, for they are slaves; but there are some thrice honorable exceptions, who, being slaves, are yet not liars; and certainly the vice results much more from the circumstances in which they are placed than from any natural tendency to untruth in their case. The truth is that they are always considered as false and deceitful, and it is very seldom that any special investigation of the facts of any particular case is resorted to in their behalf. They are always prejudged on their supposed general characteristics, and never judged after the fact on the merit of any special instance.

A question which was discussed in the real sense of the term was that of plowing the land instead of having it turned with the spade or hoe. I listened to this with great interest, for Jack and I had had some talk upon this subject, which began in his ardently expressed wish that massa would allow his land to be plowed, and his despairing conclusion that he never would, " 'cause horses more costly to keep than colored folks," and plowing, therefore, dearer than hoeing or digging. I had ventured to suggest to Mr. —— the possibility of plowing some of the fields on the island, and his reply was that the whole land was too moist, and too much interrupted with the huge masses of the cypress yam roots, which would turn the share of any plow; yet there is land belonging to our neighbor Mr. G——, on the other side of the river, where the conditions of the soil must be precisely the same, and yet which is being plowed before our faces.

On Mr. ——'s adjacent plantation the plow is also used extensively and successfully.

On my return to our own island I visited another of the hospitals, and the settlements to which it belonged. The condition of these places and of their inhabitants is, of course, the same all over the plantation, and if I were to describe them I should but weary you with a repetition of identical phenomena: filthy, wretched, almost naked, always barelegged and barefooted children; negligent, ignorant, wretched mothers, whose apparent indifference to the plight of their offspring, and utter incapacity to alter it, are the inevitable result of their slavery. It is hopeless to attempt to reform their habits or improve their condition while the women are condemned to field labor; nor is it possible to overestimate the bad moral effect of the system as regards the women entailing this enforced separation from their children, and neglect of all the cares and duties of mother, nurse, and even housewife, which are all merged in the mere physical toil of a human hoeing machine. It seems to me too—but upon this point I can not, of course, judge as well as the persons accustomed to and acquainted with the physical capacities of their slaves—that the labor is not judiciously distributed in many cases—at least not as far as the women are concerned. It is true that every able-bodied woman is made the most of in being driven afield as long as, under all and any circumstances, she is able to wield a hoe; but, on the other hand, stout, hale, hearty girls and boys, of from eight to twelve and older, are allowed to lounge about, filthy and idle, with no pretense of an occupation but what they call "tend baby," *i. e.*, see to the life and limbs of the little slave infants, to whose mothers, working in distant fields, they carry them during the day to be suckled, and for the rest of the time leave them to crawl and kick in the filthy cabins or on the broiling sand

F

which surrounds them, in which industry, excellent enough
for the poor babies, these big lazy youths and lasses emu-
late them.   Again, I find many women who have borne
from five to ten children rated as workers, precisely as
young women in the prime of their strength who have
had none; this seems a cruel carelessness.   To be sure,
while the women are pregnant their task is diminished,
and this is one of the many indirect inducements held out
to reckless propagation, which has a sort of premium offered to it in the consideration of less work and more
food, counterbalanced by none of the sacred responsibilities which hallow and ennoble the relation of parent and
child; in short, as their lives are for the most part those
of mere animals, their increase is literally mere animal
breeding, to which every encouragement is given, for it
adds to the master's live-stock and the value of his estate.

DEAR E——,—To-day I have the pleasure of announc-
ing to you a variety of improvements about to be made in
the Infirmary of the island.   There is to be a third story
—a mere loft, indeed—added to the building; but, by affording more room for the least distressing cases of sickness to be drafted off into, it will leave the ground floor
and room above it comparatively free for the most miserable of these unfortunates.   To my unspeakable satisfaction, these destitute apartments are to be furnished with
bedsteads, mattresses, pillows, and blankets; and I feel a
little comforted for the many heartaches my life here in-
flicts upon me — at least some of my twinges will have
wrought this poor alleviation of their wretchedness for
the slaves when prostrated by disease or pain.

I had hardly time to return from the hospital home this
morning before one of the most tremendous storms I ever
saw burst over the island.   Your Northern hills, with their

solemn pine woods, and fresh streams and lakes, telling
of a cold rather than a warm climate, always seem to me
as if undergoing some strange and unnatural visitation
when one of your heavy summer thunder-storms bursts
over them. Snow and frost, hail and, above all, wind,
trailing rain-clouds and brilliant northern lights, are your
appropriate sky phenomena; here, thunder and lightning
seem as if they might have been invented. Even in winter (remember, we are now in February) they appear neither astonishing nor unseasonable, and I should think in
summer (but Heaven defend me from ever making good
my supposition) lightning must be as familiar to these
sweltering lands and slimy waters as sunlight itself.

The afternoon cleared off most beautifully, and Jack
and I went out on the river to catch what might be
caught. Jack's joyful excitement was extreme at my an-
nouncing to him the fact that Mr. —— had consented to
try plowing on some of the driest portions of the island
instead of the slow and laborious process of hoeing the
fields; this is a disinterested exultation on his part, for,
at any rate, as long as I am here, he will certainly be nothing but "my boy Jack," and I should think, after my departure, will never be degraded to the rank of a field-hand
or common laborer. Indeed, the delicacy of his health, to
which his slight, slender figure and languid face bear witness, and which was one reason of his appointment to the
eminence of being "my slave," would, I should think, prevent the poor fellow's ever being a very robust or useful
working animal.

On my return from the river I had a long and painful
conversation with Mr. —— upon the subject of the flogging which had been inflicted on the wretched Teresa.
These discussions are terrible: they throw me into perfect
agonies of distress for the slaves, whose position is utterly hopeless; for myself, whose intervention in their behalf

sometimes seems to me worse than useless; for Mr. ——, whose share in this horrible system fills me by turns with indignation and pity. But, after all, what can he do? how can he help it all? Moreover, born and bred in America, how should he care or wish to help it? and, of course, he does not; and I am in despair that he does not: et voilà, it is a happy and hopeful plight for us both. He maintained that there had been neither hardship nor injustice in the case of Teresa's flogging; and that, moreover, she had not been flogged at all for complaining to me, but simply because her allotted task was not done at the appointed time. Of course this was the result of her having come to appeal to me instead of going to her labor; and as she knew perfectly well the penalty she was incurring, he maintained that there was neither hardship nor injustice in the case; the whole thing was a regularly established law, with which all the slaves were perfectly well acquainted; and this case was no exception whatever. The circumstance of my being on the island could not, of course, be allowed to overthrow the whole system of discipline established to secure the labor and obedience of the slaves; and if they chose to try experiments as to that fact, they and I must take the consequences. At the end of the day, the driver of the gang to which Teresa belongs reported her work not done, and Mr. O—— ordered him to give her the usual number of stripes, which order the driver of course obeyed, without knowing how Teresa had employed her time instead of hoeing. But Mr. O—— knew well enough, for the wretched woman told me that she had herself told him she should appeal to me about her weakness, and suffering, and inability to do the work exacted from her.

He did not, however, think proper to exceed in her punishment the usual number of stripes allotted to the non-performance of the appointed daily task, and Mr. ——

pronounced the whole transaction perfectly satisfactory and *en règle*. The common drivers are limited in their powers of chastisement, not being allowed to administer more than a certain number of lashes to their fellow-slaves. Head man Frank, as he is called, has alone the privilege of exceeding this limit; and the overseer's latitude of infliction is only curtailed by the necessity of avoiding injury to life or limb. The master's irresponsible power has no such bound. When I was thus silenced on the particular case under discussion, I resorted, in my distress and indignation, to the abstract question, as I never can refrain from doing; and to Mr. ——'s assertion of the justice of poor Teresa's punishment, I retorted the manifest injustice of unpaid and enforced labor; the brutal inhumanity of allowing a man to strip and lash a woman, the mother of ten children; to exact from her toil which was to maintain in luxury two idle young men, the owners of the plantation. I said I thought female labor of the sort exacted from these slaves, and corporal chastisement such as they endure, must be abhorrent to any manly or humane man. Mr. —— said he thought it was *disagreeable*, and left me to my reflections with that concession. My letter has been interrupted for the last three days—by nothing special, however. My occupations and interests here, of course, know no change; but Mr. —— has been anxious for a little while past that we should go down to St. Simon's, the cotton plantation.

We shall suffer less from the heat, which I am beginning to find oppressive on this swamp island; and he himself wished to visit that part of his property, whither he had not yet been since our arrival in Georgia; so the day before yesterday he departed to make the necessary arrangements for our removal thither; and my time in the mean while has been taken up in fitting him out for his departure.

In the morning Jack and I took our usual paddle, and, having the tackle on board, tried fishing. I was absorbed in many sad and serious considerations, and, wonderful to relate (for you know, ——, how keen an angler I am), had lost all consciousness of my occupation until, after I know not how long a time elapsing without the shadow of a nibble, I was recalled to a most ludicrous perception of my ill success by Jack's sudden observation, "Missis, fishing berry good fun when um fish bite." This settled the fishing for that morning, and I let Jack paddle me down the broad turbid stream, endeavoring to answer in the most comprehensible manner to his keen but utterly undeveloped intellects the innumerable questions with which he plied me about Philadelphia, about England, about the Atlantic, etc. He dilated much upon the charms of St. Simon's, to which he appeared very glad that we were going; and, among other items of description, mentioned what I was very glad to hear, that it was a beautiful place for riding, and that I should be able to indulge to my heart's content in my favorite exercise, from which I have, of course, been utterly debarred in this small dikeland of ours. He insinuated more than once his hope and desire that he might be allowed to accompany me, but as I knew nothing at all about his capacity for equestrian exercises, or any of the arrangements that might or might not interfere with such a plan, I was discreetly silent, and took no notice of his most comically turned hints on the subject. In our row we started a quantity of wild duck, and he told me there was a great deal of game at St. Simon's, but that the people did not contrive to catch much, though they laid traps constantly for it. Of course their possessing fire-arms is quite out of the question; but this abundance of what must be to them such especially desirable prey makes the fact a great hardship. I almost wonder they don't learn to shoot like savages with

bows and arrows; but these would be weapons, and equally forbidden them.

In the afternoon I saw Mr. —— off for St. Simon's; it
is fifteen miles lower down the river, and a large island
at the very mouth of the Altamaha.

The boat he went in was a large, broad, rather heavy,
though well-built craft, by no means as swift or elegant
as the narrow eight-oared long-boat in which he generally takes his walks on the water, but well adapted for
the traffic between the two plantations, where it serves the
purpose of a sort of omnibus or stage-coach for the transfer of the people from one to the other, and of a baggage-
wagon or cart for the conveyance of all sorts of household goods, chattels, and necessaries. Mr. —— sat in the
middle of a perfect chaos of such freight; and as the boat
pushed off, and the steersman took her into the stream,
the men at the oars set up a chorus, which they continued
to chant in unison with each other, and in time with their
stroke, till the voices and oars were heard no more from
the distance. I believe I have mentioned to you before
the peculiar characteristics of this veritable negro min-
strelsy—how they all sing in unison, having never, it appears, attempted or heard any thing like part-singing.
Their voices seem oftener tenor than any other quality,
and the tune and time they keep something quite wonderful; such truth of intonation and accent would make
almost any music agreeable. That which I have heard
these people sing is often plaintive and pretty, but almost
always has some resemblance to tunes with which they
must have become acquainted through the instrumentality
of white men; their overseers or masters whistling Scotch
or Irish airs, of which they have produced by ear these
rifacciamenti. The note for note reproduction of "Ah!
vous dirai-je, maman?" in one of the most popular of the
so-called negro melodies with which all America and En-

gland are familiar, is an example of this very transparent plagiarism; and the tune with which Mr. ——'s rowers started him down the Altamaha, as I stood at the steps to see him off, was a very distinct descendant of "Coming through the Rye." The words, however, were astonishingly primitive, especially the first line, which, when it burst from their eight throats in high unison, sent me into fits of laughter.

> "Jenny shake her toe at me,
>   Jenny gone away;
> Jenny shake her toe at me,
>   Jenny gone away.
> Hurrah! Miss Susy, oh!
>   Jenny gone away;
> Hurrah! Miss Susy, oh!
>   Jenny gone away."

What the obnoxious Jenny meant by shaking her toe, whether defiance or mere departure, I never could ascertain, but her going away was an unmistakable subject of satisfaction; and the pause made on the last "oh!" before the final announcement of her departure, had really a good deal of dramatic and musical effect. Except the extemporaneous chants in our honor, of which I have written to you before, I have never heard the negroes on Mr. ——'s plantation sing any words that could be said to have any sense. To one, an extremely pretty, plaintive, and original air, there was but one line, which was repeated with a sort of wailing chorus—

> "Oh! my massa told me, there's no grass in Georgia."

Upon inquiring the meaning of which, I was told it was supposed to be the lamentation of a slave from one of the more northerly states, Virginia or Carolina, where the labor of hoeing the weeds, or grass as they call it, is not nearly so severe as here, in the rice and cotton lands of

Georgia. Another very pretty and pathetic tune began with words that seemed to promise something sentimental—

> "Fare you well, and good-by, oh, oh!
> I'm goin' away to leave you, oh, oh!"

but immediately went off into nonsense verses about gentlemen in the parlor drinking wine and cordial, and ladies in the drawing-room drinking tea and coffee, etc. I have heard that many of the masters and overseers on these plantations prohibit melancholy tunes or words, and encourage nothing but cheerful music and senseless words, deprecating the effect of sadder strains upon the slaves, whose peculiar musical sensibility might be expected to make them especially excitable by any songs of a plaintive character, and having any reference to their particular hardships. If it is true, I think it a judicious precaution enough—these poor slaves are just the sort of people over whom a popular musical appeal to their feelings and passions would have an immense power.

In the evening, Mr. ——'s departure left me to the pleasures of an uninterrupted *tête-à-tête* with his cross-eyed overseer, and I endeavored, as I generally do, to atone by my conversibleness and civility for the additional trouble which, no doubt, all my outlandish ways and notions are causing the worthy man. So suggestive (to use the new-fangled jargon about books) a woman as myself is, I suspect, an intolerable nuisance in these parts; and poor Mr. O—— can not very well desire Mr. —— to send me away, however much he may wish that he would; so that figuratively, as well as literally, I fear the worthy master *me voit d'un mauvais œil*, as the French say. I asked him several questions about some of the slaves who had managed to learn to read, and by what means they had been able to do so. As teaching them is strictly prohibited by the laws, they who instructed them, and such of them as

F 2

acquired the knowledge, must have been not a little determined and persevering. This was my view of the case, of course, and of course it was not the overseer's. I asked him if many of Mr. ——'s slaves could read. He said "No ; very few, he was happy to say, but those few were just so many too many." "Why, had he observed any insubordination in those who did ?" And I reminded him of Cooper London, the Methodist preacher, whose performance of the burial service had struck me so much some time ago, to whose exemplary conduct and character there is but one concurrent testimony all over the plantation. No ; he had no special complaint to bring against the lettered members of his subject community, but he spoke by anticipation. Every step they take toward intelligence and enlightenment lessens the probability of their acquiescing in their condition. Their condition is not to be changed—ergo, they had better not learn to read ; a very succinct and satisfactory argument as far as it goes, no doubt, and one to which I had not a word to reply, at any rate, to Mr. O——, as I did not feel called upon to discuss the abstract justice or equity of the matter with him ; indeed he, to a certain degree, gave up that part of the position, starting with "I don't say whether it's right or wrong ;" and in all conversations that I have had with the Southerners upon these subjects, whether out of civility to what may be supposed to be an Englishwoman's prejudices, or a forlorn respect to their own convictions, the question of the fundamental wrong of slavery is generally admitted, or, at any rate, certainly never denied. That part of the subject is summarily dismissed, and all its other aspects vindicated, excused, and even lauded, with untiring eloquence. Of course, of the abstract question I could judge before I came here, but I confess I had not the remotest idea how absolutely my observation of every detail of the system, as a practical iniquity, would go to confirm my opinion of its abomination. Mr. O—— went on to condemn and utterly denounce all the preaching, and teaching, and moral instruction upon religious subjects which people in the South, pressed upon by Northern opinion, are endeavoring to give their slaves. The kinder and the more cowardly masters are anxious to evade the charge of keeping their negroes in brutish ignorance, and so they crumble what they suppose and hope may prove a little harmless religious enlightenment, which, mixed up with much religious authority on the subject of submission and fidelity to masters, they trust their slaves may swallow without its doing them any harm—*i. e.*, that they may be better Christians and better slaves—and so, indeed, no doubt they are; but it is a very dangerous experiment, and from Mr. O——'s point of view I quite agree with him. The letting out of water, or the letting in of light, in infinitesimal quantities, is not always easy. The half-wicked of the earth are the leaks through which wickedness is eventually swamped; compromises forerun absolute surrender in most matters, and fools and cowards are, in such cases, the instruments of Providence for their own defeat. Mr. O—— stated unequivocally his opinion that free labor would be more profitable on the plantations than the work of slaves, which, being compulsory, was of the worst possible quality and the smallest possible quantity; then the charge of them before and after they are able to work is onerous, the cost of feeding and clothing them very considerable, and, upon the whole, he, a Southern overseer, pronounced himself decidedly in favor of free labor, upon grounds of expediency. Having at the beginning of our conversation declined discussing the moral aspect of slavery, evidently not thinking that position tenable, I thought I had every right to consider Mr. ——'s slave-driver a decided Abolitionist.

I had been anxious to enlist his sympathies on behalf

of my extreme desire to have some sort of garden, but
did not succeed in inspiring him with my enthusiasm on
the subject; he said there was but one garden that he
knew of in the whole neighborhood of Darien, and that
was our neighbor, old Mr. C——'s, a Scotchman on St.
Simon's. I remembered the splendid gardinias on Tunno's Island, and referred to them as a proof of the material for ornamental gardening. He laughed, and said rice
and cotton crops were the ornamental gardening princi-
pally admired by the planters, and that, to the best of his
belief, there was not another decent kitchen or flower garden in the state but the one he had mentioned.

The next day after this conversation, I walked with my
horticultural zeal much damped, and wandered along the
dike by the broad river, looking at some pretty peach-
trees in blossom, and thinking what a curse of utter stagnation this slavery produces, and how intolerable to me a
life passed within its stifling influence would be. Think
of peach-trees in blossom in the middle of February! It
does seem cruel, with such a sun and soil, to be told that
a garden is worth nobody's while here; however, Mr.
O—— said that he believed the wife of the former overseer had made a "sort of a garden" at St. Simon's. We
shall see "what sort" it turns out to be. While I was
standing on the dike, ruminating above the river, I saw a
beautiful white bird of the crane species alight not far
from me. I do not think a little knowledge of natural
history would diminish the surprise and admiration with
which I regard the, to me, unwonted specimens of animal
existence that I encounter every day, and of which I do
not even know the names. Ignorance is an odious thing.
The birds here are especially beautiful, I think. I saw
one the other day, of what species of course I do not
know, of a warm and rich brown, with a scarlet hood and
crest—a lovely creature, about the size of your Northern
robin, but more elegantly shaped.

This morning, instead of my usual visit to the Infirmary, I went to look at the work and workers in the threshing mill: all was going on actively and orderly under the superintendence of head man Frank, with whom, and a very sagacious clever fellow who manages the steam power of the mill, and is honorably distinguished as Engineer Ned, I had a small chat. There is one among various drawbacks to the comfort and pleasure of our intercourse with these colored "men and brethren," at least in their slave condition, which certainly exercises my fortitude not a little—the swarms of fleas that cohabit with these sable dependents of ours are—well—incredible; moreover, they are by no means the only or most objectionable companions one borrows from them; and I never go to the Infirmary, where I not unfrequently am requested to look at very dirty limbs and bodies in very dirty draperies, without coming away with a strong inclination to throw myself into the water, and my clothes into the fire, which last would be expensive. I do not suppose that these hateful consequences of dirt and disorder are worse here than among the poor and neglected human creatures who swarm in the lower parts of European cities; but my call to visit them has never been such as that which constrains me to go daily among these poor people, and although on one or two occasions I have penetrated into fearfully foul and filthy abodes of misery in London, I have never rendered the same personal services to their inhabitants that I do to Mr. ——'s slaves, and so have not incurred the same amount of entomological inconvenience.

After leaving the mill I prolonged my walk, and came, for the first time, upon one of the "gangs," as they are called, in full field work. Upon my appearance and approach there was a momentary suspension of labor, and the usual chorus of screams and ejaculations of welcome, affection, and infinite desires for infinite small indulgences.

I was afraid to stop their work, not feeling at all sure that urging a conversation with me would be accepted as any excuse for an uncompleted task, or avert the fatal infliction of the usual award of stripes; so I hurried off and left them to their hoeing.

On my way home I was encountered by London, our Methodist preacher, who accosted me with a request for a Prayer-book and Bible, and expressed his regret at hearing that we were so soon going to St. Simon's. I promised him his holy books, and asked him how he had learned to read, but found it impossible to get him to tell me. I wonder if he thought he should be putting his teacher, whoever he was, in danger of the penalty of the law against instructing the slaves, if he told me who he was; it was impossible to make him do so, so that, besides his other good qualities, he appears to have that most unusual one of all in an uneducated person—discretion. He certainly is a most remarkable man.

After parting with him, I was assailed by a small gang of children, clamoring for the indulgence of some meat, which they besought me to give them. Animal food is only allowed to certain of the harder working men, hedgers and ditchers, and to them only occasionally, and in very moderate rations. My small cannibals clamored round me for flesh, as if I had had a butcher's cart in my pocket, till I began to laugh, and then to run, and away they came, like a pack of little black wolves, at my heels, shrieking, "Missis, you gib me piece meat—missis, you gib me meat," till I got home. At the door I found another petitioner, a young woman named Maria, who brought a fine child in her arms, and demanded a present of a piece of flannel. Upon my asking her who her husband was, she replied, without much hesitation, that she did not possess any such appendage. I gave another look at her bonny baby, and went into the house to get the flannel for her. I afterward heard from Mr. —— that she and two other girls of her age, about seventeen, were the only instances on the island of women with illegitimate children.

After I had been in the house a little while, I was summoned out again to receive the petition of certain poor women in the family-way to have their work lightened. I was, of course, obliged to tell them that I could not interfere in the matter; that their master was away, and that, when he came back, they must present their request to him: they said they had already begged "massa," and he had refused, and they thought, perhaps, if "missis" begged "massa" for them, he would lighten their task. Poor "missis," poor "massa," poor woman, that I am to have such prayers addressed to me! I had to tell them that, if they had already spoken to their master, I was afraid my doing so would be of no use, but that when he came back I would try; so, choking with crying, I turned away from them, and re-entered the house, to the chorus of "Oh, thank you, missis! God bless you, missis!" E——, I think an improvement might be made upon that caricature published a short time ago, called the "Chivalry of the South." I think an elegant young Carolinian or Georgian gentleman, whip in hand, driving a gang of "lusty women," as they are called here, would be a pretty version of the "Chivalry of the South"—a little coarse, I am afraid you will say. Oh! quite horribly coarse, but then so true—a great matter in works of art, which nowadays appear to be thought excellent only in proportion to their lack of ideal elevation. That would be a subject, and a treatment of it, which could not be accused of imaginative exaggeration, at any rate.

In the evening I mentioned the petitions of these poor women to Mr. O——, thinking that perhaps he had the power to lessen their tasks. He seemed evidently annoyed at their having appealed to me; said that their work was not a bit too much for them, and that constantly they were *shamming* themselves in the family-way in order to obtain a diminution of their labor. Poor creatures! I suppose some of them do; but, again, it must be a hard matter for those who do not, not to obtain the mitigation of their toil which their condition requires; for their assertion and their evidence are never received: they can't be believed, even if they were upon oath, say their white taskmasters; why? because they have never been taught the obligations of an oath, to whom made, or wherefore binding; and they are punished both directly and indirectly for their moral ignorance, as if it were a natural and incorrigible element of their character, instead of the inevitable result of their miserable position. The oath of any and every scoundrelly fellow with a white skin is received, but not that of such a man as Frank, Ned, old Jacob, or Cooper London.

DEAREST E——,—I think it right to begin this letter with an account of a most prosperous fishing expedition Jack and I achieved the other morning. It is true we still occasionally drew up huge catfish, with their detestable beards and spikes, but we also captivated some magnificent perch, and the Altamaha perch are worth one's while both to catch and to eat. On a visit I had to make on the main land the same day, I saw a tiny strip of garden ground, rescued from the sandy road called the street, perfectly filled with hyacinths, double jonquils, and snowdrops, a charming nosegay for February 11. After leaving the boat on my return home, I encountered a curious creature walking all sideways, a small cross between a lobster and a crab. One of the negroes to whom I applied for its denomination informed me that it was a land-crab, with which general description of this very peculiar multipede you must be satisfied, for I can tell you no more. I went a little farther, as the nursery rhyme says, and met with a snake; and, not being able to determine, at ignorant first sight, whether it was a malignant serpent or not, I ingloriously took to my heels, and came home on the full run. It is the first of these exceedingly displeasing animals I have encountered here; but Jack, for my consolation, tells me that they abound on St. Simon's, whither we are going — "rattlesnakes, and all kinds," says he, with an affluence of promise in his tone that is quite agreeable. Rattlesnakes will be quite enough of a treat, without the vague horrors that may be comprised in the additional "all kinds." Jack's account of the game on St. Simon's is really quite tantalizing to me, who can not carry a gun any more than if I were a slave. He says that partridges, woodcocks, snipe, and wild duck abound, so that, at any rate, our table ought to be well supplied. His account of the bears that are still to be found in the woods of the main land is not so pleasant, though he says they do no harm to the people if they are not meddled with, but that they steal the corn from the fields when it is ripe, and actually swim the river to commit their depredations on the islands. It seems difficult to believe this, looking at this wide and heavy stream, though, to be sure, I did once see a young horse swim across the St. Lawrence, between Montreal and Quebec, a feat of natation which much enlarged my belief in what quadrupeds may accomplish when they have no choice between swimming and sinking.

You can not imagine how great a triumph the virtue next to godliness is making under my auspices and a judicious system of small bribery. I can hardly stir now without being assailed with cries of "Missis, missis, me mind chile, me bery clean," or the additional gratifying fact, "and chile too, him bery clean." This virtue, however, if painful to the practisers, as no doubt it is, is expensive, too, to me, and I shall have to try some moral influence equivalent in value to a cent current coin of the realm. What a poor chance, indeed, the poor abstract idea runs! however, it is really a comfort to see the poor little woolly heads now, in most instances, stripped of their additional filthy artificial envelopes.

In my afternoon's row to-day I passed a huge dead alligator, lying half in and half out of the muddy slime of the river bank — a most hideous object it was, and I was glad to turn my eyes to the beautiful surface of the mid stream, all burnished with sunset glories, and broken with the vivacious gambols of a school of porpoises. It is curious, I think, that these creatures should come fifteen miles from the sea to enliven the waters round our little rice swamp.

While rowing this evening, I was led by my conversation with Jack to some of those reflections with which my mind is naturally incessantly filled here, but which I am obliged to be very careful not to give any utterance to. The testimony of no negro is received in a Southern court of law, and the reason commonly adduced for this is, that the state of ignorance in which the negroes are necessarily kept renders them incapable of comprehending the obligations of an oath, and yet, with an inconsistency which might be said to border on effrontery, these same people are admitted to the most holy sacrament of the Church, and are certainly thereby supposed to be capable of assuming the highest Christian obligations, and the entire fulfillment of God's commandments, including, of course, the duty of speaking the truth at all times.

As we were proceeding down the river, we met the flat, as it is called, a huge sort of clumsy boat, more like a raft than any other species of craft, coming up from St. Simon's with its usual swarthy freight of Mr. ——'s dependents from that place. I made Jack turn our canoe, because the universal outcries and exclamations very distinctly intimated that I should be expected to be at home to receive the homage of this cargo of "massa's people." No sooner, indeed, had I disembarked and reached the house, than a dark cloud of black life filled the piazza and swarmed up the steps, and I had to shake hands, like a popular president, till my arm ached at the shoulder-joint.

When this tribe had dispersed itself, a very old woman, with a remarkably intelligent, nice-looking young girl, came forward and claimed my attention. The old woman, who must, I think, by her appearance, have been near seventy, had been one of the house servants on St. Simon's Island in Major ——'s time, and retained a certain dignified courtesy and respectfulness of manner which is by no means an uncommon attribute of the better class of slaves, whose intercourse with their masters, while tending to expand their intelligence, cultivates, at the same time, the natural turn for good manners which is, I think, a distinctive peculiarity of negroes, if not in the kingdom of Dahomey, certainly in the United States of America. If it can be for a moment attributed to the beneficent influence of slavery on their natures (and I think slaveowners are quite likely to imagine so), it is curious enough that there is hardly any alloy whatever of cringing servility, or even humility, in the good manners of the blacks, but a rather courtly and affable condescension which, combined with their affection for, and misapplication of, long words, produces an exceedingly comical effect. Old House Molly, after congratulating herself, with many thanks to heaven, for having spared her to see "massa's" wife and children, drew forward her young companion, and informed me she was one of her numerous grandchildren. The damsel, ycleped Louisa, made rather a shamefaced obeisance, and her old grandmother went on to inform

me that she had only lately been forgiven by the overseer
for an attempt to run away from the plantation. I inquired the cause of her desire to do so—a "thrashing"
she had got for an unfinished task—" but lor, missis," explained the old woman, "taint no use—what use nigger
run away?—de swamp all round; dey get in dar, an' dey
starve to def, or de snakes eat 'em up—massa's nigger,
dey don't neber run away;" and if the good lady's account of their prospects in doing so is correct (which,
substituting biting for eating on the part of the snakes, it
undoubtedly is), one does not see exactly what particular
merit the institution of slavery as practiced on Mr. ——'s
plantation derives from the fact that his "nigger don't
neber run away."

After dismissing Molly and her granddaughter, I was
about to re-enter the house, when I was stopped by Betty, head man Frank's wife, who came with a petition that
she might be baptized. As usual with all requests involving any thing more than an immediate physical indulgence, I promised to refer the matter to Mr. ——, but expressed some surprise that Betty, now by no means a
young woman, should have postponed a ceremony which
the religious among the slaves are apt to attach much importance to. She told me she had more than once applied for this permission to Massa K—— (the former overseer), but had never been able to obtain it, but that now
she thought she would ask " de missis."*

* Of this woman's life on the plantation I subsequently learned the
following circumstances: She was the wife of head man Frank, the
most intelligent and trustworthy of Mr. ——'s slaves; the head driver
—second in command to the overseer, and, indeed, second to none during the pestilential season, when the rice swamps can not with impunity be inhabited by any white man, and when, therefore, the whole force
employed in its cultivation on the island remains entirely under his
authority and control. His wife—a tidy, trim, intelligent woman, with
a pretty figure, but a decidedly negro face—was taken from him by the

Yesterday afternoon I received a visit from the wife of our neighbor, Dr. T——. As usual, she exclaimed at my good fortune in having a white woman with my children when she saw M——, and, as usual, went on to expatiate on the utter impossibility of finding a trustworthy nurse any where in the South, to whom your children could be safely confided for a day or even an hour; as usual, too, the causes of this unworthiness or incapacity for a confidential servant's occupation were ignored, and the fact laid to the natural defects of the negro race. I am sick and weary of this cruel and ignorant folly. This afternoon I went out to refresh myself with a row on the broad Altamaha and the conversation of my slave Jack, which is, I assure you, by no means devoid of interest of various kinds, pathetic and humorous. I do not know that Jack's scientific information is the most valuable in the world,

---

overseer left in charge of the plantation by the Messrs. ——, the all-efficient and all-satisfactory Mr. K——, and she had a son by him, whose straight features and diluted color, no less than his troublesome, discontented, and insubmissive disposition, bear witness to his Yankee descent. I do not know how long Mr. K——'s occupation of Frank's wife continued, or how the latter endured the wrong done to him. When I visited the island Betty was again living with her husband—a grave, sad, thoughtful-looking man, whose admirable moral and mental qualities were extolled to me by no worse a judge of such matters than Mr. K—— himself, during the few days he spent with Mr. ——, while we were on the plantation. This outrage upon this man's rights was perfectly notorious among all the slaves; and his hopeful offspring, Renty, alluding very unmistakably to his superior birth on one occasion when he applied for permission to have a gun, observed that, though the people in general on the plantation were not allowed fire-arms, he thought he might, *on account of his color*, and added that he thought Mr. K—— might have left him his. This precious sample of the mode in which the vices of the whites procure the intellectual progress of the blacks to their own endangerment was, as you will easily believe, a significant chapter to me in the black history of oppression which is laid before my eyes in this place.

and I sometimes marvel with perhaps unjust incredulity at the facts in natural history which he imparts to me; for instance, to-day he told me, as we rowed past certain mud islands, very like children's mud puddings on a rather larger scale than usual, that they were inaccessible, and that it would be quite impossible to land on one of them even for the shortest time. Not understanding why people who did not mind being up to their knees in mud should not land there if they pleased, I demurred to his assertion, when he followed it up by assuring me that there were what he called sand-sinks under the mud, and that whatever was placed on the surface would not only sink through the mud, but also into a mysterious quicksand of unknown depth and extent below it. This may be true, but sounds very strange, although I remember that the frequent occurrence of large patches of quicksand was found to be one of the principal impediments in the way of the canal speculators at Brunswick. I did not, however, hear that these sinks, as Jack called them, were found below a thick stratum of heavy mud.

In remonstrating with him upon the want of decent cleanliness generally among the people, and citing to him one among the many evils resulting from it, the intolerable quantity of fleas in all the houses, he met me full with another fact in natural history which, if it be fact and not fiction, certainly gave him the best of the argument: he declared, with the utmost vehemence, that the sand of the pine woods on the main land across the river literally swarmed with fleas; that, in the uninhabited places, the sand itself was full of them; and that, so far from being a result of human habitation, they were found in less numbers round the negro huts on the main land than in the lonely woods around them.

The plowing is at length fully inaugurated, and there is a regular jubilee among the negroes thereat. After discoursing fluently on the improvements likely to result from the measure, Jack wound up by saying he had been afraid it would not be tried on account of the greater scarcity, and consequently greater value, of horses over men in these parts—a modest and slave-like conclusion.

DEAREST E——,—I walked up to-day, *February* 14*th*, to see that land of promise, the plowed field: it did not look to me any thing like as heavy soil as the cold, wet, sour, stiff clay I have seen turned up in some of the swampy fields round Lenox; and as for the cypress roots which were urged as so serious an impediment, they are not much more frequent, and certainly not as resisting, as the granite knees and elbows that stick out through the scanty covering of the said clay, which mother earth allows herself as sole garment for her old bones in many a Berkshire patch of córn. After my survey, as I walked home, I came upon a gang of lusty women, as the phrase is here for women in the family-way; they were engaged in burning stubble, and I was nearly choked while receiving the multitudinous complaints and compliments with which they overwhelmed me. After leaving them, I wandered along the river side of the dike homeward, rejoicing in the buds and green things putting forth their tender shoots on every spray, in the early bees and even the less amiable wasps busy in the sunshine with flowers (weeds I suppose they should be called), already opening their sweet temptations to them, and giving the earth a spring aspect, such as it does not wear with you in Massachusetts till late in May.

In the afternoon I took my accustomed row: there had been a tremendous ebb tide, the consequence of which was to lay bare portions of the banks which I had not seen before. The cypress roots form a most extraordinary mass of intertwined wood-work, so closely matted and joined together that the separate roots, in spite of their individual peculiarities, appeared only like divisions of a continuous body; they presented the appearance in several places of jagged pieces of splintered rock, with their huge teeth pointing downward into the water. Their decay is so slow that the protection they afford the soft spongy banks against the action of the water is likely to be prolonged until the gathering and deposit of successive layers of alluvium will remove them from the margin of which they are now most useful supports. On my return home I was met by a child (as she seemed to me) carrying a baby, in whose behalf she begged me for some clothes. On making some inquiry, I was amazed to find that the child was her own: she said she was married, and fourteen years old; she looked much younger even than that, poor creature. Her mother, who came up while I was talking to her, said she did not herself know the girl's age; how horridly brutish it all did seem, to be sure.

The spring is already here with her hands full of flowers. I do not know who planted some straggling pyrus japonica near the house, but it is blessing my eyes with a hundred little flame-like buds, which will presently burst into a blaze: there are clumps of narcissus roots sending up sheaves of ivory blossoms, and I actually found a monthly rose in bloom on the sunny side of one of the dikes; what a delight they are in the slovenly desolation of this abode of mine! what a garden one might have on the banks of these dikes, with the least amount of trouble and care!

In the afternoon I rowed over to Darien, and there procuring the most miserable vehicle calling itself a carriage that I had ever seen (the dirtiest and shabbiest London hackney-coach were a chariot of splendor and ease to it),

we drove some distance into the sandy wilderness that
surrounds the little town, to pay a visit to some of the
resident gentry who had called upon us. The road was
a deep, wearisome sandy track, stretching wearisomely
into the wearisome pine forest—a species of wilderness
more oppressive a thousand times to the senses and imagination than any extent of monotonous prairie, barren
steppe, or boundless desert can be; for the horizon there
at least invites and detains the eye, suggesting beyond its
limit possible change; the lights, and shadows, and enchanting colors of the sky afford some variety in their
movement and change, and the reflections of their tints;
while in this hideous and apparently boundless pine barren you are deprived alike of horizon before you and heav-
en above you: nor sun nor star appears through the thick
covert, which, in the shabby dinginess of its dark blue-
green expanse, looks like a gigantic cotton umbrella
stretched immeasurably over you. It is true that over
that sandy soil a dark green cotton umbrella is a very
welcome protection from the sun, and when the wind
makes music in the tall pine-tops and refreshment in the
air beneath them. The comparison may seem ungrateful
enough: to-day, however, there was neither sound above
nor motion below, and the heat was perfectly stifling, as
we plowed our way through the resinous-smelling sand
solitudes.

From time to time a thicket of exquisite evergreen
shrubs broke the monotonous lines of the countless pine
shafts rising round us, and still more welcome were the
golden garlands of the exquisite wild jasmine, hanging,
drooping, trailing, clinging, climbing through the dreary
forest, joining to the warm aromatic smell of the fir-trees
a delicious fragrance as of acres of heliotrope in bloom.
I wonder if this delightful creature is very difficult of cultivation out of its natural region; I never remember to

G

have seen it, at least not in blossom, in any collection of
plants in the Northern states or in Europe, where it certainly deserves an honorable place for its grace, beauty,
and fragrance.

On our drive we passed occasionally a tattered man or
woman, whose yellow mud complexion, straight features,
and singularly sinister countenance bespoke an entirely
different race from the negro population in the midst of
which they lived. These are the so-called pine-landers of
Georgia, I suppose the most degraded race of human beings claiming an Anglo-Saxon origin that can be found on
the face of the earth—filthy, lazy, ignorant, brutal, proud,
penniless savages, without one of the nobler attributes
which have been found occasionally allied to the vices of
savage nature. They own no slaves, for they are almost
without exception abjectly poor; they will not work, for
that, as they conceive, would reduce them to an equality
with the abhorred negroes; they squat, and steal, and
starve, on the outskirts of this lowest of all civilized societies, and their countenances bear witness to the squalor
of their condition and the utter degradation of their natures. To the crime of slavery, though they have no profitable part or lot in it, they are fiercely accessory, because
it is the barrier that divides the black and white races, at
the foot of which they lie wallowing in unspeakable degradation, but immensely proud of the base freedom which
still separates them from the lash-driven tillers of the
soil.*

* Of such is the white family so wonderfully described in Mrs.
Stowe's "Dred," whose only slave brings up the orphaned children of
his masters with such exquisitely grotesque and pathetic tenderness.
From such the conscription which has fed the Southern army in the
deplorable civil conflict now raging in America has drawn its rank and
file.   Better "food for powder" the world could scarcely supply.
Fierce and idle, with hardly one of the necessities or amenities that
belong to civilized existence, they are hardy endurers of hardship, and

The house at which our call was paid was set down in the midst of the Pine Barren, with half-obliterated roads and paths round it, suggesting that it might be visited and was inhabited. It was large and not unhandsome, though curiously dilapidated, considering that people were actually living in it; certain remnants of carving on the cornices and paint on the panels bore witness to some former stage of existence less neglected and deteriorated than the present. The old lady mistress of this most forlorn abode amiably inquired if so much exercise did not fatigue me; at first I thought she imagined I must have walked through the pine forest all the way from Darien, but she explained that she considered the drive quite an effort; and it is by no means uncommon to hear people in America talk of being dragged over bad roads in uneasy carriages as exercise, showing how very little they know the meaning of the word, and how completely they identify it with the idea of mere painful fatigue instead of pleasurable exertion.

Returning home, my reflections ran much on the possible future destiny of these vast tracts of sandy soil. It seems to me that the ground capable of supporting the evergreen growth, the luxuriant gardinia bushes, the bay myrtle, the beautiful magnolia grandiflora, and the powerful and gnarled live oaks, that find their sustenance in this

reckless to a savage degree of the value of life, whether their own or others. The soldier's pay, received or promised, exceeds in amount per month any thing they ever earned before per year, and the war they wage is one that enlists all their proud and ferocious instincts. It is against the Yankees—the Northern sons of free soil, free toil and intelligence, the hated Abolitionists whose success would sweep away slavery and reduce the Southern white men to work—no wonder they are ready to fight to the death against this detestable alternative, especially as they look to victory as the certain promotion of the refuse of the "poor white" population of the South, of which they are one and all members, to the coveted dignity of slaveholders.

earth and under this same sky as the fir-trees, must be convertible into a prosperous habitation for other valuable vegetable growth that would add immensely to the wealth of the Southern states. The orange thrives and bears profusely along this part of the sea-board of Georgia; and I can not conceive that the olive, the mulberry, and the vine might not be acclimated, and successfully and profitably cultivated throughout the whole of this region, the swampy lower lands alone remaining as rice plantations. The produce of these already exceeds in value that of the once gold-growing cotton-fields; and I can not help believing that silk, and wine, and oil may, and will, hereafter become, with the present solitary cotton crop, joint possessors of all this now but half-reclaimed wilderness. The soil all round Sorrento is very nearly as light, and dry, and sandy as this, and vineyards, and olive orchards, and cocooneries are part of the agricultural wealth there. Our neighbor, Mr. C——, has successfully cultivated the date-palm in his garden on the edge of the sea at St. Simon's, and certainly the ilex, orange, and myrtle abounding here suggest natural affinities between the Italian soil and climate and this.

I must tell you something funny which occurred yesterday at dinner, which will give you some idea of the strange mode in which we live. We have now not unfrequently had mutton at table, the flavor of which is quite excellent, as indeed it may well be, for it is raised under all the conditions of the famous *Prè salé* that the French gourmands especially prize, and which are reproduced on our side of the Channel in the peculiar qualities of our best South Down. The mutton we have here grazes on the short sweet grass at St. Simon's within sea-salt influence, and is some of the very best I have ever tasted, but it is invariably brought to table in lumps or chunks of no particular shape or size, and in which it is utterly impossible to recognize any part of the quadruped creature sheep with which my eyes have hitherto become acquainted. Eat it, one may and does thankfully; name it, one could not by any possibility. Having submitted to this for some time, I at length inquired why a decent usual Christian joint of mutton—leg, shoulder, or saddle—was never brought to table: the reply was that the *carpenter* always cut up the meat, and that he did not know how to do it otherwise than by dividing it into so many thick square pieces, and proceeding to chop it up on that principle; and the consequence of this is, that *four lumps* or *chunks* are all that a whole sheep ever furnishes to our table by this artistic and economical process.

This morning I have been to the hospital to see a poor woman who has just enriched Mr. —— by *borning* him another slave. The poor little pickaninny, as they called it, was not one bit uglier than white babies under similarly novel circumstances, except in one particular, that it had a head of hair like a trunk, in spite of which I had all the pains in the world in persuading its mother not to put a cap upon it. I bribed her finally by the promise of a pair of socks instead, with which I undertook to endow her child, and, moreover, actually prevailed upon her to forego the usual swaddling and swathing process, and let her poor baby be dressed at its first entrance into life as I assured her both mine had been.

On leaving the hospital I visited the huts all along the street, confiscating sundry refractory baby caps among shrieks and outcries, partly of laughter and partly of real ignorant alarm for the consequences. I think, if this infatuation for hot head-dresses continues, I shall make shaving the children's heads the only condition upon which they shall be allowed to wear caps.

On Sunday morning I went over to Darien to church. Our people's church was closed, the minister having gone to officiate elsewhere. With laudable liberality, I walked into the opposite church of a different, not to say opposite sect: here I heard a sermon, the opening of which will probably edify you as it did me, viz., that if a man was *just in all his dealings,* he was apt to think he did all that could be required of him — and no wide mistake either, one might suppose. But is it not wonderful how such words can be spoken here, with the most absolute unconsciousness of their tremendous bearing upon the existence of every slaveholder who hears them? Certainly the use that is second nature has made the awful injustice in the daily practice of which these people live a thing of which they are as little aware as you or I of the atmospheric air that we inhale each time we breathe. The bulk of the congregation in this church was white. The negroes are, of course, not allowed to mix with their masters in the house of God, and there is no special place set apart for them. Occasionally one or two are to be seen in the corners of the singing gallery, but any more open pollution by them of their owners' church could not be tolerated. Mr. ——'s people have petitioned very vehemently that he would build a church for them on the island. I doubt, however, his allowing them such a luxury as a place of worship all to themselves. Such a privilege might not be thought well of by the neighboring planters; indeed, it is almost what one might call a whity-brown idea, dangerous, demoralizing, inflammatory, incendiary. I should not wonder if I should be suspected of being the chief cornerstone of it, and yet I am not: it is an old hope and entreaty of these poor people, which I am afraid they are not destined to see fulfilled.

DEAREST E——,—Passing the rice mill this morning in my walk, I went in to look at the machinery, the large steam mortars which shell the rice, and which work under the intelligent and reliable supervision of Engineer Ned. I was much surprised, in the course of conversation with him this morning, to find how much older a man he was than he appeared. Indeed, his youthful appearance had hitherto puzzled me much in accounting for his very superior intelligence and the important duties confided to him. He is, however, a man upward of forty years old, although he looks ten years younger. He attributed his own uncommonly youthful appearance to the fact of his never having done what he called field-work, or been exposed, as the common gang negroes are, to the hardships of their all but brutish existence. He said his former master had brought him up very kindly, and he had learned to tend the engines, and had never been put to any other work, but he said this was not the case with his poor wife. He wished she was as well off as he was, but she had to work in the rice-fields, and was "most broke in two" with labor, and exposure, and hard work while with child, and hard work just directly after childbearing; he said she could hardly crawl, and he urged me very much to speak a kind word for her to massa. She was almost all the time in hospital, and he thought she could not live long.

Now, E——, here is another instance of the horrible injustice of this system of slavery. In my country or in yours, a man endowed with sufficient knowledge and capacity to be an engineer would, of course, be in the receipt of considerable wages; his wife would, together with himself, reap the advantages of his ability, and share the well-being his labor earned; he would be able to procure for her comfort in sickness or in health, and beyond the necessary household work, which the wives of most

artisans are inured to, she would have no labor to encounter; in case of sickness even these would be alle-
viated by the assistance of some stout girl of all work or
kindly neighbor, and the tidy parlor or snug bedroom
would be her retreat if unequal to the daily duties of her
own kitchen.   Think of such a lot compared with that of
the head engineer of Mr. ——'s plantation, whose sole
wages are his coarse food and raiment and miserable
hovel, and whose wife, covered with one filthy garment
of ragged texture and dingy color, barefooted and bareheaded, is daily driven afield to labor with aching pain-
racked joints, under the lash of a driver, or lies languishing on the earthen floor of the dismal plantation hospital
in a condition of utter physical destitution and degradation such as the most miserable dwelling of the poorest
inhabitant of your free Northern villages never beheld
the like of.   Think of the rows of tidy tiny houses in the
long suburbs of Boston and Philadelphia, inhabited by
artisans of just the same grade as this poor Ned, with
their white doors and steps, their hydrants of inexhaustible fresh flowing water, the innumerable appliances for
decent comfort of their cheerful rooms, the gay wardrobe
of the wife, her cotton prints for daily use, her silk for
Sunday church-going; the careful comfort of the children's clothing, the books and newspapers in the little
parlor, the daily district school, the weekly parish church:
imagine if you can—but you are happy that you can not
—the contrast between such an existence and that of the
best mechanic on a Southern plantation.

Did you ever read (but I am sure you never did, and
no more did I) an epic poem on fresh-water fish?   Well,
such a one was once written, I have forgotten by whom,
but assuredly the heroine of it ought to have been the
Altamaha shad—a delicate creature, so superior to the
animal you Northerners devour with greedy thankfulness

when the spring sends back their finny drove to your
colder waters, that one would not suppose these were of
the same family, instead of being, as they really are, precisely the same fish. Certainly the mud of the Altamaha
must have some most peculiar virtues; and, by-the-by, I
have never any where tasted such delicious tea as that
which we make with this same turbid stream, the water
of which, duly filtered of course, has some peculiar softness which affects the tea (and it is the same we always
use) in a most curious and agreeable manner.

On my return to the house I found a terrible disturb-
ance in consequence of the disappearance from under cook
John's safe keeping of a ham Mr. —— had committed to
his charge. There was no doubt whatever that the unfortunate culinary slave had made away in some inscrut-
able manner with the joint intended for our table: the
very lies he told about it were so curiously shallow, child-
like, and transparent, that while they confirmed the fact
of his theft quite as much, if not more, than an absolute
confession would have done, they provoked at once my
pity and my irrepressible mirth to a most painful degree.
Mr. —— was in a state of towering anger and indignation, and, besides a flogging, sentenced the unhappy cook
to degradation from his high and dignified position (and,
alas! all its sweets of comparatively easy labor and good
living from the remains of our table) to the hard toil,
coarse scanty fare, and despised position of a common
field-hand. I suppose some punishment was inevitably
necessary in such a plain case of deliberate theft as this,
but, nevertheless, my whole soul revolts at the injustice
of visiting upon these poor wretches a moral darkness
which all possible means are taken to increase and per-
petuate.

In speaking of this and the whole circumstance of
John's trespass to Mr. —— in the evening, I observed

G 2

that the ignorance of these poor people ought to screen
them from punishment. He replied that they knew well
enough what was right and wrong. I asked how they
could be expected to know it? He replied, by the means
of Cooper London, and the religious instruction he gave
them. So that, after all, the appeal is to be made against
themselves to that moral and religious instruction which
is withheld from them, and which, if they obtain it at all,
is the result of their own unaided and unencouraged exertion. The more I hear, and see, and learn, and ponder
the whole of this system of slavery, the more impossible
I find it to conceive how its practisers and upholders are
to justify their deeds before the tribunal of their own conscience or God's law. It is too dreadful to have those
whom we love accomplices to this wickedness; it is too
intolerable to find myself an involuntary accomplice to it.

I had a conversation the next morning with Abraham,
cook John's brother, upon the subject of his brother's
theft; and only think of the *slave* saying that "this action had brought disgrace upon the family." Does not
that sound very like the very best sort of free pride, the
pride of character, the honorable pride of honesty, integrity, and fidelity? But this was not all, for this same
Abraham, a clever carpenter and much valued *hand* on
the estate, went on, in answer to my questions, to tell me
such a story that I declare to you I felt as if I could have
howled with helpless indignation and grief when he departed and went to resume his work. His grandfather
had been an old slave in Darien, extremely clever as a carpenter, and so highly valued for his skill and good character that his master allowed him to purchase his liberty
by money which he earned by working for himself at odd
times, when his task-work was over. I asked Abraham
what sum his grandfather paid for his freedom: he said
he did not know, but he supposed a large one, because of

his being a "skilled carpenter," and so a peculiarly valuable chattel. I presume, from what I remember Major M—— and Dr. H—— saying on the subject of the market value of negroes in Charleston and Savannah, that such a man in the prime of life would have been worth from 1500 to 2000 dollars. However, whatever the man paid for his ransom, by his grandson's account, fourteen years after he became free, when he died, he had again amassed money to the amount of 700 dollars, which he left among his wife and children, the former being a slave on Major ——'s estate, where the latter remained by virtue of that fact slaves also. So this man not only bought his own freedom at a cost of *at least* 1000 dollars, but left a little fortune of 700 more at his death ; and then we are told of the universal idleness, incorrigible sloth, and brutish incapacity of this inferior race of creatures, whose only fitting and Heaven-appointed condition is that of beasts of burden to the whites. I do not believe the whole low white population of the State of Georgia could furnish such an instance of energy, industry, and thrift as the amassing of this laborious little fortune by this poor slave, who left, nevertheless, his children and grandchildren to the lot from which he had so heroically ransomed himself; and yet the white men with whom I live and talk tell me, day after day, that there is neither cruelty nor injustice in this accursed system.

About half past five I went to walk on the dikes, and met a gang of the field-hands going to the tide-mill, as the water served them for working then. I believe I have told you that besides the great steam mill there is this, which is dependent on the rise and fall of the tide in the river, and where the people are therefore obliged to work by day or night, at whatever time the water serves to impel the wheel. They greeted me with their usual profusion of exclamations, petitions, and benedictions, and I parted from them to come and oversee my slave Jack, for whom I had bought a spade, and to whom I had intrusted the task of turning up some ground for me, in which I wanted to establish some of the narcissus and other flowers I had remarked about the ground and the house. Jack, however, was a worse digger than Adam could have been when first he turned his hand to it, after his expulsion from Paradise. I think I could have managed a spade with infinitely more efficiency, or rather less incapacity, than he displayed. Upon my expressing my amazement at his performance, he said the people here never used spades, but performed all their agricultural operations with the hoe. Their soil must be very light and their agriculture very superficial, I should think. However, I was obliged to terminate Jack's spooning process, and abandon, for the present, my hopes of a flower-bed created by his industry, being called into the house to receive the return visit of old Mrs. S——. As usual, the appearance, health, vigor, and good management of the children were the theme of wondering admiration; as usual, my possession of a white nurse the theme of envious congratulation; as usual, I had to hear the habitual senseless complaints of the inefficiency of colored nurses. If you are half as tired of the sameness and stupidity of the conversation of my Southern female neighbors as I am, I pity you; but not as much as I pity them for the stupid sameness of their most vapid existence, which would deaden any amount of intelligence, obliterate any amount of instruction, and render torpid and stagnant any amount of natural energy and vivacity. I would rather die—rather a thousand times—than live the lives of these Georgia planters' wives and daughters.

Mrs. S—— had brought me some of the delicious wild jasmine that festoons her dreary pine-wood drive, and most grateful I was for the presence of the sweet wild

nosegay in my highly unornamental residence. When
my visitors had left me, I took the refreshment of a row
over to Darien; and as we had the tide against us coming back, the process was not so refreshing for the rowers. The evening was so extremely beautiful, and the
rising of the moon so exquisite, that instead of retreating
to the house when I reached the island, I got into the
Dolphin, my special canoe, and made Jack paddle me
down the great river to meet the Lily, which was coming
back from St. Simon's with Mr. ——, who has been preparing all things for our advent thither.

My letter has been interrupted, dear E——, by the
breaking up of our residence on the rice plantation, and
our arrival at St. Simon's, whence I now address you.
We came down yesterday afternoon, and I was thankful
enough of the fifteen miles' row to rest in, from the labor
of leave-taking, with which the whole morning was taken
up, and which, combined with packing and preparing all
our own personalities and those of the children, was no
sinecure. At every moment one or other of the poor people rushed in upon me to bid me good-by; many of their
farewells were grotesque enough, some were pathetic, and
all of them made me very sad. Poor people! how little
I have done, how little I can do for them. I had a long
talk with that interesting and excellent man, Cooper London, who made an earnest petition that I would send him
from the North a lot of Bibles and Prayer-books; certainly the science of reading must be much more common
among the negroes than I supposed, or London must look
to a marvelously increased spread of the same hereafter.
There is, however, considerable reticence upon this point,
or else the poor slaves must consider the mere possession
of the holy books as good for salvation and as effectual
for spiritual assistance to those who can not as to those
who can comprehend them. Since the news of our de-

parture has spread, I have had repeated eager entreaties for presents of Bibles and Prayer-books, and to my demurrer of " But you can't read, can you?" have generally received for answer a reluctant acknowledgment of ignorance, which, however, did not always convince me of the fact. In my farewell conversation with London I found it impossible to get him to tell me how he had learned to read : the penalties for teaching them are very severe— heavy fines, increasing in amount for the first and second offense, and imprisonment for the third.* Such a man as London is certainly aware that to teach the slaves to read is an illegal act, and he may have been unwilling to betray whoever had been his preceptor even to my knowledge; at any rate, I got no answers from him but " Well, missis, me learn ; well, missis, me try;" and finally, " Well, missis, me 'spose Heaven help me ;" to which I could only reply that I knew Heaven was helpful, but very hardly to the tune of teaching folks their letters.   I got no satisfaction. Old Jacob, the father of Abraham, cook John, and poor Psyche's husband, took a most solemn and sad leave of me, saying he did not expect ever to see me again.   I could not exactly tell why, because, though he is aged and infirm, the fifteen miles between the rice plantation and St. Simon's do not appear so insuperable a barrier between the inhabitants of the two places, which I represented to him as a suggestion of consolation.

I have worked my fingers nearly off with making, for the last day or two, innumerable rolls of coarse little baby-clothes, layettes for the use of small new-born slaves;

---

* These laws have been greatly increased in stringency and severity since these letters were written, and *death* has not been reckoned too heavy a penalty for those who should venture to offer these unfortunate people the fruit of that forbidden tree of knowledge, their access to which has appeared to their owners the crowning danger of their own precarious existence among their terrible dependents.

M—— diligently cutting and shaping, and I as diligently stitching. We leave a good supply for the hospitals, and for the individual clients besides who have besieged me ever since my departure became imminent.

Our voyage from the rice to the cotton plantation was performed in the Lily, which looked like a soldier's baggage-wagon and an emigrant transport combined. Our crew consisted of eight men. Forward in the bow were miscellaneous live-stock, pots, pans, household furniture, kitchen utensils, and an indescribable variety of heterogeneous necessaries. Enthroned upon beds, bedding, tables, and other chattels, sat that poor pretty chattel Psyche, with her small chattel children. Midships sat the two tiny free women and myself, and in the stern Mr. —— steering. And "all in the blue unclouded weather" we rowed down the huge stream, the men keeping time and tune to their oars with extemporaneous chants of adieu to the rice-island and its denizens. Among other poetical and musical comments on our departure recurred the assertion, as a sort of burden, that we were "parted in body, but not in mind," from those we left behind. Having relieved one set of sentiments by this reflection, they very wisely betook themselves to the consideration of the blessings that remained to them, and performed a spirited chant in honor of Psyche and our bouncing black housemaid, Mary.

At the end of a fifteen miles' row we entered one among a perfect labyrinth of arms or branches, into which the broad river ravels like a fringe as it reaches the sea, a dismal navigation along a dismal tract, called "Five Pound," through a narrow cut or channel of water divided from the main stream. The conch was sounded, as at our arrival at the rice-island, and we made our descent on the famous long staple cotton island of St. Simon's, where we presently took up our abode in what had all the appearance of an old, half-decayed, rattling farm-house.

This morning, Sunday, I peeped round its immediate neighborhood, and saw, to my inexpressible delight, within hail, some noble-looking evergreen oaks, and close to the house itself a tiny would-be garden, a plot of ground with one or two peach-trees in full blossom, tufts of silver narcissus and jonquils, a quantity of violets and an exquisite myrtle bush; wherefore I said my prayers with especial gratitude.

DEAREST E——,—The fame of my peculiar requisitions has, I find, preceded me here, for the babies that have been presented to my admiring notice have all been without caps; also, however, without socks to their opposite little wretched extremities, but that does not signify quite so much. The people, too, that I saw yesterday were remarkably clean and tidy; to be sure, it was Sunday. The whole day, till quite late in the afternoon, the house was surrounded by a crowd of our poor dependents, waiting to catch a glimpse of Mr. ——, myself, or the children; and until, from sheer weariness, I was obliged to shut the doors, an incessant stream poured in and out, whose various modes of salutation, greeting, and welcome were more grotesque and pathetic at the same time than any thing you can imagine. In the afternoon I walked with —— to see a new house in process of erection, which, when it is finished, is to be the overseer's abode and our residence during any future visits we may pay to the estate. I was horrified at the dismal site selected, and the hideous house erected on it. It is true that the central position is the principal consideration in the overseer's location; but both position and building seemed to me to witness to an inveterate love of ugliness, or, at any rate, a deadness to every desire of beauty, nothing short of horrible; and, for my own part, I think it is intolerable to have to leave the

point where the waters meet, and where a few fine picturesque old trees are scattered about, to come to this place
even for the very short time I am ever likely to spend
here.

In every direction our view, as we returned, was bounded by thickets of the most beautiful and various evergreen
growth, which beckoned my inexperience most irresistibly. —— said, to my unutterable horror, that they were
perfectly infested with rattlesnakes, and I must on no account go "beating about the bush" in these latitudes, as
the game I should be likely to start would be any thing
but agreeable to me. We saw quantities of wild plum-
trees all silvery with blossoms, and in lovely companionship and contrast with them a beautiful shrub covered
with delicate pink bloom like flowering peach-trees. After that life in the rice-swamp, where the Altamaha kept
looking over the dike at me all the time as I sat in the
house writing or working, it is pleasant to be on *terra
firma* again, and to know that the river is at the conventional, not to say natural, depth below its banks, and under my feet instead of over my head. The two plantations are of diametrically opposite dispositions—that is all
swamp, and this all sand; or, to speak more accurately,
that is all swamp, and all of this that is not swamp is sand.

On our way home we met a most extraordinary creature of the negro kind, who, coming toward us, halted,
and caused us to halt straight in the middle of the path,
when, bending himself down till his hands almost touched
the ground, he exclaimed to Mr. ——, "Massa ——, your
most obedient;" and then, with a kick and a flourish altogether indescribable, he drew to the side of the path to
let us pass, which we did perfectly shouting with laughter, which broke out again every time we looked at each
other and stopped to take breath: so sudden, grotesque,
uncouth, and yet dexterous a gambado never came into

the brain or out of the limbs of any thing but a "nig-gar."

I observed, among the numerous groups that we passed or met, a much larger proportion of mulattoes than at the rice-island; upon asking Mr. —— why this was so, he said that there no white person could land without his or the overseer's permission, whereas on St. Simon's, which is a large island containing several plantations belonging to different owners, of course the number of whites, both re-siding on and visiting the place, was much greater, and the opportunity for intercourse between the blacks and whites much more frequent. While we were still on this subject, a horrid-looking filthy woman met us with a little child in her arms, a very light mulatto, whose extraordi-nary resemblance to Driver Bran (one of the officials who had been duly presented to me on my arrival, and who was himself a mulatto) struck me directly. I pointed it out to Mr. ——, who merely answered, "Very likely his child." "And," said I, " did you never remark that Driver Bran is the exact image of Mr. K——?" "Very likely his brother," was the reply: all which rather unpleasant state of relationships seemed accepted as such a complete matter of course, that I felt rather uncomfortable, and said no more about who was like who, but came to certain con-clusions in my own mind as to a young lad who had been among our morning visitors, and whose extremely light color and straight, handsome features and striking resem-blance to Mr. K—— had suggested suspicions of a rather unpleasant nature to me, and whose sole-acknowledged parent was a very black negress of the name of Minda. I have no doubt at all, now, that he is another son of Mr. K——, Mr. ——'s paragon overseer.

As we drew near the house again we were gradually joined by such a numerous escort of Mr. ——'s slaves that it was almost with difficulty we could walk along the path. They buzzed, and hummed, and swarmed round us like flies, and the heat and dust consequent upon this friendly companionship were a most unpleasant addition to the labor of walking in the sandy soil through which we were plowing. I was not sorry when we entered the house and left our body-guard outside. In the evening I looked over the plan of the delightful residence I had visited in the morning, and could not help suggesting to Mr. —— the advantage to be gained in point of picturesqueness by merely turning the house round. It is but a wooden frame one after all, and your folks " down East" would think no more of inviting it to face about than if it was built of cards; but the fact is, here nothing signifies except the cotton crop, and whether one's nose is in a swamp and one's eyes in a sand-heap is of no consequence whatever either to one's self (if one's self was not I) or any one else.

I find here an immense proportion of old people; the work and the climate of the rice plantation require the strongest of the able-bodied men and women of the estate. The cotton crop is no longer by any means as paramount in value as it used to be, and the climate, soil, and labor of St. Simon's are better adapted to old, young, and feeble cultivators than the swamp fields of the rice-island. I wonder if I ever told you of the enormous decrease in value of this same famous sea-island long staple cotton. When Major ——, Mr. ——'s grandfather, first sent the produce of this plantation where we now are to England, it was of so fine a quality that it used to be quoted by itself in the Liverpool cotton market, and was then worth half a guinea a pound; it is now not worth a shilling a pound. This was told me by the gentleman in Liverpool who has been factor for this estate for thirty years. Such a decrease as this in the value of one's crop, and the steady increase at the same time of a slave population, now numbering between 700 and 800 bodies to clothe and house, mouths to feed, while the land is being exhausted by the careless and wasteful nature of the agriculture itself, suggests a pretty serious prospect of declining prosperity; and, indeed, unless these Georgia cotton-planters can command more land, or lay abundant capital (which they have not, being almost all of them over head and ears in debt) upon that which has already spent its virgin vigor, it is a very obvious thing that they must all very soon be eaten up by their own property. The rice plantations are a great thing to fall back upon under these circumstances, and the rice crop is now quite as valuable, if not more so, than the cotton one on Mr. ——'s estates, once so famous and prosperous through the latter.

I find any number of all but superannuated men and women here, whose tales of the former grandeur of the estate and family are like things one reads of in novels. One old woman, who crawled to see me, and could hardly lift her poor bowed head high enough to look in my face, had been in Major ——'s establishment in Philadelphia, and told with infinite pride of having waited upon his daughters and granddaughters, Mr. ——'s sisters. Yet here she is, flung by like an old rag, crippled with age and disease, living, or rather dying by slow degrees in a miserable hovel, such as no decent household servant would at the North, I suppose, ever set their foot in. The poor old creature complained bitterly to me of all her ailments and all her wants. I can do little, alas! for either. I had a visit from another tottering old crone called Dorcas, who all but went on her knees as she wrung and kissed my hands; with her came my friend Molly, the grandmother of the poor runaway girl Louisa, whose story I wrote you some little time ago. I had to hear it all over again, it being the newest event evidently in Molly's life; and it ended as before with the highly reasonable proposition:

"Me say, missis, what for massa's niggar run away? Snake eat 'em up, or dey starve to def in a swamp. Massa's niggars dey don't neber run away." If I was "massa's niggars," I "spose" I shouldn't run away either, with only those alternatives; but when I look at these wretches and at the sea that rolls round this island, and think how near the English West Indies and freedom are, it gives me a pretty severe twinge at the heart.

DEAREST E——,—I am afraid my letters must be becoming very wearisome to you; for if, as the copy-book runs, "Variety is charming," they certainly can not be so unless monotony is also charming, a thing not impossible to some minds, but of which the copy-book makes no mention. But what will you? as the French say; my days are no more different from one another than peas in a dish, or sands on the shore: 'tis a pleasant enough life to live for one who, like myself, has a passion for dullness, but it affords small matter for epistolary correspondence. I suppose it is the surfeit of excitement that I had in my youth that has made a life of quiet monotony so extremely agreeable to me; it is like stillness after loud noise, twilight after glare, rest after labor. There is enough strangeness, too, in every thing that surrounds me here to interest and excite me agreeably and sufficiently, and I should like the wild savage loneliness of the far away existence extremely if it were not for the one small item of "the slavery."

I had a curious visit this morning from half a dozen of the women, among whom were Driver Morris's wife and Venus (a hideous old gooddess she was, to be sure), Driver Bran's mother. They came especially to see the children, who are always eagerly asked for, and hugely admired by their sooty dependents. These poor women went into ecstasies over the little white pickaninnies, and were loud and profuse in their expressions of gratitude to Massa —— for getting married and having children, a matter of thankfulness which, though it always makes me laugh very much, is a most serious one to them; for the continuance of the family keeps the estate and slaves from the hammer, and the poor wretches, besides seeing in every new child born to their owners a security against their own banishment from the only home they know, and separation from all ties of kindred and habit, and dispersion to distant plantations, not unnaturally look for a milder rule from masters who are the children of their fathers' masters. The relation of owner and slave may be expected to lose some of its harsher features, and, no doubt, in some instances, does so, when it is on each side the inheritance of successive generations. And so ——'s slaves laud, and applaud, and thank, and bless him for having married, and endowed their children with two little future mistresses. One of these women, a Diana by name, went down on her knees, and uttered in a loud voice a sort of extemporaneous prayer of thanksgiving at our advent, in which the sacred and the profane were most ludicrously mingled : her " tanks to de good Lord God Almighty that missus had come, what give de poor niggar sugar and flannel," and dat " Massa ——, him hab brought de missis and de two little misses down among de people," were really too grotesque, and yet certainly more sincere acts of thanksgiving are not often uttered among the solemn and decorous ones that are offered up to heaven for " benefits received."

I find the people here much more inclined to talk than those on the rice-island; they have less to do and more leisure, and bestow it very liberally on me ; moreover, the poor old women, of whom there are so many turned out to grass here, and of whom I have spoken to you before, though they are past work, are by no means past gossip, and the stories they have to tell of the former government of the estate under old Massa K—— are certainly pretty tremendous illustrations of the merits of slavery as a moral institution. This man, the father of the late owner, Mr. R—— K——, was Major ——'s agent in the management of this property, and a more cruel and unscrupulous one as regards the slaves themselves, whatever he may have been in his dealings with the master, I should think it would be difficult to find, even among the cruel and unscrupulous class to which he belonged.

In a conversation with old "House Molly," as she is called, to distinguish her from all other Mollies on the estate, she having had the honor of being a servant in Major ——'s house for many years, I asked her if the relation between men and women who are what they call married, i. e., who have agreed to live together as man and wife (the only species of marriage formerly allowed on the estate, I believe now London may read the Marriage Service to them), was considered binding by the people themselves and by the overseer. She said "not much formerly," and that the people couldn't be expected to have much regard to such an engagement, utterly ignored as it was by Mr. K——, whose invariable rule, if he heard of any disagreement between a man and woman calling themselves married, was immediately to bestow them in " marriage" on other parties, whether they chose it or not, by which summary process the slightest " incompatibility of temper" received the relief of a divorce more rapid and easy than even Germany could afford, and the estate lost nothing by any prolongation of celibacy on either side. Of course, the misery consequent upon such arbitrary destruction of voluntary and imposition of involuntary ties was nothing to Mr. K——.

I was very sorry to hear to-day that Mr. O——, the

overseer at the rice-island, of whom I have made mention
to you more than once in my letters, had had one of the
men flogged very severely for getting his wife baptized.
I was quite unable, from the account I received, to understand what his objection had been to the poor man's desire to make his wife at least a formal Christian; but it
does seem dreadful that such an act should be so visited.
I almost wish I was back again at the rice-island; for,
though this is every way the pleasanter residence, I hear
so much more that is intolerable of the treatment of the
slaves from those I find here, that my life is really made
wretched by it. There is not a single natural right that
is not taken away from these unfortunate people, and the
worst of all is, that their condition does not appear to me,
upon farther observation of it, to be susceptible of even
partial alleviation as long as the fundamental evil, the slavery itself, remains.

My letter was interrupted as usual by clamors for my
presence at the door, and petitions for sugar, rice, and
baby-clothes from a group of women who had done their
tasks at three o'clock in the afternoon, and had come to
say, "Ha do, missis?" (How do you do?), and beg something on their way to their huts. Observing one among
them whose hand was badly maimed, one finger being reduced to a mere stump, she told me it was in consequence
of the bite of a rattlesnake, which had attacked and bitten
her child, and then struck her as she endeavored to kill
it; her little boy had died, but one of the drivers cut off
her finger, and so she had escaped with the loss of that
member only. It is yet too early in the season for me to
make acquaintance with these delightful animals, but the
accounts the negroes give of their abundance is full of
agreeable promise for the future. It seems singular, considering how very common they are, that there are not
more frequent instances of the slaves being bitten by

them; to be sure, they seem to me to have a holy horror of ever setting their foot near either tree or bush, or any where but on the open road and the fields where they labor; and, of course, the snakes are not so frequent in open and frequented places as in their proper coverts. The Red Indians are said to use successfully some vegetable cure for the bite, I believe the leaves of the slippery ash or elm; the only infallible remedy, however, is suction, but of this the ignorant negroes are so afraid that they never can be induced to have recourse to it, being, of course, immovably persuaded that the poison which is so fatal to the blood must be equally so to the stomach. They tell me that the cattle wandering into the brakes and bushes are often bitten to death by these deadly creatures; the pigs, whose fat, it seems, does not accept the venom into its tissues with the same effect, escape unhurt for the most part—so much for the anti-venomous virtue of adipose matter—a consolatory consideration for such of us as are inclined to take on flesh more than we think graceful.

Monday morning, 25th. This letter has been long on the stocks, dear E——. I have been busy all day, and tired, and lazy in the evening latterly, and, moreover, feel as if such very dull matter was hardly worth sending all the way off to where you are happy to be. However, that is nonsense; I know well enough that you are glad to hear from me, be it what it will, and so I resume my chronicle. Some of my evenings have been spent in reading Mr. Clay's anti-abolition speech, and making notes on it, which I will show you when we meet. What a cruel pity and what a cruel shame it is that such a man should either know no better or do no better for his country than he is doing now!

Yesterday I for the first time bethought me of the riding privileges of which Jack used to make such magnificent mention when he was fishing with me at the rice-

H

island; and desiring to visit the remoter parts of the plantation and the other end of the island, I inquired into the resources of the stable. I was told I could have a mare with foal; but I declined adding my weight to what the poor beast already carried, and my only choice then was between one who had just foaled, or a fine stallion used as a plow-horse on the plantation. I determined for the latter, and shall probably be handsomely shaken whenever I take my rides abroad.

Tuesday, the 26th. My dearest E——, I write to you to-day in great depression and distress. I have had a most painful conversation with Mr. ——, who has declined receiving any of the people's petitions through me. Whether he is wearied with the number of these prayers and supplications, which he would escape but for me, as they probably would not venture to come so incessantly to him, and I, of course, feel bound to bring every one confided to me to him, or whether he has been annoyed at the number of pitiful and horrible stories of misery and oppression under the former rule of Mr. K——, which have come to my knowledge since I have been here, and the grief and indignation caused, but which can not, by any means, always be done away with, though their expression may be silenced by his angry exclamations of "Why do you listen to such stuff?" or "Why do you believe such trash? don't you know the niggers are all d—d liars?" etc., I do not know; but he desired me this morning to bring him no more complaints or requests of any sort, as the people had hitherto had no such advocate, and had done very well without, and I was only kept in an incessant state of excitement with all the falsehoods they "found they could make me believe." How well they have done without my advocacy, the conditions which I see with my own eyes, even more than their pitiful petitions, demonstrate; it is indeed true that the sufferings

of those who come to me for redress, and, still more, the
injustice done to the great majority who can not, have
filled my heart with bitterness and indignation that have
overflowed my lips, till, I suppose, —— is weary of hearing what he has never heard before, the voice of passionate expostulation and importunate pleading against
wrongs that he will not even acknowledge, and for creatures whose common humanity with his own I half think
he does not believe; but I must return to the North, for
my condition would be almost worse than theirs—condemned to hear and see so much wretchedness, not only
without the means of alleviating it, but without permission even to represent it for alleviation : this is no place
for me, since I was not born among slaves, and can not
bear to live among them.

Perhaps, after all, what he says is true : when I am
gone they will fall back into the desperate uncomplaining
habit of suffering, from which my coming among them,
willing to hear and ready to help, has tempted them; he
says that bringing their complaints to me, and the sight
of my credulous commiseration, only tend to make them
discontented and idle, and brings renewed chastisement
upon them; and that so, instead of really befriending
them, I am only preparing more suffering for them whenever I leave the place, and they can no more cry to me for
help. And so I see nothing for it but to go and leave
them to their fate; perhaps, too, he is afraid of the mere
contagion of freedom which breathes from the very existence of those who are free; my way of speaking to the
people, of treating them, of living with them, the appeals
I make to their sense of truth, of duty, of self-respect, the
infinite compassion and the human consideration I feel for
them—all this, of course, makes my intercourse with them
dangerously suggestive of relations far different from any
thing they have ever known; and, as Mr. Q—— once al-

most hinted to me, my existence among slaves was an element of danger to the "institution." If I should go away, the human sympathy that I have felt for them will certainly never come near them again.

I was too unhappy to write any more, my dear friend, and you have been spared the rest of my paroxysm, which hereabouts culminated in the blessed refuge of abundant tears. God will provide. He has not forgotten, nor will He forsake these His poor children; and if I may no longer minister to them, they yet are in His hand, who cares for them more and better than I can.

Toward the afternoon yesterday I rowed up the river to the rice-island by way of refreshment to my spirits, and came back to-day, Wednesday, the 27th, through rather a severe storm. Before going to bed last night I finished Mr. Clay's speech, and ground my teeth over it. Before starting this morning I received from head man Frank a lesson on the various qualities of the various sorts of rice, and should be (at any rate till I forget all he told me, which I "feel in my bones" will be soon) a competent judge and expert saleswoman. The dead white speck, which shows itself sometimes in rice as it does in teeth, is in the former, as in the latter, a sign of decay; the finest quality of rice is what may be called flinty, clear and unclouded, and a pretty, clean, sparkling-looking thing it is.

I will tell you something curious and pleasant about my row back. The wind was so high and the river so rough when I left the rice-island, that just as I was about to get into the boat I thought it might not be amiss to carry my life-preserver with me, and ran back to the house to fetch it. Having taken that much care for my life, I jumped into the boat, and we pushed off. The fifteen miles' row with a furious wind, and part of the time the tide against us, and the huge broad, turbid river broken into a foaming sea of angry waves, was a pretty severe task for the men. They pulled with a will, however, but I had to forego the usual accompaniment of their voices, for the labor was tremendous, especially toward the end of our voyage, where, of course, the nearness of the sea increased the roughness of the water terribly. The men were in great spirits, however (there were eight of them rowing, and one behind was steering); one of them said something which elicited an exclamation of general assent, and I asked what it was; the steerer said they were pleased because there was not another planter's lady in all Georgia who would have gone through the storm all alone with them in a boat; *i. e.*, without the protecting presence of a white man. "Why," said I, "my good fellows, if the boat capsized, or any thing happened, I am sure I should have nine chances for my life instead of one;" at this there was one shout of "So you would, missis; true for dat, missis;" and in great mutual good-humor we reached the landing at Hampton Point.

As I walked home I pondered over this compliment of Mr. ——'s slaves to me, and did not feel quite sure that the very absence of the fear which haunts the Southern women in their intercourse with these people, and prevents them from trusting themselves ever with them out of reach of white companionship and supervision, was not one of the circumstances which makes my intercourse with them unsafe and undesirable. The idea of apprehending any mischief from them never yet crossed my brain; and in the perfect confidence with which I go among them, they must perceive a curious difference between me and my lady neighbors in these parts; all have expressed unbounded astonishment at my doing so.

The spring is fast coming on, and we shall, I suppose, soon leave Georgia. How new and sad a chapter of my life this winter here has been!

DEAR E——,—I can not give way to the bitter impatience I feel at my present position, and come back to the North without leaving my babies; and though I suppose their stay will not in any case be much prolonged in these regions of swamp and slavery, I must, for their sakes, remain where they are, and learn this dreary lesson of human suffering to the end. The record, it seems to me, must be utterly wearisome to you, as the instances themselves, I suppose, in a given time (thanks to that dreadful reconciler to all that is evil—habit), would become to me.

This morning I had a visit from two of the women, Charlotte and Judy, who came to me for help and advice for a complaint, which it really seems to me every other woman on the estate is cursed with, and which is a direct result of the conditions of their existence; the practice of sending women to labor in the fields in the third week after their confinement is a specific for causing this infirmity, and I know no specific for curing it under these circumstances. As soon as these poor things had departed with such comfort as I could give them, and the bandages they especially begged for, three other sable graces introduced themselves, Edie, Louisa, and Diana; the former told me she had had a family of seven children, but had lost them all through "ill luck," as she denominated the ignorance and ill treatment which were answerable for the loss of these, as of so many other poor little creatures their fellows. Having dismissed her and Diana with the sugar and rice they came to beg, I detained Louisa, whom I had never seen but in the presence of her old grandmother, whose version of the poor child's escape to, and hiding in the woods, I had a desire to compare with the heroine's own story. She told it very simply, and it was most pathetic. She had not finished her task one day, when she said she felt ill, and unable to do so, and had been severely flogged by Driver Bran, in whose "gang" she then was. The next day, in spite of this encouragement to labor, she had again been unable to complete her appointed work; and Bran having told her that he'd tie her up and flog her if she did not get it done, she had left the field and run into the swamp. "Tie you up, Louisa!" said I; "what is that?" She then described to me that they were fastened up by their wrists to a beam or a branch of a tree, their feet barely touching the ground, so as to allow them no purchase for resistance or evasion of the lash, their clothes turned over their heads, and their backs scored with a leather thong, either by the driver himself, or, if he pleases to inflict their punishment by deputy, any of the men he may choose to summon to the office; it might be father, brother, husband, or lover, if the overseer so ordered it. I turned sick, and my blood curdled listening to these details from the slender young slip of a lassie, with her poor piteous face and murmuring, pleading voice. "Oh," said I, "Louisa; but the rattlesnakes—the dreadful rattlesnakes in the swamps; were you not afraid of those horrible creatures?" "Oh, missis," said the poor child, "me no tink of dem; me forget all 'bout dem for de fretting." "Why did you come home at last?" "Oh, missis, me starve with hunger, me most dead with hunger before me come back." "And were you flogged, Louisa?" said I, with a shudder at what the answer might be. "No, missis, me go to hospital; me almost dead and sick so long, 'spec Driver Bran him forgot 'bout de flogging." I am getting perfectly savage over all these doings, E——, and really think I should consider my own throat and those of my children well cut if some night the people were to take it into their heads to clear off scores in that fashion.

The Calibanish wonderment of all my visitors at the exceedingly coarse and simple furniture and rustic means of comfort of my abode is very droll. I have never inhabited any apartment so perfectly devoid of what we should consider the common decencies of life; but to them, my rude chintz-covered sofa and common pine-wood table, with its green baize cloth, seem the adornings of a palace; and often in the evening, when my bairns are asleep, and M—— up stairs keeping watch over them, and I sit writing this daily history for your edification, the door of the great barn-like room is opened stealthily, and one after another, men and women come trooping silently in, their naked feet falling all but inaudibly on the bare boards as they betake themselves to the hearth, where they squat down on their hams in a circle, the bright blaze from the huge pine logs, which is the only light of this half of the room, shining on their sooty limbs and faces, and making them look like a ring of ebony idols surrounding my domestic hearth. I have had as many as fourteen at a time squatting silently there for nearly half an hour, watching me writing at the other end of the room. The candles on my table give only light enough for my own occupation, the fire-light illuminates the rest of the apartment; and you can not imagine any thing stranger than the effect of all these glassy whites of eyes and grinning white teeth turned toward me, and shining in the flickering light. I very often take no notice of them at all, and they seem perfectly absorbed in contemplating me. My evening dress probably excites their wonder and admiration no less than my rapid and continuous writing, for which they have sometimes expressed compassion, as if they thought it must be more laborious than hoeing; sometimes at the end of my day's journal I look up and say suddenly, "Well, what do you want?" when each black figure springs up at once, as if moved by machinery; they all answer, "Me come say ha do (how d'ye do), missis;" and then they troop out as noiselessly as they entered, like a procession of sable dreams, and I go off in search, if possible, of whiter ones.

Two days ago I had a visit of great interest to me from several lads from twelve to sixteen years old, who had come to beg me to give them work. To make you understand this, you must know that, wishing very much to cut some walks and drives through the very picturesque patches of woodland not far from the house, I announced, through Jack, my desire to give employment in the wood-cutting line to as many lads as chose, when their unpaid task was done, to come and do some work for me, for which I engaged to pay them. At the risk of producing a most dangerous process of reflection and calculation in their brains, I have persisted in paying what I considered wages to every slave that has been my servant; and these my laborers must, of course, be free to work or no, as they like, and if they work for me must be paid by me. The proposition met with unmingled approbation from my " gang ;" but I think it might be considered dangerously suggestive of the rightful relation between work and wages; in short, very involuntarily no doubt, but, nevertheless, very effectually I am disseminating ideas among Mr. ——'s dependents, the like of which have certainly never before visited their wool-thatched brains.

Friday, March 1. Last night, after writing so much to you, I felt weary, and went out into the air to refresh my spirit. The scene just beyond the house was beautiful; the moonlight slept on the broad river, which here is almost the sea, and on the masses of foliage of the great Southern oaks; the golden stars of German poetry shone in the purple curtains of the night, and the measured rush of the Atlantic unfurling its huge skirts upon the white sands of the beach (the sweetest and most awful lullaby in nature) resounded through the silent air.

I have not felt well, and have been much depressed for

H 2

some days past.   I think I should die if I had to live here. This morning, in order not to die yet, I thought I had better take a ride, and accordingly mounted the horse which I told you was one of the equestrian alternatives offered me here; but no sooner did he feel my weight, which, after all, is mere levity and frivolity to him, than he thought proper to rebel, and find the grasshopper a burden, and rear and otherwise demonstrate his disgust.   I have not ridden for a long time now; but Montreal's opposition very presently aroused the Amazon which is both natural and acquired in me, and I made him comprehend that, though I object to slaves, I expect obedient servants; which views of mine being imparted by a due administration of both spur and whip, attended with a judicious combination of coaxing pats on his great crested neck, and endearing commendations of his beauty, produced the desired effect.   Montreal accepted me as inevitable, and carried me very wisely and well up the island to another of the slave settlements on the plantation, called Jones's Creek.

On my way I passed some magnificent evergreen oaks,* and some thickets of exquisite evergreen shrubs, and one or two beautiful sites for a residence, which made me gnash my teeth when I thought of the one we had chosen. To be sure, these charming spots, instead of being conveniently in the middle of the plantation, are at an out of the way end of it, and so hardly eligible for the one quality desired for the overseer's abode, viz., being central.

All the slaves' huts on St. Simon's are far less solid, comfortable, and habitable than those at the rice-island.   I do

---

* The only ilex-trees which I have seen comparable in size and beauty with those of the sea-board of Georgia are some to be found in the Roman Campagna, at Passerano, Lunghegna, Castel Fusano, and other of its great princely farms, but especially in the magnificent woody wilderness of Valerano.

not know whether the laborer's habitation bespeaks the alteration in the present relative importance of the crops, but certainly the cultivators of the once far-famed long staple sea-island cotton of St. Simon's are far more miserably housed than the rice-raisers of the other plantation. These ruinous shielings, that hardly keep out wind or weather, are deplorable homes for young or aged people, and poor shelters for the hard-working men and women who cultivate the fields in which they stand. Riding home I passed some beautiful woodland, with charming pink and white blossoming peach and plum trees, which seemed to belong to some orchard that had been attempted, and afterward delivered over to wildness. On inquiry, I found that no fruit worth eating was ever gathered from them. What a pity it seems! for in this warm, delicious winter climate any and every species of fruit might be cultivated with little pains and to great perfection. As I was cantering along the side of one of the cotton-fields I suddenly heard some inarticulate vehement cries, and saw what seemed to be a heap of black limbs tumbling and leaping toward me, renewing the screams at intervals as it approached. I stopped my horse, and the black ball bounded almost into the road before me, and, suddenly straightening itself up into a haggard hag of a half-naked negress, exclaimed, with panting, eager breathlessness, "Oh, missis, missis, you no hear me cry, you no hear me call. Oh, missis, me call, me cry, and me run ; make me a gown like dat. Do, for massy's sake, only make me a gown like dat." This modest request for a riding habit in which to hoe the cotton-fields served for an introduction to sundry other petitions for rice, and sugar, and flannel, all which I promised the petitioner, but not the "gown like dat;" whereupon I rode off, and she flung herself down in the middle of the road to get her wind and rest.

The passion for dress is curiously strong in these people, and seems as though it might be made an instrument in converting them, outwardly at any rate, to something like civilization ; for, though their own native taste is decidedly both barbarous and ludicrous, it is astonishing how very soon they mitigate it in imitation of their white models. The fine figures of the mulatto women in Charleston and Savannah are frequently as elegantly and tastefully dressed as those of any of their female superiors; and here on St. Simon's, owing, I suppose, to the influence of the resident lady proprietors of the various plantations, and the propensity to imitate in their black dependents, the people that I see all seem to me much tidier, cleaner, and less fantastically dressed than those on the rice plantation, where no such influences reach them.

On my return from my ride I had a visit from Captain F——, the manager of a neighboring plantation, with whom I had a long conversation about the present and past condition of the estate, the species of feudal magnificence in which its original owner, Major ——, lived, the iron rule of old overseer K—— which succeeded to it, and the subsequent sovereignty of his son, Mr. R—— K——, the man for whom Mr. —— entertains such a cordial esteem, and of whom every account I receive from the negroes seems to me to indicate a merciless sternness of disposition that may be a virtue in a slave-driver, but is hardly a Christian grace. Captain F—— was one of our earliest visitors at the rice plantation on our arrival, and I think I told you of his mentioning, in speaking to me of the orange-trees which formerly grew all round the dikes there, that he had taken Basil Hall there once in their blossoming season, and that he had said the sight was as well worth crossing the Atlantic for as Niagara. To-day he referred to that again. He has resided for a great many years on a plantation here, and is connected with our neighbor, old Mr. C——, whose daughter, I believe, he married. He interested me extremely by his description of the house Major —— had many years ago on a part of the island called St. Clair. As far as I can understand, there must have been an indefinite number of "masters'" residences on this estate in the old major's time; for, what with the one we are building, and the ruined remains of those not quite improved off the face of the earth, and the tradition of those that have ceased to exist, even as ruins, I make out no fewer than seven. How gladly would I exchange all that remain and all that do not for the smallest tenement in your blessed Yankee mountain village!

Captain F—— told me that at St. Clair General Oglethorpe, the good and brave English governor of the State of Georgia in its colonial days, had his residence, and that among the magnificent live oaks which surround the site of the former settlement, there was one especially venerable and picturesque, which in his recollection always went by the name of General Oglethorpe's Oak. If you remember the history of the colony under his benevolent rule, you must recollect how absolutely he and his friend and counselor Wesley opposed the introduction of slavery in the colony. How wrathfully the old soldier's spirit ought to haunt these cotton-fields and rice-swamps of his old domain, with their population of wretched slaves! I will ride to St. Clair and see his oak; if I should see him, he can not have much to say to me on the subject that I should not cry amen to.

Saturday, March 2. I have made a gain, no doubt, in one respect in coming here, dear E——, for, not being afraid of a rearing stallion, I can ride; but, on the other hand, my aquatic diversions are all likely, I fear, to be much curtailed. Well may you, or any other Northern Abolitionist, consider this a heaven-forsaken region—why, I can not even get worms to fish with, and was solemnly

assured by Jack this morning that the whole " Point," *i.
e.*, neighborhood of the house, had been searched in vain
for these useful and agreeable animals. I must take to
some more sportsman-like species of bait; but, in my total ignorance of even the kind of fish that inhabit these
waters, it is difficult for me to adapt my temptations to
their taste.

Yesterday evening I had a visit that made me very sorrowful, if any thing connected with these poor people can
be called more especially sorrowful than their whole condition; but Mr. ——'s declaration that he will receive no
more statements of grievances or petitions for redress
through me makes me as desirous now of shunning the
vain appeals of these unfortunates as I used to be of receiving and listening to them. The imploring cry, " Oh
missis!" that greets me whichever way I turn, makes me
long to stop my ears now; for what can I say or do any
more for them? The poor little favors—the rice, the sugar, the flannel—that they beg for with such eagerness,
and receive with such exuberant gratitude, I can, it is true,
supply, and words and looks of pity, and counsel of patience, and such instruction in womanly habits of decency
and cleanliness as may enable them to better, in some degree, their own hard lot; but to the entreaty, " Oh, missis, you speak to massa for us! Oh, missis, you beg massa
for us! Oh, missis, you tell massa for we, he sure do as
you say!" I can not now answer as formerly, and I turn
away choking and with eyes full of tears from the poor
creatures, not even daring to promise any more the faithful transmission of their prayers.

The women who visited me yesterday evening were all
in the family-way, and came to entreat of me to have the
sentence (what else can I call it?) modified which con-
demns them to resume their labor of hoeing in the fields
three weeks after their confinement. They knew, of

course, that I can not interfere with their appointed labor, and therefore their sole entreaty was that I would use my influence with Mr. —— to obtain for them a month's respite from labor in the field after childbearing. Their principal spokeswoman, a woman with a bright sweet face, called Mary, and a very sweet voice, which is by no means an uncommon excellence among them, appealed to my own experience; and while she spoke of my babies, and my carefully tended, delicately nursed, and tenderly watched confinement and convalescence, and implored me to have a kind of labor given to them less exhausting during the month after their confinement, I held the table before me so hard in order not to cry that I think my fingers ought to have left a mark on it. At length I told them that Mr. —— had forbidden me to bring him any more complaints from them, for that he thought the ease with which I received and believed their stories only tended to make them discontented, and that, therefore, I feared I could not promise to take their petitions to him; but that he would be coming down to "the Point" soon, and that they had better come then some time when I was with him, and say what they had just been saying to me; and with this, and various small bounties, I was forced, with a heavy heart, to dismiss them; and when they were gone, with many exclamations of, "Oh yes, missis, you will, you will speak to massa for we; God bless you, missis, we sure you will!" I had my cry out for them, for myself, for us. All these women had had large families, and *all* of them had lost half their children, and several of them had lost more. How I do ponder upon the strange fate which has brought me here, from so far away, from surroundings so curiously different—how my own people in that blessed England of my birth would marvel if they could suddenly have a vision of me as I sit here, and how sorry some of them would be for me!

I am helped to bear all that is so very painful to me here by my constant enjoyment of the strange, wild scenery in the midst of which I live, and which my resumption of my equestrian habits gives me almost daily opportunity of observing. I rode to-day to some new-cleared and plowed ground that was being prepared for the precious cotton-crop. I crossed a salt marsh upon a raised causeway that was perfectly alive with land-crabs, whose desperately active endeavors to avoid my horse's hoofs were so ludicrous that I literally laughed alone and aloud at them. The sides of this road across the swamp were covered with a thick and close embroidery of creeping moss, or rather lichens of the most vivid green and red: the latter made my horse's path look as if it was edged with an exquisite pattern of coral; it was like a thing in a fairy tale, and delighted me extremely.

I suppose, E——, one secret of my being able to suffer as acutely as I do, without being made either ill or absolutely miserable, is the childish excitability of my temperament, and the sort of ecstasy which any beautiful thing gives me. No day, almost no hour, passes without some enjoyment of the sort this coral-bordered road gave me, which not only charms my senses completely at the time, but returns again and again before my memory, delighting my fancy, and stimulating my imagination. I sometimes despise myself for what seems to me an inconceivable rapidity of emotion, that almost makes me doubt whether any one who feels so many things can really be said to feel any thing; but I generally recover from this perplexity by remembering whither invariably every impression of beauty leads my thoughts, and console myself for my contemptible facility of impression by the reflection that it is, upon the whole, a merciful system of compensation by which my whole nature, tortured as it was last night, can be absorbed this morning in a perfectly pleasurable contemplation of the capers of crabs and the color of mosses as if nothing else existed in creation. One thing, however, I think, is equally certain, and that is, that I need never expect much sympathy, and perhaps this special endowment will make me, to some degree, independent of it; but I have no doubt that to follow me through half a day with any species of lively participation in my feelings would be a severe breathless moral calisthenic to most of my friends — what Shakspeare calls "sweating labor." As far as I have hitherto had opportunities of observing, children and maniacs are the only creatures who would be capable of sufficiently rapid transitions of thought and feeling to keep pace with me.

And so I rode through the crabs and the coral. There is one thing, however, I beg to commend to your serious consideration as a trainer of youth, and that is, the expediency of cultivating in all the young minds you educate an equal love of the good, the beautiful, and the absurd (not an easy task, for the latter is apt in its development to interfere a little with the two others) : doing this, you command all the resources of existence. The love of the good and beautiful of course you are prepared to cultivate—that goes without saying, as the French say; the love of the ludicrous will not appear to you as important, and yet you will be wrong to undervalue it. In the first place, I might tell you that it was almost like cherishing the love of one's fellow-creatures — at which, no doubt, you shake your head reprovingly; but, leaving aside the enormous provision for the exercise of this natural faculty which we offer to each other, why should crabs scuttle from under my horse's feet in such a way as to make me laugh again every time I think of it, if there is not an inherent propriety in laughter, as the only emotion which certain objects challenge—an emotion wholesome for the soul and body of man ? After all, *why* are we contrived to laugh at all, if laughter is not essentially befitting and beneficial? and most people's lives are too lead-colored to afford to lose one sparkle on them, even the smallest twinkle of light gathered from a flash of nonsense. Hereafter point out for the "appreciative" study of your pupils all that is absurd in themselves, others, and the universe in general; 'tis an element largely provided, of course, to meet a corresponding and grateful capacity for its enjoyment.

After my crab and coral causeway I came to the most exquisite thickets of evergreen shrubbery you can imagine. If I wanted to paint Paradise I would copy this undergrowth, passing through which I went on to the settlement at St. Annie's, traversing another swamp on another raised causeway. The thickets through which I next rode were perfectly draped with the beautiful wild jasmine of these woods. Of all the parasitical plants I ever saw, I do think it is the most exquisite in form and color, and its perfume is like the most delicate heliotrope.

I stopped for some time before a thicket of glittering evergreens, over which hung, in every direction, streaming garlands of these fragrant golden cups, fit for Oberon's banqueting service. These beautiful shrubberies were resounding with the songs of mocking-birds. I sat there on my horse in a sort of dream of enchantment, looking, listening, and inhaling the delicious atmosphere of those flowers; and suddenly my eyes opened, as if I had been asleep, on some bright red bunches of spring leaves on one of the winter-stripped trees, and I as suddenly thought of the cold Northern skies and earth, where the winter was still inflexibly tyrannizing over you all, and, in spite of the loveliness of all that was present, and the harshness of all that I seemed to see at that moment, no first tokens of the spring's return were ever more welcome to me than those bright leaves that reminded me how soon I should leave this scene of material beauty and moral degradation, where the beauty itself is of an appropriate character to the human existence it surrounds: above all, loveliness, brightness, and fragrance; but below! it gives one a sort of melusina feeling of horror—all swamp and poisonous stagnation, which the heat will presently make alive with venomous reptiles.

I rode on, and the next object that attracted my attention was a very startling and by no means agreeable one —an enormous cypress-tree which had been burnt stood charred and blackened, and leaning toward the road so as to threaten a speedy fall across it, and on one of the limbs of this great charcoal giant hung a dead rattlesnake. If I tell you that it looked to me at least six feet long, you will say you only wonder I did not say twelve; it was a hideous-looking creature, and some negroes I met soon after told me they had found it in the swamp, and hung it dead on the burning tree. Certainly the two together made a dreadful trophy, and a curious contrast to the lovely bowers of bloom I had just been contemplating with such delight.

This settlement at St. Annie's is the remotest on the whole plantation, and I found there the wretchedest huts, and most miserably squalid, filthy, and forlorn creatures I had yet seen here—certainly the condition of the slaves on this estate is infinitely more neglected and deplorable than that on the rice plantation. Perhaps it may be that the extremely unhealthy nature of the rice cultivation makes it absolutely necessary that the physical condition of the laborers should be maintained at its best to enable them to abide it; and yet it seems to me that even the process of soaking the rice can hardly create a more dangerous miasma than the poor creatures must inhale who live in the midst of these sweltering swamps, half sea, half river slime. Perhaps it has something to do with the fact that the climate on St. Simon's is generally considered peculiarly mild and favorable, and so less protection of clothes and shelter is thought necessary here for the poor residents; perhaps, too, it may be because the cotton crop is now, I believe, hardly as valuable as the rice crop, and the plantation here, which was once the chief source of its owner's wealth, is becoming a secondary one, and so not worth so much care or expense in repairing and constructing negro huts and feeding and clothing the slaves. More pitiable objects than some of those I saw at the St. Annie's settlement to-day I hope never to see: there was an old crone called Hannah, a sister, as well as I could understand what she said, of old House Molly, whose face and figure, seamed with wrinkles, and bowed and twisted with age and infirmity, really hardly retained the semblance of those of a human creature, and as she crawled to me almost half her naked body was exposed through the miserable tatters that she held on with one hand, while the other eagerly clutched my hand, and her poor blear eyes wandered all over me as if she was bewildered by the strange aspect of any human being but those whose sight was familiar to her. One or two forlorn creatures like herself, too old or too infirm to be compelled to work, and the half-starved and more than half-naked children apparently left here under their charge, were the only inmates I found in these wretched hovels.

I came home without stopping to look at any thing, for I had no heart any longer for what had so charmed me on my way to this place. Galloping along the road after leaving the marshes, I scared an ox who was feeding leisurely, and, to my great dismay, saw the foolish beast betake himself with lumbering speed into the "bush:" the slaves will have to hunt after him, and perhaps will discover more rattlesnakes six or twelve feet long.

After reaching home I went to the house of the overseer to see his wife, a tidy, decent, kind-hearted little woman, who seems to me to do her duty by the poor people she lives among as well as her limited intelligence and still more limited freedom allow. The house her husband lives in is the former residence of Major ——, which was the great mansion of the estate. It is now in a most ruinous and tottering condition, and they inhabit but a few rooms in it; the others are gradually mouldering to pieces, and the whole edifice will, I should think, hardly stand long enough to be carried away by the river, which in its yearly inroads on the bank on which it stands has already approached within a perilous proximity to the old dilapidated planter's palace. Old Molly, of whom I have often before spoken to you, who lived here in the days of the prosperity and grandeur of "Hampton," still clings to the relics of her old master's former magnificence, and with a pride worthy of old Caleb of Ravenswood showed me through the dismantled decaying rooms and over the remains of the dairy, displaying a capacious fish-box or well, where, in the good old days, the master's supply was kept in fresh salt water till required for table. Her prideful lamentations over the departure of all this quondam glory were ludicrous and pathetic; but, while listening with some amusement to the jumble of grotesque descriptions, through which her impression of the immeasurable grandeur and nobility of the house she served was the predominant feature, I could not help contrasting the present state of the estate with that which she described, and wondering why it should have become, as it undoubtedly must have done, so infinitely less productive a property than in the old major's time.

Before closing this letter, I have a mind to transcribe to you the entries for to-day recorded in a sort of day-book, where I put down very succinctly the number of people who visit me, their petitions and ailments, and also such special particulars concerning them as seem to me worth recording. You will see how miserable the physical condition of many of these poor creatures is; and their physical condition, it is insisted by those who uphold this evil system, is the only part of it which is prosperous, happy, and compares well with that of Northern laborers. Judge from the details I now send you; and never forget, while reading them, that the people on this plantation are well off, and consider themselves well off, in comparison with the slaves on some of the neighboring estates.

Fanny has had six children; all dead but one. She came to beg to have her work in the field lightened.

Nanny has had three children; two of them are dead. She came to implore that the rule of sending them into the field three weeks after their confinement might be altered.

Leah, Cæsar's wife, has had six children; three are dead.

Sophy, Lewis's wife, came to beg for some old linen. She is suffering fearfully; has had ten children; five of them are dead. The principal favor she asked was a piece of meat, which I gave her.

Sally, Scipio's wife, has had two miscarriages and three children born, one of whom is dead. She came complaining of incessant pain and weakness in her back. This woman was a mulatto daughter of a slave called Sophy, by a white man of the name of Walker, who visited the plantation.

Charlotte, Renty's wife, had had two miscarriages, and was with child again. She was almost crippled with rheumatism, and showed me a pair of poor swollen knees that made my heart ache. I have promised her a pair of flannel trowsers, which I must forthwith set about making.

Sarah, Stephen's wife—this woman's case and history were alike deplorable. She had had four miscarriages, had brought seven children into the world, five of whom were dead, and was again with child. She complained of dreadful pains in the back, and an internal tumor which swells with the exertion of working in the fields; probably, I think, she is ruptured. She told me she had once been mad and had ran into the woods, where she contrived to elude discovery for some time, but was at last tracked and brought back, when she was tied up by the arms, and heavy logs fastened to her feet, and was severely flogged. After this she contrived to escape again, and lived for some time skulking in the woods, and she supposes mad, for when she was taken again she was entirely naked. She subsequently recovered from this derangement, and seems now just like all the other poor creatures who come to me for help and pity. I suppose her constant childbearing and hard labor in the fields at the same time may have produced the temporary insanity.

Sukey, Bush's wife, only came to pay her respects. She had had four miscarriages; had brought eleven children into the world, five of whom are dead.

Molly, Quambo's wife, also only came to see me. Hers was the best account I have yet received; she had had nine children, and six of them were still alive.

This is only the entry for to-day, in my diary, of the people's complaints and visits. Can you conceive a more wretched picture than that which it exhibits of the conditions under which these women live? Their cases are in no respect singular, and though they come with pitiful entreaties that I will help them with some alleviation of their pressing physical distresses, it seems to me marvelous with what desperate patience (I write it advisedly, patience of utter despair) they endure their sorrow-laden existence. Even the poor wretch who told that miserable story of insanity, and lonely hiding in the swamps, and scourging when she was found, and of her renewed

madness and flight, did so in a sort of low, plaintive,
monotonous murmur of misery, as if such sufferings were
all "in the day's work."

I ask these questions about their children because I
think the number they bear as compared with the number they rear a fair gauge of the effect of the system on
their own health and that of their offspring. There was
hardly one of these women, as you will see by the details
I have noted of their ailments, who might not have been
a candidate for a bed in a hospital, and they had come to
me after working all day in the fields.

DEAREST E——,—When I told you in my last letter of
the encroachments which the waters of the Altamaha are
daily making on the bank at Hampton Point and immediately in front of the imposing-looking old dwelling of
the former master, I had no idea how rapid this crumbling process has been of late years; but to-day, standing
there with Mrs. G——, whom I had gone to consult about
the assistance we might render to some of the poor creatures whose cases I sent you in my last letter, she told me
that within the memory of many of the slaves now living
on the plantation, a grove of orange-trees had spread its
fragrance and beauty between the house and the river.
Not a vestige remains of them. The earth that bore
them was gradually undermined, slipped, and sank down
into the devouring flood; and when she saw the astonished incredulity of my look, she led me to the ragged
and broken bank, and there, immediately below it, and
just covered by the turbid waters of the in-rushing tide,
were the heads of the poor drowned orange-trees, sway-
ing like black twigs in the briny flood, which had not yet
dislodged all of them from their hold upon the soil which
had gone down beneath the water wearing its garland of

bridal blossom. As I looked at those trees a wild wish rose in my heart that the river and the sea would swallow up and melt in their salt waves the whole of this accursed property of ours. I am afraid the horror of slavery with which I came down to the South, the general theoretic abhorrence of an Englishwoman for it, has gained, through the intensity it has acquired, a morbid character of mere desire to be delivered from my own share in it. I think so much of these wretches that I see, that I can hardly remember any others; and my zeal for the general emancipation of the slave has almost narrowed itself to this most painful desire that I and mine were freed from the responsibility of our share in this huge misery; and so I thought, "Beat, beat, the crumbling banks and sliding shores, wild waves of the Atlantic and the Altamaha! Sweep down and carry hence this evil earth and these homes of tyranny, and roll above the soil of slavery, and wash my soul and the souls of those I love clean from the blood of our kind!" But I have no idea that Mr. —— and his brother would cry amen to any such prayer. Sometimes, as I stand and listen to the roll of the great ocean surges on the farther side of little St. Simon's Island, a small green screen of tangled wilderness that interposes between this point and the Atlantic, I think how near our West Indian Islands and freedom are to these unfortunate people, many of whom are expert and hardy boatmen, as far as the mere mechanical management of a boat goes; but, unless Providence were compass and steersman too, it avails nothing that they should know how near their freedom might be found, nor have I any right to tell them if they could find it, for the slaves are not mine, they are Mr. ——'s.

The mulatto woman, Sally, accosted me again to-day, and begged that she might be put to some other than field labor. Supposing she felt herself unequal to it, I

I

asked her some questions, but the principal reason she
urged for her promotion to some less laborious kind of
work was, that hoeing in the field was so hard to her on
" *account of her color*," and she therefore petitions to be
allowed to learn a trade. I was much puzzled at this
reason for her petition, but was presently made to understand that, being a mulatto, she considered field labor a
degradation; her white bastardy appearing to her a title
to consideration in my eyes. The degradation of these
people is very complete, for they have accepted the contempt of their masters to that degree that they profess,
and really seem to feel it for themselves, and the faintest
admixture of white blood in their black veins appears at
once, by common consent of their own race, to raise them
in the scale of humanity. I had not much sympathy for
this petition. The woman's father had been a white man
who was employed for some purpose on the estate. In
speaking upon this subject to Mrs. G——, she said that,
as far as her observation went, the lower class of white
men in the South lived with colored women precisely as
they would at the North with women of their own race;
the outcry that one hears against amalgamation appears
therefore to be something educated and acquired rather
than intuitive. I can not perceive, in observing my children, that they exhibit the slightest repugnance or dislike
to these swarthy dependents of theirs, which they surely
would do if, as is so often pretended, there is an inherent,
irreconcilable repulsion on the part of the white toward
the negro race. All the Southern children that I have
seen seem to have a special fondness for these good-na-
tured, childish human beings, whose mental condition is
kin in its simplicity and proneness to impulsive emotion
to their own, and I can detect in them no trace of the abhorrence and contempt for their dusky skins which all
questions of treating them with common justice is so apt
to elicit from American men and women.

To-day, for the first time since I left the rice-island, I went out fishing, but had no manner of luck. Jack rowed me up Jones's Creek, a small stream which separates St. Simon's from the main, on the opposite side from the great waters of the Altamaha. The day was very warm. It is becoming almost too hot to remain here much longer, at least for me, who dread and suffer from heat so much. The whole summer, however, is passed by many members of the Georgia families on their estates by the sea. When the heat is intense, the breeze from the ocean and the salt air, I suppose, prevent it from being intolerable or hurtful. Our neighbor, Mr. C——, and his family reside entirely, the year round, on their plantations here without apparently suffering in their health from the effects of the climate. I suppose it is the intermediate region between the sea-board and the mountains that becomes so pestilential when once the warm weather sets in. I remember the Belgian minister, M. de ——, telling me that the mountain country of Georgia was as beautiful as Paradise, and that the climate, as far as his experience went, was perfectly delicious. He was, however, only there on an exploring expedition, and, of course, took the most favorable season of the year for the purpose.

I have had several women with me this afternoon more or less disabled by chronic rheumatism. Certainly, either their labor or the exposure it entails must be very severe, for this climate is the last that ought to engender rheumatism. This evening I had a visit from a bright young woman, calling herself Minda, who came to beg for a little rice or sugar. I inquired from which of the settlements she had come down, and found that she has to walk three miles every day to and from her work. She made no complaint whatever of this, and seemed to think her laborious tramp down to the Point after her day of labor on the field well rewarded by the pittance of rice and sugar she obtained. Perhaps she consoled herself for the exertion by the reflection which occurred to me while talking to her, that many women who have borne children, and many women with child, go the same distance to and from their task-ground—that seems dreadful!

I have let my letter lie from a stress of small interruptions. Yesterday, Sunday, 3d, old Auber, a stooping, halting hag, came to beg for flannel and rice. As usual, of course, I asked various questions concerning her condition, family, etc.; she told me she had never been married, but had had five children, two of whom were dead. She complained of flooding, of intolerable backache, and said that with all these ailments she considered herself quite recovered, having suffered horribly from an abscess in her neck, which was now nearly well. I was surprised to hear of her other complaints, for she seemed to me like quite an old woman; but constant childbearing, and the life of labor, exposure, and privation which they lead, ages these poor creatures prematurely.

Dear E——, how I do defy you to guess the novel accomplishment I have developed within the last two days; what do you say to my turning butcher's boy, and cutting up the carcase of a sheep for the instruction of our butcher and cook, and benefit of our table? You know, I have often written you word that we have mutton here—thanks to the short salt grass on which it feeds—that compares with the best South Down or *Prè salé;* but such is the barbarous ignorance of the cook, or rather the butcher who furnishes our kitchen supplies, that I defy the most expert anatomist to pronounce on any piece (joints they can not be called) of mutton brought to our table to what part of the animal sheep it originally belonged. I have often complained bitterly of this, and in vain implored Abraham the cook to send me some dish of mutton to which I might with safety apply the familiar name of leg, shoulder, or haunch. These remonstrances and expostulations have produced no result whatever, however, but an increase of eccentricity in the *chunks* of sheeps' flesh placed upon the table; the squares, diamonds, cubes, and rhomboids of mutton have been more ludicrously and hopelessly unlike any thing we see in a Christian butcher's shop, with every fresh endeavor Abraham has made to find out " zackly wot de missis do want;" so the day before yesterday, while I was painfully dragging S——through the early intellectual science of the alphabet and first reading lesson, Abraham appeared at the door of the room brandishing a very long thin knife, and with many bows, grins, and apologies for disturbing me, begged that I would go and cut up a sheep for him. My first impulse, of course, was to decline the very unusual task offered me with mingled horror and amusement. Abraham, however, insisted and besought, extolled the fineness of his sheep, declared his misery at being unable to cut it as I wished, and his readiness to conform for the future to whatever *patterns* of mutton " de missis would only please to give him." Upon reflection, I thought I might very well contrive to indicate upon the sheep the size and form of the different joints of civilized mutton, and so, for the future, save much waste of good meat; and, moreover, the lesson, once taught, would not require to be repeated, and I have ever held it expedient to accept every opportunity of learning to do any thing, no matter how unusual, which presented itself to be done; and so I followed Abraham to the kitchen, when, with a towel closely pinned over my silk dress, and knife in hand, I stood for a minute or two meditating profoundly before the rather unsightly object which Abraham had pronounced " de beautifullest sheep de missis eber saw." The sight and smell of raw meat are especially odious to me, and I have often thought that if I had had to be my own cook, I should inevitably be-

come a vegetarian, probably, indeed, return entirely to my
green and salad days. Nathless, I screwed my courage
to the sticking-point, and slowly and delicately traced out
with the point of my long carving-knife two shoulders,
two legs, a saddle, and a neck of mutton; not probably
in the most thoroughly artistic and butcherly style, but as
nearly as my memory and the unassisted light of nature
would enable me; and having instructed Abraham in the
various boundaries, sizes, shapes, and names of the several
joints, I returned to S—— and her belles-lettres, rather
elated, upon the whole, at the creditable mode in which I
flattered myself I had accomplished my unusual task, and
the hope of once more seeing roast mutton of my acquaintance. I will confess to you, dear E——, that the *neck*
was not a satisfactory part of the performance, and I have
spent some thoughts since in trying to adjust in my own
mind its proper shape and proportions.

As an accompaniment to "de beautifullest mutton de
missis eber see," we have just received from my neighbor
Mr. C—— the most magnificent supply of fresh vegetables, green peas, salad, etc. He has a garden, and a Scotchman's real love for horticulture, and I profit by them in
this very agreeable manner.

I have been interrupted by several visits, my dear E——,
among other, one from a poor creature called Judy, whose
sad story and condition affected me most painfully. She
had been married, she said, some years ago to one of the
men called Temba, who, however, now has another wife,
having left her because she went mad. While out of her
mind she escaped into the jungle, and contrived to secrete
herself there for some time, but was finally tracked and
caught, and brought back and punished by being made to
sit, day after day, for hours in the stocks—a severe punishment for a man, but for a woman perfectly barbarous.
She complained of chronic rheumatism, and other terrible

ailments, and said she suffered such intolerable pain while laboring in the fields, that she had come to entreat me to have her work lightened. She could hardly crawl, and cried bitterly all the time she spoke to me.

She told me a miserable story of her former experience on the plantation under Mr. K——'s overseership. It seems that Jem Valiant (an extremely difficult subject, a mulatto lad, whose valor is sufficiently accounted for now by the influence of the mutinous white blood) was her first-born, the son of Mr. K——, who forced her, flogged her severely for having resisted him, and then sent her off, as a farther punishment, to Five Pound—a horrible swamp in a remote corner of the estate, to which the slaves are sometimes banished for such offenses as are not sufficiently atoned for by the lash. The dismal loneliness of the place to these poor people, who are as dependent as children upon companionship and sympathy, makes this solitary exile a much-dreaded infliction; and this poor creature said that, bad as the flogging was, she would sooner have taken that again than the dreadful lonely days and nights she spent on the penal swamp of Five Pound.

I make no comment on these terrible stories, my dear friend, and tell them to you as nearly as possible in the perfectly plain, unvarnished manner in which they are told to me. I do not wish to add to, or perhaps I ought to say take away from, the effect of such narrations by amplifying the simple horror and misery of their bare details.

My dearest E——, —I have had an uninterrupted stream of women and children flowing in the whole morning to say " Ha de, missis ?" Among others, a poor woman called Mile, who could hardly stand for pain and swelling in her limbs; she had had fifteen children and two miscarriages; nine of her children had died; for the last three years she had become almost a cripple with chronic rheumatism, yet she is driven every day to work in the field. She held my hands, and stroked them in the most appealing way while she exclaimed, " Oh my missis! my missis! me neber sleep till day for de pain," and with the day her labor must again be resumed. I gave her flannel and sal volatile to rub her poor swelled limbs with; rest I could not give her—rest from her labor and her pain—this mother of fifteen children.

Another of my visitors had a still more dismal story to tell; her name was Die; she had had sixteen children, fourteen of whom were dead; she had had four miscarriages: one had been caused with falling down with a very heavy burden on her head, and one from having her arms strained up to be lashed. I asked her what she meant by having her arms tied up. She said their hands were first tied together, sometimes by the wrists, and sometimes, which was worse, by the thumbs, and they were then drawn up to a tree or post, so as almost to swing them off the ground, and then their clothes rolled round their waist, and a man with a cowhide stands and stripes them. I give you the woman's words. She did not speak of this as of any thing strange, unusual, or especially horrid and abominable; and when I said, "Did they do that to you when you were with child?" she simply replied, " Yes, missis." And to all this I listen—I, an English woman, the wife of the man who owns these wretches, and I can not say, "That thing shall not be done again; that cruel shame and villainy shall never be known here again." I gave the woman meat and flannel, which were what she came to ask for, and remained choking with indignation and grief long after they had all left me to my most bitter thoughts.

I went out to try and walk off some of the weight of horror and depression which I am beginning to feel daily more and more, surrounded by all this misery and degradation that I can neither help nor hinder. The blessed spring is coming very fast, the air is full of delicious wildwood fragrances, and the wonderful songs of Southern birds; the wood paths are as tempting as paths into Paradise, but Jack is in such deadly terror about the snakes, which are now beginning to glide about with a freedom and frequency certainly not pleasing, that he will not follow me off the open road, and twice to-day scared me back from charming wood paths I ventured to explore with his exclamations of terrified warning.

I gathered some exquisite pink blossoms, of a sort of waxen texture, off a small shrub which was strange to me, and for which Jack's only name was dye-bush; but I could not ascertain from him whether any dyeing substance was found in its leaves, bark, or blossoms.

I returned home along the river side, stopping to admire a line of noble live oaks beginning, alas! to be smothered with the treacherous white moss under whose pale trailing masses their verdure gradually succumbs, leaving them, like huge hoary ghosts, perfect mountains of parasitical vegetation, which, strangely enough, appears only to hang upon and swing from their boughs without adhering to them. The mixture of these streams of gray-white filaments with the dark foliage is extremely beautiful as long as the leaves of the tree survive in sufficient masses to produce the rich contrast of color; but when the moss has literally conquered the whole tree, and, after stripping its huge limbs bare, clothed them with its own wan masses, they always looked to me like so many gigantic Druid ghosts, with flowing robes and beards, and locks all of one ghastly gray, and I would not have broken a twig off them for the world, lest a sad voice, like that which reproached Dante, should have moaned out of it to me,

I 2

"Non hai tu spirto di pietade alcuno?"

A beautiful mass of various woodland skirted the edge
of the stream, and mingled in its foliage every shade of
green, from the pale, stiff spikes and fans of the dwarf palmetto to the dark canopy of the magnificent ilex—bowers
and brakes of the loveliest wildness, where one dare not
tread three steps for fear.   What a tantalization ! it is like
some wicked enchantment.

DEAREST E——,—I have found growing along the edge
of the dreary inclosure where the slaves are buried such
a lovely wild flower; it is a little like the euphrasia or
eyebright of the English meadows, but grows quite close
to the turf, almost into it, and consists of clusters of tiny
white flowers that look as if they were made of the finest
porcelain.   I took up a root of it yesterday, with a sort
of vague idea that I could transplant it to the North;
though I can not say that I should care to transplant any
thing thither that could renew to me the associations of
this place—not even the delicious wild flowers, if I could.
The woods here are full of wild plum-trees, the delicate
white blossoms of which twinkle among the evergreen
copses, and, besides illuminating them with a faint starlight, suggest to my mind a possible liqueur like kirsch,
which I should think could quite as well be extracted from
wild plums as wild cherries, and the trees are so numerous
that there ought to be quite a harvest from them.   You
may, and, doubtless, have seen palmetto plants in Northern green and hot houses, but you never saw palmetto
roots; and what curious things they are ! huge, hard, yel-
lowish-brown stems, as thick as my arm, or thicker, ex-
tending and ramifying under the ground in masses that
seem hardly justified or accounted for by the elegant,
light, spiky fans of dusky green foliage with which they

fill the under part of the woods here. They look very tropical and picturesque, but both in shape and color suggest something metallic rather than vegetable; the bronze-green hue and lance-like form of their foliage has an arid, hard character, that makes one think they could be manufactured quite as well as cultivated. At first I was extremely delighted with the novelty of their appearance; but now I feel thirsty when I look at them, and the same with their kinsfolk, the yuccas and their intimate friends, if not relations, the prickly pears, with all of which once strange growth I have grown contemptuously familiar now.

Did it ever occur to you what a strange affinity there is between the texture and color of the wild vegetables of these sandy Southern soils, and the texture and color of shells? The prickly pear, and especially the round little cactus plants all covered with hairy spikes, are curiously suggestive of a family of round spiked shells, with which you, as well as myself, are doubtless familiar; and though the splendid flame-color of some cactus blossoms never suggests any nature but that of flowers, I have seen some of a peculiar shade of yellow-pink, that resembles the mingled tint on the inside of some elaborately colored shell, and the pale white and rose flowers of another kind have the coloring and almost texture of shell, much rather than of any vegetable substance.

To-day I walked out without Jack, and, in spite of the terror of snakes with which he has contrived slightly to inoculate me, I did make a short exploring journey into the woods. I wished to avoid a plowed field, to the edge of which my wanderings had brought me; but my dash into the woodland, though unpunished by an encounter with snakes, brought me only into a marsh as full of land-crabs as an ant-hill is of ants, and from which I had to retreat ingloriously, finding my way home at last by the beach.

I have had, as usual, a tribe of visitors and petitioners ever since I came home. I will give you an account of those cases which had any thing beyond the average of interest in their details. One poor woman, named Molly, came to beg that I would, if possible, get an extension of their exemption from work after childbearing. The close of her argument was concise and forcible. "Missis, we hab um pickanniny — tree weeks in de ospital, and den right out upon the hoe again — *can we strong* dat way, missis ? No!" And truly I do not see that they can. This poor creature has had eight children and two miscarriages. All her children were dead but one. Another of my visitors was a divinely named but not otherwise divine Venus; it is a favorite name among these sable folk, but, of course, must have been given originally in derision. The Aphrodite in question was a dirt-colored (convenient color I should say for these parts) mulatto. I could not understand how she came on this property, for she was the daughter of a black woman and the overseer of an estate to which her mother formerly belonged, and from which I suppose she was sold, exchanged, or given, as the case may be, to the owners of this plantation. She was terribly crippled with rheumatism, and came to beg for some flannel. She had had eleven children, five of whom had died, and two miscarriages. As she took her departure, the vacant space she left on the other side of my writing-table was immediately filled by another black figure with a bowed back and piteous face, one of the thousand "Mollies" on the estate, where the bewildering redundancy of their name is avoided by adding that of their husband; so when the question, "Well, who are you ?" was answered with the usual genuflexion, and "I'se Molly, missis!" I, of course, went on with "whose Molly," and she went on to refer herself to the ownership (under Mr. —— and heaven) of one Tony, but proceeded to say that

he was not her *real* husband. This appeal to an element
of reality in the universally accepted fiction which passes
here by the title of marriage surprised me; and on asking
her what she meant, she replied that her real husband had
been sold from the estate for repeated attempts to run
away. He had made his escape several times, and skulked
starving in the woods and morasses, but had always been
tracked and brought back, and flogged almost to death,
and finally sold as an incorrigible runaway. What a
spirit of indomitable energy the wretched man must have
had, to have tried so often that hideously hopeless attempt
to fly! I do not write you the poor woman's jargon,
which was ludicrous; for I can not write you the sighs,
and tears, and piteous looks, and gestures, that made it
pathetic; of course she did not know whither or to whom
her *real* husband had been sold; but in the mean time
Mr. K——, that merciful Providence of the estate, had
provided her with the above-named Tony, by whom she
had had nine children, six of whom were dead; she, too,
had miscarried twice. She came to ask me for some flannel for her legs, which were all swollen with constant
rheumatism, and to beg me to give her something to cure
some bad sores and ulcers, which seemed to me dreadful
enough in their present condition, but which she said
break out afresh and are twice as bad every summer.

I have let my letter lie since the day before yesterday,
dear E——, having had no leisure to finish it. Yesterday
morning I rode out to St. Clair's, where there used formerly to be another negro settlement, and another house
of Major ——'s. I had been persuaded to try one of the
mares I had formerly told you of, and to be sure a more
"curst" quadrup d, and one more worthy of a Petruchio
for a rider I did never back. Her temper was furious,
her gait intolerable, her mouth the most obdurate that
ever tugged against bit and bridle. It is not wise any

where — here it is less wise than any where else in the
world—to say, " Jamais de cette eau je ne boirai ;" but I
think I will never ride that delightful creature Miss Kate
again.

I wrote you of my having been to a part of the estate
called St. Clair's, where there was formerly another residence of Major ——'s ; nothing remains now of it but a
ruined chimney of some of the offices, which is standing
yet in the middle of what has become a perfect wilderness.
At the best of times, with a large house, numerous household, and paths, and drives of approach, and the usual external conditions of civilization about it, a residence here
would have been the loneliest that can well be imagined ;
now it is the shaggiest desert of beautiful wood that I
ever saw. The magnificent old oaks stand round the
place in silent solemn grandeur ; and among them I had
no difficulty in recognizing, by the description Captain
F—— had given me of it, the crumbling, shattered relic
of a tree called Oglethorpe's oak. That worthy, valiant
old governor had a residence here himself in the early
days of the colony, when, under the influence of Wesley,
he vainly made such strenuous efforts to keep aloof from
his infant province the sore curse of slavery.

I rode almost the whole way through a grove of perfect
evergreen. I had with me one of the men of the name of
Hector, who has a good deal to do with the horses, and
so had volunteered to accompany me, being one of the
few negroes on the estate who can sit a horse. In the
course of our conversation, Hector divulged certain opinions relative to the comparative gentility of driving in a
carriage and the vulgarity of walking, which sent me into
fits of laughing ; at which he grinned sympathetically, and
opened his eyes very wide, but certainly without attaining
the least insight into what must have appeared to him
my very unaccountable and unreasonable merriment.

Among various details of the condition of the people on the several estates in the island, he told me that a great number of the men on all the different plantations had *wives* on the neighboring estates as well as on that to which they properly belonged. "Oh, but," said I, "Hector, you know that can not be; a man has but one lawful wife." Hector knew this, he said, and yet seemed puzzled himself, and rather puzzled me to account for the fact, that this extensive practice of bigamy was perfectly well known to the masters and overseers, and never in any way found fault with or interfered with. Perhaps this promiscuous mode of keeping up the slave population finds favor with the owners of creatures who are valued in the market at so much per head. This was a solution which occurred to me, but which I left my Trojan hero to discover, by dint of the profound pondering into which he fell.

Not far from the house, as I was cantering home, I met S——, and took her up on the saddle before me, an operation which seemed to please her better than the vicious horse I was riding, whose various demonstrations of dislike to the arrangement afforded my small equestrian extreme delight and triumph. My whole afternoon was spent in shifting my bed and bedroom furniture from a room on the ground floor to one above; in the course of which operation a brisk discussion took place between M—— and my boy Jack, who was nailing on the vallence of the bed, and whom I suddenly heard exclaim, in answer to something she had said, "Well, den, I do tink so; and dat's the speech of a man, whether um bond or free." A very trifling incident, and insignificant speech; and yet it came back to my ears very often afterward—"the speech of a *man*, whether bond or free." They might be made conscious—some of them are evidently conscious—of an inherent element of manhood superior to the bitter accident of slavery, and to which, even in their degraded

condition, they might be made to refer that vital self-respect which can survive all external pressure of mere circumstance, and give their souls to that service of God,
which is perfect freedom, in spite of the ignoble and cruel
bondage of their bodies.

My new apartment is what I should call decidedly airy;
the window, unless when styled by courtesy shut, which
means admitting of draught enough to blow a candle out,
must be wide open, being incapable of any intermediate
condition; the latch of the door, to speak the literal truth,
does shut; but it is the only part of it that does—that is,
the latch and the hinges; every where else its configuration is traced by a distinct line of light and air. If what
old Dr. Physic used to say be true, that a draught which
will not blow out a candle will blow out a man's life (a
Spanish proverb originally I believe), my life is threatened
with extinction in almost every part of this new room of
mine, wherein, moreover, I now discover to my dismay,
having transported every other article of bedroom furniture to it, it is impossible to introduce the wardrobe for
my clothes. Well, our stay here is drawing to a close,
and therefore these small items of discomfort can not af-
flict me much longer.

Among my visitors to-day was a poor woman named
Oney, who told me her husband had gone away from her
now for four years; it seems he was the property of Mr.
K——, and when that gentleman went to slave-driving
on his own account, and ceased to be the overseer of this
estate, he carried her better half, who was his chattel,
away with him, and she never expects to see him again.
After her departure I had a most curious visitor, a young
lad of the name of Renty, whose very decidedly mulatto
tinge accounted, I suppose, for the peculiar disinvoltura
of his carriage and manner; he was evidently, in his own
opinion, a very superior creature, and yet, as his conver-

sation with me testified, he was conscious of some flaw in the honor of his "yellow" complexion. "Who is your mother, Renty?" said I (I give you our exact dialogue). "Betty, head man Frank's wife." I was rather dismayed at the promptness of this reply, and hesitated a little at my next question, "Who is your father?" My sprightly young friend, however, answered, without an instant's pause, "Mr. K——." Here I came to a halt, and, willing to suggest some doubt to the lad, because for many peculiar reasons this statement seemed to me shocking, I said, "What, old Mr. K——?" "No, Massa R——." "Did your mother tell you so?" "No, missis, me ashamed to ask her; Mr. C——'s children told me so, and I 'spect they know it." Renty, you see, did not take Falconbridge's view of such matters; and as I was by no means sorry to find that he considered his relation to Mr. K—— a disgrace to his mother, which is an advance in moral perception not often met with here, I said no more upon the subject.

Tuesday, March 3. This morning, old House Molly, coming from Mr. G——'s upon some errand to me, I asked her if Renty's statement was true; she confirmed the whole story, and, moreover, added that this connection took place after Betty was married to head man Frank. Now he, you know, E——, is the chief man at the rice-island, second in authority to Mr. O——, and, indeed, for a considerable part of the year, absolute master and guardian during the night of all the people and property at the rice plantation; for, after the early spring, the white overseer himself is obliged to betake himself to the main land to sleep, out of the influence of the deadly malaria of the rice swamp, and Frank remains sole sovereign of the island from sunset to sunrise—in short, during the whole period of his absence. Mr. —— bestowed the highest commendations upon his fidelity and intelligence, and, during the visit Mr. R—— K—— paid us at the island, he was emphatic in his praise of both Frank and his wife, the latter having, as he declared, by way of climax to his eulogies, quite the principles of a white woman. Perhaps she imbibed them from his excellent influence over her. Frank is a serious, sad, sober-looking, very intelligent man; I should think he would not relish having his wife borrowed from him even by the white gentleman who admired her principles so much; and it is quite clear, from poor Renty's speech about his mother, that by some of these people (and if by any, then very certainly by Frank) the disgrace of such an injury is felt and appreciated much after the fashion of white men.

This old woman Molly is a wonderfully intelligent, active, energetic creature, though considerably over seventy years old; she was talking to me about her former master, Major ——, and what she was pleased to call the *revelation* war (*i. e.*, revolution war), during which that gentleman, having embraced the side of the rebellious colonies in their struggle against England, was by no means on a bed of roses. He bore King George's commission, and was a major in the British army; but having married a great Carolina heiress, and become proprietor of these plantations, sided with the country of his adoption, and not that of his birth, in the war between them, and was a special object of animosity on that account to the English officers who attacked the sea-board of Georgia, and sent troops on shore and up the Altamaha to fetch off the negroes, or incite them to rise against their owners. "De British," said Molly, "make old massa run about bery much in de great revelation war." He ran effectually, however, and contrived to save both his life and property from the invader.

Molly's account was full of interest, in spite of the grotesque lingo in which it was delivered, and which once or twice nearly sent me into convulsions of laughing, where-upon she apologized with great gravity for her mispro-nunciation, modestly suggesting that *white words* were impossible to the organs of speech of black folks. It is curious how universally any theory, no matter how ab-surd, is accepted by these people; for any thing in which the contemptuous supremacy of the dominant race is ad-mitted, and their acquiescence in the theory of their own incorrigible baseness is so complete, that this, more than any other circumstance in their condition, makes me doubt-ful of their rising from it.

In order to set poor dear old Molly's notions straight with regard to the negro incapacity for speaking plain the noble white words, I called S—— to me and set her talk-ing; and having pointed out to Molly how very imperfect her mode of pronouncing many words was, convinced the worthy old negress that want of training, and not any ab-solute original impotence, was the reason why she disfig-ured the *white words*, for which she had such a profound respect. In this matter, as in every other, the slaves pay back to their masters the evil of their own dealings with usury, though unintentionally. No culture, however slight, simple, or elementary, is permitted to these poor creatures, and the utterance of many of them is more like what Prospero describes Caliban's to have been, than the speech of men and women in a Christian and civilized land: the children of their owners, brought up among them, acquire their negro mode of talking—slavish speech surely it is—and it is distinctly perceptible in the utterances of all Southerners, particularly of the women, whose avocations, taking them less from home, are less favorable to their throwing off this ignoble trick of pronunciation than the more varied occupation and the more extended and pro-miscuous business relations of men. The Yankee twang of the regular down Easter is not more easily detected by

any ear, nice in enunciation and accent, than the thick negro speech of the Southerners: neither is lovely or melodious; but, though the Puritan snuffle is the harsher of
the two, the slave *slobber* of the language is the more ignoble, in spite of the softer voices of the pretty Southern
women who utter it.

I rode out to-day upon Miss Kate again, with Jack for
my esquire. I made various vain attempts to ride through
the woods, following the cattle-tracks; they turned round
and round into each other, or led out into the sandy pine
barren, the eternal frame in which all nature is set here,
the inevitable limit to the prospect, turn landward which
way you will. The wood paths which I followed between
evergreen thickets, though little satisfactory in their ulti-
mate result, were really more beautiful than the most perfect arrangement of artificial planting that I ever saw in
an English park; and I thought, if I could transplant the
region which I was riding through bodily into the midst
of some great nobleman's possessions on the other side of
the water, how beautiful an accession it would be thought
to them. I was particularly struck with the elegant
growth of a profuse wild shrub I passed several times to-
day, the leaves of which were pale green underneath, and
a deep red, varnished brown above.

I must give you an idea of the sort of service one is liable to obtain from one's most intelligent and civilized
servants hereabouts, and the consequent comfort and luxury of one's daily existence. Yesterday Aleck, the youth
who fulfills the duties of what you call a waiter, and we
in England a footman, gave me a salad for dinner, mixed
with so large a portion of the soil in which it had grown
that I requested him to-day to be kind enough to wash
the lettuce before he brought it to table. M—— later in
the day told me that he had applied to her very urgently
for soap and a brush, "as missis wished de lettuce scrub-

bed," a fate from which my second salad was saved by her refusal of these desired articles, and farther instructions upon the subject.

DEAREST E——,—I have been long promising poor old House Molly to visit her in her own cabin, and so the day before yesterday I walked round the settlement to her dwelling, and a most wretched hovel I found it. She has often told me of the special directions left by her old master for the comfort and well-being of her old age, and certainly his charge has been but little heeded by his heirs, for the poor faithful old slave is most miserably off in her infirm years. She made no complaint, however, but seemed overjoyed at my coming to see her. She took me to the hut of her brother, old Jacob, where the same wretched absence of every decency and every comfort prevailed; but neither of them seemed to think the condition that appeared so wretched to me one of peculiar hardship—though Molly's former residence in her master's house might reasonably have made her discontented with the lot of absolute privation to which she was now turned over—but, for the moment, my visit seemed to compensate for all sublunary sorrows, and she and poor old Jacob kept up a duet of rejoicing at my advent, and that I had brought " de little missis among um people afore they die."

Leaving them, I went on to the house of Jacob's daughter Hannah, with whom Psyche, the heroine of the rice-island story, and wife of his son Joe, lives. I found their cabin as tidy and comfortable as it could be made, and their children, as usual, neat and clean; they are capital women, both of them, with an innate love of cleanliness and order most uncommon among these people. On my way home I overtook two of my daily suppliants, who were going to the house in search of me, and meat, flannel, rice, and sugar, as the case might be; they were both old and infirm-looking women, and one of them, called Scylla, was extremely lame, which she accounted for by an accident she had met with while carrying a heavy weight of rice on her head; she had fallen on a sharp stake, or snag, as she called it, and had never recovered the injury she had received. She complained also of falling of the womb. Her companion (who was not Charybdis, however, but Phœbe) was a cheery soul who complained of nothing, but begged for flannel. I asked her about her family and children; she had no children left, nothing but grandchildren; she had had nine children, and seven of them died quite young; the only two who grew up left her to join the British when they invaded Georgia in the last war, and their children, whom they left behind, were all her family now.

In the afternoon I made my first visit to the hospital of the estate, and found it, as indeed I find every thing else here, in a far worse state even than the wretched establishments on the rice-island, dignified by that name; so miserable a place for the purpose to which it was dedicated I could not have imagined on a property belonging to Christian owners. The floor (which was not boarded, but merely the damp hard earth itself) was strewn with wretched women, who, but for their moans of pain, and uneasy, restless motions, might very well each have been taken for a mere heap of filthy rags; the chimney refusing passage to the smoke from the pine-wood fire, it puffed out in clouds through the room, where it circled and hung, only gradually oozing away through the windows, which were so far well adapted to the purpose that there was not a single whole pane of glass in them. My eyes, unaccustomed to the turbid atmosphere, smarted and watered, and refused to distinguish at first the different dismal forms, from which cries and wails assailed me in every corner of the place. By degrees I was able to endure for a few minutes what they were condemned to live their hours and days of suffering and sickness through; and, having given what comfort kind words and promises of help in more substantial forms could convey, I went on to what seemed a yet more wretched abode of wretchedness. This was a room where there was no fire because there was no chimney, and where the holes made for windows had no panes or glasses in them. The shutters being closed, the place was so dark that, on first entering it, I was afraid to stir lest I should fall over some of the deplorable creatures extended upon the floor. As soon as they perceived me, one cry of " Oh missis !" rang through the darkness; and it really seemed to me as if I was never .to exhaust the pity, and amazement, and disgust which this receptacle of suffering humanity was to excite in me. The poor dingy supplicating sleepers upraised themselves as I cautiously advanced among them ; those who could not rear their bodies from the earth held up piteous beseeching hands, and as I passed from one to the other I felt more than one imploring clasp laid upon my dress, to solicit my attention to some new form of misery. One poor woman, called Tressa, who was unable to speak above a whisper from utter weakness and exhaustion, told me she had had nine children, was suffering from incessant flooding, and felt "as if her back would split open." There she lay, a mass of filthy tatters, without so much as a blanket under her or over her, on the bare earth in this chilly darkness. I promised them help and comfort, beds and blankets, and light and fire—that is, I promised to ask Mr. —— for all this for them; and, in the very act of doing so, I remembered with a sudden pang of anguish that I was to urge no more petitions for his slaves to their master. I groped my way out, and, emerging on the piazza, all the choking tears and sobs I had controlled broke forth, and I leaned there crying over the lot of these unfortunates till I heard a feeble voice of " Missis, you no cry; missis, what for you cry ?" and, looking up, saw that I had not yet done with this intolerable infliction. A poor crippled old man, lying in the corner of the piazza, unable even to crawl toward me, had uttered this word of consolation, and by his side (apparently too idiotic, as he was too impotent, to move) sat a young woman, the expression of whose face was the most suffering, and, at the same time, the most horribly repulsive I ever saw.   I found she was, as I supposed, half-witted ; and, on coming nearer to inquire into her ailments and what I could do for her, found her uffering from that horrible disease—I believe some form of scrofula—to which the negroes are subject, which attacks and eats away the joints of their hands and fingers —a more hideous and loathsome object I never beheld ; her name was Patty, and she was granddaughter to the old crippled creature by whose side she was squatting.

I wandered home, stumbling with crying as I went, and feeling so utterly miserable that I really hardly saw where I was going, for I as nearly as possible fell over a great heap of oyster-shells left in the middle of the path. This is a horrid nuisance, which results from an indulgence which the people here have and value highly ; the waters round the island are prolific in shell-fish, oysters, and the most magnificent prawns I ever saw. The former are a considerable article of the people's diet, and the shells are allowed to accumulate, as they are used in the composition of which their huts are built, and which is a sort of combination of mud and broken oyster-shells, which forms an agglomeration of a kind very solid and durable for such building purposes ; but, instead of being all carried to some specified place out of the way, these great heaps of oyster-shells are allowed to be piled up any where and every where, forming the most unsightly obstructions in every direction. Of course, the cultivation of order for the sake of its own seemliness and beauty is not likely to be an element of slave existence; and as masters have been scarce on this plantation for many years now, a mere unsightliness is not a matter likely to trouble any body much; but, after my imminent overthrow by one of these disorderly heaps of refuse, I think I may make bold to request that the paths along which I am likely to take my daily walks may be kept free from them.

On my arrival at home—at the house—I can not call any place here my home!—I found Renty waiting to exhibit to me an extremely neatly-made leather pouch, which he has made by my order, of fitting size and dimensions to receive Jack's hatchet and saw. Jack and I have set up a sort of Sir Walter and Tom Purdie companionship of clearing and cutting paths through the woods nearest to the house; thinning the overhanging branches, clearing the small evergreen thickets which here and there close over and across the grassy track. To me this occupation was especially delightful until quite lately, since the weather began to be rather warmer and the snakes to slide about. Jack has contrived to inoculate me with some portion of his terror of them; but I have still a daily hankering after the lovely green wood walks; perhaps, when once I have seen a live rattlesnake, my enthusiasm for them will be modified to the degree that his is.

DEAR E——,—This letter has remained unfinished, and my journal interrupted for more than a week. Mr. —— has been quite unwell, and I have been traveling to and fro daily between Hampton and the rice-island in the

K

long-boat to visit him; for the last three days I have remained at the latter place, and only returned here this
morning early. My daily voyages up and down the river
have introduced me to a great variety of new musical performances of our boatmen, who invariably, when the rowing is not too hard, moving up or down with the tide,
accompany the stroke of their oars with the sound of
their voices. I told you formerly that I thought I could
trace distinctly some popular national melody with which
I was familiar in almost all their songs; but I have been
quite at a loss to discover any such foundation for many
that I have heard lately, and which have appeared to me
extraordinarily wild and unaccountable. The way in
which the chorus strikes in with the burden, between
each phrase of the melody chanted by a single voice, is
very curious and effective, especially with the rhythm of
the rowlocks for accompaniment. The high voices all in
unison, and the admirable time and true accent with which
their responses are made, always make me wish that some
great musical composer could hear these semi-savage performances. With a very little skillful adaptation and in-
strumentation, I think one or two barbaric chants and
choruses might be evoked from them that would make
the fortune of an opera.

The only exception that I have met with yet among
our boat voices to the high tenor which they seem all to
possess is in the person of an individual named Isaac, a
basso profondo of the deepest dye, who nevertheless never
attempts to produce with his different register any different effects in the chorus by venturing a second, but sings
like the rest in unison, perfect unison, of both time and
tune. By-the-by, this individual *does* speak, and therefore I presume he is not an ape, orang-outang, chimpan-
zee, or gorilla; but I could not, I confess, have conceived
it possible that the presence of articulate sounds, and the

absence of an articulate tail, should make, externally at least, so completely the only appreciable difference between a man and a monkey, as they appear to do in this individual " black brother." Such stupendous long thin hands, and long flat feet, I did never see off a large quadruped of the ape species. But, as I said before, Isaac *speaks*, and I am much comforted thereby.

You can not think (to return to the songs of my boatmen) how strange some of their words are : in one, they repeatedly chanted the " sentiment" that " God made man, and man makes"—what do you think ?—" money !" Is not that a peculiar poetical proposition ? Another ditty to which they frequently treat me they call Cæsar's song; it is an extremely spirited war-song, beginning " The trumpets blow, the bugles sound—Oh, stand your ground !" It has puzzled me not a little to determine in my own mind whether this title of Cæsar's song has any reference to the great Julius, and, if so, what may be the negro notion of him, and whence and how derived. One of their songs displeased me not a little, for it embodied the opinion that " twenty-six black girls not make mulatto yellow girl ;" and as I told them I did not like it, they have omitted it since. This desperate tendency to despise and undervalue their own race and color, which is one of the very worst results of their abject condition, is intolerable to me.

While rowing up and down the broad waters of the Altamaha to the music of these curious chants, I have been reading Mr. Moore's speech about the abolition of slavery in the District of Columbia, and I confess I think his the only defensible position yet taken, and the only consistent argument yet used in any of the speeches I have hitherto seen upon the subject.

I have now settled down at Hampton again ; Mr. —— is quite recovered, and is coming down here in a day or two for change of air; it is getting too late for him to stay on the rice plantation even in the day, I think. You can not imagine any thing so exquisite as the perfect curtains of yellow jasmine with which this whole island is draped; and as the boat comes sweeping down toward the Point, the fragrance from the thickets hung with their golden garlands greets one before one can distinguish them; it is really enchanting.

I have now to tell you of my hallowing last Sunday by gathering a congregation of the people into my big sitting-room, and reading prayers to them. I had been wishing very much to do this for some time past, and obtained Mr. ——'s leave while I was with him at the rice-island, and it was a great pleasure to me. Some of the people are allowed to go up to Darien once a month to church; but, with that exception, they have no religious service on Sunday whatever for them. There is a church on the island of St. Simon, but they are forbidden to frequent it, as it leads them off their own through neighboring plantations, and gives opportunities for meetings between the negroes of the different estates, and very likely was made the occasion of abuses and objectionable practices of various kinds; at any rate, Mr. K—— forbade the Hampton slaves resorting to the St. Simon's church, and so for three Sundays in the month they are utterly without Christian worship or teaching, or any religious observance of God's day whatever.

I was very anxious that it should not be thought that I *ordered* any of the people to come to prayers, as I particularly desired to see if they themselves felt the want of any Sabbath service, and would of their own accord join in any such ceremony; I therefore merely told the house servants that if they would come to the sitting-room at eleven o'clock, I would read prayers to them, and that they might tell any of their friends or any of the people that I should be very glad to see them if they liked to come. Accordingly, most of those who live at the Point, *i. e.*, in the immediate neighborhood of the house, came, and it was encouraging to see the very decided efforts at cleanliness and decorum of attire which they had all made. I was very much affected and impressed myself by what I was doing, and I suppose must have communicated some of my own feeling to those who heard me. It is an extremely solemn thing to me to read the Scriptures aloud to any one, and there was something in my relation to the poor people by whom I was surrounded that touched me so deeply while thus attempting to share with them the best of my possessions, that I found it difficult to command my voice, and had to stop several times in order to do so. When I had done, they all with one accord uttered the simple words, " We thank you, missis," and instead of overwhelming me as usual with petitions and complaints, they rose silently and quietly, in a manner that would have become the most orderly of Christian congregations accustomed to all the impressive decorum of civilized church privileges. Poor people! They are said to have what a very irreligious young English clergyman once informed me I had—a " *turn* for religion." They seem to me to have a " turn" for instinctive good manners too ; and certainly their mode of withdrawing from my room after our prayers bespoke either a strong feeling of their own, or a keen appreciation of mine.

I have resumed my explorations in the woods with renewed enthusiasm, for during my week's absence they have become more lovely and enticing than ever : unluckily, however, Jack seems to think that fresh rattlesnakes have budded together with the tender spring foliage, and I see that I shall either have to give up my wood walks and rides, or go without a guide. Lovely blossoms are springing up every where—weeds, of course, wild things, impertinently so called. Nothing is cultivated here but cotton; but in some of the cotton-fields beautiful creatures are peeping into blossom, which I suppose will all be duly hoed off the surface of the soil in proper season; meantime I rejoice in them, and in the splendid, magnificent thistles, which would be in flower-gardens in other parts of the world, and in the wonderful, strange, beautiful butterflies that seem to me almost as big as birds, that go zigzagging in the sun. I saw yesterday a lovely monster, who thought proper, for my greater delectation, to alight on a thistle I was admiring, and as the flower was purple, and he was all black velvet fringed with gold, I was exceedingly pleased with his good inspiration.

This morning I drove up to the settlement at St. Annie's, having various bundles of benefaction to carry in the only equipage my estate here affords — an exceedingly small, rough, and uncomfortable cart, called the sick-house wagon, inasmuch as it is used to convey to the hospital such of the poor people as are too ill to walk there. Its tender mercies must be terrible indeed for the sick, for I, who am sound, could very hardly abide them; however, I suppose Montreal's pace is moderated for them: to-day he went rollicking along with us behind him, shaking his fine head and mane, as if he thought the more we were jolted the better we should like it. We found, on trying to go on to Cartwright's Point, that the state of the tide would not admit of our getting thither, and so had to return, leaving it unvisited. It seems to me strange that, where the labor of so many hands might be commanded, piers, and wharves, and causeways are not thrown out (wooden ones, of course, I mean) wherever the common traffic to or from different parts of the plantation is thus impeded by the daily rise and fall of the river; the trouble and expense would be nothing, and the gain in convenience very considerable. However, perhaps the nature of the tides, and of the banks and shores themselves, may not be propitious for such constructions, and I rather incline, upon reflection, to think this may be so, because to go from Hampton to our neighbor Mr. C——'s plantation, it is necessary to consult the tide in order to land conveniently. Driving home to-day by Jones's Creek, we saw an immovable row of white cranes, all standing with imperturbable gravity upon one leg. I thought of Boccaccio's cook, and had a mind to say Ha! at them, to try if they had two. I have been over to Mr. C——'s, and was very much pleased with my visit, but will tell you of it in my next.

Dear E——,—I promised to tell you of my visit to my neighbor Mr. C——, which pleased and interested me very much. He is an old Glasgow man, who has been settled here many years. It is curious how many of the people round this neighborhood have Scotch names; it seems strange to find them thus gathered in the vicinity of a new Darien; but those in our immediate neighborhood seem to have found it a·far less fatal region than their countrymen did its namesake of the Isthmus. Mr. C——'s house is a roomy, comfortable, handsomely laid-out mansion, to which he received me with very cordial kindness, and where I spent part of a very pleasant morning, talking with him, hearing all he could tell me of the former history of Mr. ——'s plantation. His description of its former master, old Major ——, and of his agent and overseer Mr. K——, and of that gentleman's worthy son and successor the late overseer, interested me very much; of the two latter functionaries his account was terrible, and much what I had supposed any impartial account of them would be; because, let the propensity to lying of the poor wretched slaves be what it will, they could not invent, with a common consent, the things that they one and all tell me with reference to the manner in which they have been treated by the man who has just left the estate, and his father, who for the last nineteen years have been sole sovereigns of their bodies and souls. The crops have satisfied the demands of the owners, who, living in Philadelphia, have been perfectly contented to receive a large income from their estate without apparently caring how it was earned. The stories that the poor people tell me of the cruel tyranny under which they have lived are not complaints, for they are of things past and gone, and very often, horridly as they shock and affect me, they themselves seem hardly more than half conscious of the misery their condition exhibits to me, and they speak of things which I shudder to hear of almost as if they had been matters of course with them.

Old Mr. C—— spoke with extreme kindness of his own people, and had evidently bestowed much humane and benevolent pains upon endeavors to better their condition. I asked him if he did not think the soil and climate of this part of Georgia admirably suited to the cultivation of the mulberry and the rearing of the silkworm; for it has appeared to me that hereafter silk may be made one of the most profitable products of this whole region: he said that that had long been his opinion, and he had at one time had it much at heart to try the experiment, and had proposed to Major —— to join him in it, on a scale large enough to test it satisfactorily; but he said Mr. K—— opposed the scheme so persistently that of course it was impossible to carry it out, as his agency and co-operation were indispensable; and that in like manner he had suggested sowing turnip crops, and planting peach-trees for the benefit and use of the people on the Hampton estate, experiments which he had tried with excellent success on his own; but all these plans for the amelioration and progress of the people's physical condition had been obstructed and finally put entirely aside by old Mr. K—— and his son, who, as Mr. C—— said, appeared to give satisfaction to their employers, so it was not his business to find fault with them; he said, however, that the whole condition and treatment of the slaves had changed from the time of Major ——'s death, and that he thought it providential for the poor people that Mr. K—— should have left the estate, and the young gentleman, the present owner, come down to look after the people.

He showed me his garden, from whence come the beautiful vegetables he had more than once supplied me with; in the midst of it was a very fine and flourishing date-palm-tree, which he said bore its fruit as prosperously here as it would in Asia. After the garden we visited a charming, nicely-kept poultry-yard, and I returned home much delighted with my visit and the kind good-humor of my host.

In the afternoon I sat as usual at the receipt of custom, hearing of aches and pains till I ached myself sympathetically from head to foot.

Yesterday morning, dear E——, I went on horseback to St. Annie's, exploring on my way some beautiful woods, and in the afternoon I returned thither in a wood-wagon, with Jack to drive and a mule to draw me, Montreal being quite beyond his management; and then and there, the hatchet and saw being in company, I compelled my slave Jack, all the rattlesnakes in creation to the contrary notwithstanding, to cut and clear a way for my chariot through the charming copse.

My letter has been lying unfinished for the last three days. I have been extraordinarily busy, having emancipated myself from the trammels of Jack and all his terror, and as I fear no serpents on horseback, have been daily

K 2

riding through new patches of woodland without any guide, taking my chance of what I might come to in the shape of impediments. Last Tuesday I rode through a whole wood of burned and charred trees, cypresses and oaks, that looked as if they had been each of them blasted by a special thunderbolt, and whole thickets of young trees and shrubs perfectly black and brittle from the effect of fire, I suppose the result of some carelessness of the slaves. As this charcoal woodland extended for some distance, I turned out of it, and round the main road through the plantation, as I could not ride through the blackened boughs and branches without getting begrimed. It had a strange, wild, desolate effect, not without a certain gloomy picturesqueness.

In the afternoon I made Israel drive me through Jack's new-made path to break it down and open it still more, and Montreal's powerful trampling did good service to that effect, though he did not seem to relish the narrow wood road with its grass path by any means as much as the open way of what may be called the high road. After this operation I went on to visit the people at the Busson Hill settlement. I here found, among other noteworthy individuals, a female named Judy, whose two children belong to an individual called (not Punch, but) Joe, who has another wife, called Mary, at the rice-island. In one of the huts I went to leave some flannel, and rice, and sugar for a poor old creature called Nancy, to whom I had promised such indulgences : she is exceedingly infirm and miserable, suffering from sore limbs and an ulcerated leg so cruelly that she can hardly find rest in any position from the constant pain she endures, and is quite unable to lie on her hard bed at night. As I bent over her to-day, trying to prop her into some posture where she might find some ease, she took hold of my hand, and with the tears streaming over her face, said, "I have worked every day through dew and damp, and sand and heat, and done good work; but oh, missis, me old and broken now; no tongue can tell how much I suffer." In spite of their curious thick utterance and comical jargon, these people sometimes use wonderfully striking and pathetic forms of speech. In the next cabin, which consisted of an inclosurê called by courtesy a room, certainly not ten feet square, and owned by a woman called Dice—that is, not owned, of course, but inhabited by her—three grown-up human beings and eight children stow themselves by day and night, which may be called close packing, I think. I presume that they must take turns to be inside and outside the house, but they did not make any complaint about it, though I should think the aspect of my countenance, as I surveyed their abode and heard their numbers, might have given them a hint to that effect; but I really do find these poor creatures patient of so much misery, that it inclines me the more to heed as well as hear their petitions and complaints when they bring them to me.

After my return home I had my usual evening reception, and, among other pleasant incidents of plantation life, heard the following agreeable anecdote from a woman named Sophy, who came to beg for some rice. In asking her about her husband and children, she said she had never had any husband; that she had had two children by a white man of the name of Walker, who was employed at the mill on the rice-island; she was in the hospital after the birth of the second child she bore this man, and at the same time two women, Judy and Sylla, of whose children Mr. K—— was the father, were recovering from their confinements. It was not a month since any of them had been delivered, when Mrs. K—— came to the hospital, had them all three severely flogged, a process which *she* personally superintended, and then sent them to Five Pound — the swamp Botany Bay of the plantation, of which I have told you—with farther orders to the drivers to flog them every day for a week. Now, E——, if I make you sick with these disgusting stories, I can not help it; they are the life itself here; hitherto I have thought these details intolerable enough, but this apparition of a female fiend in the middle of this hell I confess adds an element of cruelty which seems to me to surpass all the rest. Jealousy is not an uncommon quality in the feminine temperament; and just conceive the fate of these unfortunate women between the passions of their masters and mistresses, each alike armed with power to oppress and torture them. Sophy went on to say that Isaac was her son by Driver Morris, who had forced her while she was in her miserable exile at Five Pound. Almost beyond my patience with this string of detestable details, I exclaimed—foolishly enough, heaven knows—"Ah! but don't you know—did nobody ever tell or teach any of you that it is a sin to live with men who are not your husbands?" Alas! E——, what could the poor creature answer but what she did, seizing me at the same time vehemently by the wrist: "Oh yes, missis, we know—we know all about dat well enough; but we do any thing to get our poor flesh some rest from de whip; when he made me follow him into de bush, what use me tell him no? he have strength to make me." I have written down the woman's words; I wish I could write down the voice and look of abject misery with which they were spoken. Now you will observe that the story was not told to me as a complaint; it was a thing long past and over, of which she only spoke in the natural course of accounting for her children to me. I make no comment; what need, or can I add, to such stories? But how is such a state of things to endure? and again, how is it to end? While I was pondering, as it seemed to me, at the very bottom of the Slough of Despond, on this miserable creature's story, an-

other woman came in (Tema), carrying in her arms a child
the image of the mulatto Bran; she came to beg for flannel. I asked her who was her husband. She said she
was not married. Her child is the child of Bricklayer
Temple, who has a wife at the rice-island. By this time,
what do you think of the moralities, as well as the amenities, of slave life? These are the conditions which can
only be known to one who lives among them; flagrant
acts of cruelty may be rare, but this ineffable state of utter degradation, this really *beastly* existence, is the nor-
mal condition of these men and women, and of that no one
seems to take heed, nor have I ever heard it described, so
as to form any adequate conception of it, till I found myself plunged into it; where and how is one to begin the
cleansing of this horrid pestilential immondezzio of an existence?

It is Wednesday, the 20th of March; we can not stay
here much longer; I wonder if I shall come back again!
and whether, when I do, I shall find the trace of one idea
of a better life left in these poor people's minds by my sojourn among them.

One of my industries this morning has been cutting out
another dress for one of our women, who had heard of my
tailoring prowess at the rice-island. The material, as
usual, was a miserable cotton, many-colored like the scarf
of Iris. While shaping it for my client, I ventured to suggest the idea of the possibility of a change of the nether-
most as well as the uppermost garment. This, I imagine,
is a conception that has never dawned upon the female
slave mind on this plantation. They receive twice a year
a certain supply of clothing, and wear them (as I have
heard some nasty fine ladies do their stays, for fear they
should get out of shape), without washing, till they receive
the next suit. Under these circumstances I think it is
unphilosophical, to say the least of it, to speak of the ne-

groes as a race whose unfragrance is heaven-ordained, and the result of special organization.

I must tell you that I have been delighted, surprised, and the very least perplexed, by the sudden petition on the part of our young waiter, Aleck, that I will teach him to read. He is a very intelligent lad of about sixteen, and preferred his request with an urgent humility that was very touching. I told him I would think about it. I mean to do it. I will do it; and yet, it is simply breaking the laws of the government under which I am living. Unrighteous laws are made to be broken—*perhaps*—but then, you see, I am a woman, and Mr. —— stands between me and the penalty. If I were a man, I would do that and many a thing besides, and doubtless should be shot some fine day from behind a tree by some good neighbor, who would do the community a service by quietly getting rid of a mischievous incendiary; and I promise you, in such a case, no questions would be asked, and my lessons would come to a speedy and silent end; but teaching slaves to read is a finable offense, and I am *feme couverte*, and my fines must be paid by my legal owner, and the first offense of the sort is heavily fined, and the second more heavily fined, and for the third, one is sent to prison. What a pity it is I can't begin with Aleck's third lesson, because going to prison can't be done by proxy, and that penalty would light upon the right shoulders! I certainly intend to teach Aleck to read. I certainly won't tell Mr. —— any thing about it. I'll leave him to find it out, as slaves, and servants, and children, and all oppressed, and ignorant, and uneducated and unprincipled people do; then, if he forbids me, I can stop—perhaps before then the lad may have learned his letters. I begin to perceive one most admirable circumstance in this slavery: you are absolute on your own plantation. No slaves' testimony avails against you, and no white testimony exists but such as you choose to admit. Some owners have a fancy for maiming their slaves, some brand them, some pull out their teeth, some shoot them a little here and there (all details gathered from advertisements of runaway slaves in Southern papers); now they do all this on their plantations, where nobody comes to see, and I'll teach Aleck to read, for nobody is here to see, at least nobody whose seeing I mind; and I'll teach every other creature that wants to learn. I haven't much more than a week to remain in this blessed purgatory; in that last week perhaps I may teach the boy enough to go on alone when I am gone.

Thursday, 21*st.* I took a long ride to-day all through some new woods and fields, and finally came upon a large space sown with corn for the people. Here I was accosted by such a shape as I never beheld in the worst of my dreams; it looked at first, as it came screaming toward me, like a live specimen of the arms of the Isle of Man, which, as you may or may not know, are three legs joined together, and kicking in different directions. This uncouth device is not an invention of the Manxmen, for it is found on some very ancient coins—Greek, I believe; but, at any rate, it is now the device of our subject Island of Man, and, like that set in motion, and nothing else, was the object that approached me, only it had a head where the three legs were joined, and a voice came out of the head to this effect: " Oh, missis, you hab to take me out of dis here bird-field; me no able to run after birds, and ebery night me lick because me no run after dem." When this apparition reached me and stood as still as it could, I perceived it consisted of a boy who said his name was "Jack de bird-driver." I suppose some vague idea of the fitness of things had induced them to send this living scarecrow into the cornfield, and if he had been set up in the midst of it, nobody, I am sure, would have imagined he was any thing else; but it seems he was expected to run after the feathered fowl who alighted on the grain-field, and I do not wonder that he did not fulfill this expectation. His feet, legs, and knees were all maimed and distorted, his legs were nowhere thicker than my wrist, his feet were a yard apart from each other, and his knees swollen and knocking together. What a creature to run after birds! He implored me to give him some meat, and have him sent back to Little St. Simon's Island, from which he came, and where he said his poor limbs were stronger and better.

Riding home, I passed some sassafras-trees, which are putting forth deliciously fragrant tassels of small leaves and blossoms, and other exquisite flowering shrubs, which are new to me, and enchant me perhaps all the more for their strangeness. Before reaching the house I was stopped by one of our multitudinous Jennies with a request for some meat, and that I would help her with some clothes for Ben and Daphne, of whom she had the sole charge; these are two extremely pretty and interesting-looking mulatto children, whose resemblance to Mr. K—— had induced me to ask Mr. ——, when first I saw them, if he did not think they must be his children. He said they were certainly like him, but Mr. K—— did not acknowledge the relationship. I asked Jenny who their mother was. "Minda." "Who their father?" "Mr. K——." "What! old Mr. K——?" "No, Mr. R—— K——." "Who told you so?" "Minda, who ought to know." "Mr. K—— denies it." "That's because he never has looked upon them, nor done a thing for them." "Well, but he acknowledged Renty as his son, why should he deny these?" "Because old master was here then when Renty was born, and he made Betty tell all about it, and Mr. K—— had to own it; but nobody knows any thing about this, and so he denies it"—with which information I rode home. I always give you an exact report of any conversation I may have with any of the people, and you see from this that the people on the plantation themselves are much of my worthy neighbor Mr. C——'s mind, that the death of Major —— was a great misfortune for the slaves on his estate.

I went to the hospital this afternoon to see if the condition of the poor people was at all improved since I had been last there; but nothing had been done. I suppose Mr. G—— is waiting for Mr. —— to come down in order to speak to him about it. I found some miserable new cases of women disabled by hard work. One poor thing, called Priscilla, had come out of the fields to-day scarcely able to crawl; she has been losing blood for a whole fortnight without intermission, and, until to-day, was laboring in the fields. Leah, another new face since I visited the hospital last, is lying quite helpless from exhaustion; she is advanced in her pregnancy, and doing task-work in the fields at the same time. What piteous existences, to be sure! I do .wonder, as I walk among them, well fed, well clothed, young, strong, idle, doing nothing but ride and drive about all day, a woman, a creature like themselves, who have borne children too, what sort of feeling they have toward me. I wonder it is not one of murderous hate—that they should lie here almost dying with unrepaid labor for me. I stand and look at them, and these thoughts work in my mind and heart, till I feel as if I must tell them how dreadful and how monstrous it seems to me myself, and how bitterly ashamed and grieved I feel for it all.

To-day I rode in the morning round poor Cripple Jack's bird-field again, through the sweet, spicy-smelling pine land, and home by my new road cut through Jones's wood, of which I am as proud as if I had made instead of found it—the grass, flowering shrubs, and all. In the afternoon I drove in the wood-wagon back to Jones's, and visited Busson Hill on .the way, with performances of certain promises of flannel, quarters of dollars, etc., etc. At Jones's, the women to-day had all done their work at a quarter past three, and had swept their huts out very scrupulously for my reception. Their dwellings are shockingly dilapidated and overcrammed—poor creatures!—and it seems hard that, while exhorting them to spend labor in cleaning and making them tidy, I can not promise them that they shall be repaired and made habitable for them.

In driving home through my new wood cut, Jack gave me a terrible account of a flogging that a negro called Glasgow had received yesterday. He seemed awfully impressed with it, so I suppose it must have been an unusually severe punishment; but he either would not or could not tell me what the man had done. On my return to the house I found Mr. —— had come down from the rice plantation, whereat I, was much delighted on all accounts. I am sure it is getting much too late for him to remain in that pestilential swampy atmosphere; besides, I want him to see my improvements in the new wood paths, and I want him to come and hear all these poor people's complaints and petitions himself. They have been flocking in to see him ever since it was known he had arrived. I met coming on that errand Dandy, the husband of the woman for whom I cut out the gown the other day; and asking him how it had answered, he gave a piteous account of its tearing all to pieces the first time she put it on; it had appeared to me perfectly rotten and good for nothing, and, upon questioning him as to where he bought it and what he paid for it, I had to hear a sad account of hardship and injustice. I have told you that the people collect moss from the trees and sell it to the shopkeepers in Darien for the purpose of stuffing furniture; they also raise poultry, and are allowed to dispose of the eggs in the same way. It seems that poor Dandy had taken the miserable material Edie's gown was made of as payment for a quantity of moss and eggs furnished by him at various times to one of the Darien storekeepers, who refused him payment in any other shape, and the poor fellow had no redress; and this, he tells me, is a frequent experience with all the slaves both here and at the rice-island. Of course, the rascally shopkeepers can cheat these poor wretches to any extent they please with perfect impunity.

Mr. —— told me of a visit Renty paid him, which was not a little curious in some of its particulars. You know none of the slaves are allowed the use of fire-arms; but Renty put up a petition to be allowed Mr. K——'s gun, which it seems that gentleman left behind him. Mr. —— refused this petition, saying at the same time to the lad that he knew very well that none of the people were allowed guns. Renty expostulated on the score of his *white blood*, and finding his master uninfluenced by that consideration, departed with some severe reflections on Mr. K——, his father, for not having left him his gun as a keepsake, in token of (paternal) affection, when he left the plantation.

It is quite late, and I am very tired, though I have not done much more than usual to-day, but the weather is beginning to be oppressive to me, who hate heat; but I find the people, and especially the sick in the hospital, speak of it as cold. I will tell you hereafter of a most comical account Mr. —— has given me of the prolonged and still protracted pseudo-pregnancy of a woman called Markie, who for many more months than are generally required for the process of continuing the human species, pretended to be what the Germans pathetically and poetically call "in good hope," and continued to reap increased rations as the reward of her expectation, till she finally had to disappoint the estate and receive a flogging.

He told me, too, what interested me very much, of a

conspiracy among Mr. C——'s slaves some years ago.
I can not tell you about it now; I will some other time.
It is wonderful to me that such attempts are not being
made the whole time among these people to regain their
liberty; probably because many are made ineffectually,
and never known beyond the limits of the plantation
where they take place.

———————

DEAR E——,—We have been having something like
Northern March weather—blinding sun, blinding wind,
and blinding dust, through all which, the day before yesterday, Mr. —— and I rode together round most of the
fields, and over the greater part of the plantation. It was
a detestable process, the more so that he rode Montreal
and I Miss Kate, and we had no small difficulty in managing them both. In the afternoon we had an equally detestable drive through the new wood paths to St. Annie's,
and having accomplished all my errands among the people there, we crossed over certain sounds, and seas, and
separating waters, to pay a neighborly visit to the wife
of one of our adjacent planters.

How impossible it would be for you to conceive, even
if I could describe, the careless desolation which pervaded
the whole place; the shaggy unkempt grounds we passed
through to approach the house; the ruinous, rackrent,
tumble-down house itself; the untidy, slatternly, all but
beggarly appearance of the mistress of the mansion herself. The smallest Yankee farmer has a tidier estate, a
tidier house, and a tidier wife than this member of the
proud Southern chivalry, who, however, inasmuch as he
has slaves, is undoubtedly a much greater personage in
his own estimation than those capital fellows W—— and
B——, who walk in glory and in joy behind their plows
upon your mountain sides. The Brunswick Canal project

was descanted upon, and pronounced, without a shadow of dissent, a scheme the impracticability of which all but convicted its projectors of insanity. Certainly, if, as I hear, the moneyed men of Boston have gone largely into this speculation, their habitual sagacity must have been seriously at fault, for here on the spot nobody mentions the project but as a subject of utter derision.

While the men discussed about this matter, Mrs. B—— favored me with the congratulations I have heard so many times on the subject of my having a white nursery-maid for my children. Of course, she went into the old subject of the utter incompetency of negro women to discharge such an office faithfully; but, in spite of her multiplied examples of their utter inefficiency, I believe the discussion ended by simply our both agreeing that ignorant negro girls of twelve years old are not as capable or trustworthy as well-trained white women of thirty.

Returning home, our route was changed, and Quash the boatman took us all the way round by water to Hampton. I should have told you that our exit was as wild as our entrance to this estate, and was made through a broken wooden fence, which we had to climb partly over and partly under, with some risk and some obloquy, in spite of our dexterity, as I tore my dress, and very nearly fell flat on my face in the process. Our row home was perfectly enchanting; for, though the morning's wind and (I suppose) the state of the tide had roughened the waters of the great river, and our passage was not as smooth as it might have been, the wind had died away, the evening air was deliciously still, and mild, and soft. A young slip of a moon glimmered just above the horizon, and "the stars climbed up the sapphire steps of heaven," while we made our way over the rolling, rushing, foaming waves, and saw to right and left the marsh fires burning in the swampy meadows, adding another colored light in the landscape to the amber-tinted lower sky and the violet arch above, and giving wild picturesqueness to the whole scene by throwing long flickering rays of flame upon the distant waters.

Sunday, the 14th. I read service again to-day to the people. You can not conceive any thing more impressive than the silent devotion of their whole demeanor while it lasted, nor more touching than the profound thanks with which they rewarded me when it was over, and they took their leave; and to-day they again left me with the utmost decorum of deportment, and without pressing a single petition or complaint such as they ordinarily thrust upon me on all other occasions, which seems to me an instinctive feeling of religious respect for the day and the business they have come upon, which does them infinite credit.

In the afternoon I took a long walk with the chicks in the woods—long at least for the little legs of S—— and M——, who carried baby. We came home by the shore, and I stopped to look at a jutting point, just below which a sort of bay would have afforded the most capital position for a bathing-house. If we staid here late in the season, such a refreshment would become almost a necessary of life, and any where along the bank just where I stopped to examine it to-day an establishment for that purpose might be prosperously founded.

I am amused, but by no means pleased, at an entirely new mode of pronouncing which S—— has adopted. Apparently the negro jargon has commended itself as euphonious to her infantile ears, and she is now treating me to the most ludicrous and accurate imitations of it every time she opens her mouth. Of course I shall not allow this, comical as it is, to become a habit. This is the way the Southern ladies acquire the thick and inelegant pronunciation which distinguishes their utterances from the Northern snuffle, and I have no desire that S—— should adorn her mother tongue with either peculiarity. It is a curious and sad enough thing to observe, as I have frequent opportunities of doing, the unbounded insolence and tyranny (of manner, of course it can go no farther) of the slaves toward each other. "Hi! you boy!" and "Hi! you girl!" shouted in an imperious scream, is the civilest mode of apostrophizing those at a distance from them; more frequently it is "You niggar, you hear? hi! you niggar!" And I assure you no contemptuous white intonation ever equaled the *prepotenza* of the despotic insolence of this address of these poor wretches to each other.

I have left my letter lying for a couple of days, dear E——. I have been busy and tired; my walking and riding is becoming rather more laborious to me, for, though nobody here appears to do so, I am beginning to feel the relaxing influence of the spring.

The day before yesterday I took a disagreeable ride, all through swampy fields, and charred, blackened thickets, to discover nothing either picturesque or beautiful; the woods in one part of the plantation have been on fire for three days, and a whole tract of exquisite evergreens has been burnt down to the ground. In the afternoon I drove in the wood-wagon to visit the people at St. Annie's. There has been rain these last two nights, and their wretched hovels do not keep out the weather; they are really miserable abodes for human beings. I think pigs who were at all particular might object to some of them. There is a woman at this settlement called Sophy, the wife of a driver, Morris, who is so pretty that I often wonder if it is only by contrast that I admire her so much, or if her gentle, sweet, refined face, in spite of its dusky color, would not approve itself any where to any one with an eye for beauty. Her manner and voice, too, are peculiarly soft and gentle; but, indeed, the voices of all these poor people, men as well as women, are much pleasanter and more melodious than the voices of white people in general. Most of the wretched hovels had been swept and tidied out in expectation of my visit, and many were the consequent petitions for rations of meat, flannel, osna-burgs, etc.; promising all which, in due proportion to the cleanliness of each separate dwelling, I came away. On my way home I called for a moment at Jones's settlement to leave money and presents promised to the people there for similar improvement in the condition of their huts. I had not time to stay and distribute my benefactions my-self, and so appointed a particularly bright, intelligent-looking woman, called Jenny, paymistress in my stead, and her deputed authority was received with the utmost cheerfulness by them all.

I have been having a long talk with Mr. —— about Ben and Daphne, those two young mulatto children of Mr. K——'s, whom I mentioned to you lately. Poor pret-ty children! they have refined and sensitive faces as well as straight, regular features; and the expression of the girl's countenance, as well as the sound of her voice, and the sad humility of her deportment, are indescribably touching. Mr. B—— expressed the strongest interest in and pity for them, *because of their color:* it seems unjust almost to the rest of their fellow-unfortunates that this should be so, and yet it is almost impossible to resist the impression of the unfitness of these two forlorn young creatures for the life of coarse labor and dreadful degra-dation to which they are destined. In any of the South-ern cities the girl would be pretty sure to be reserved for a worse fate; but even here, death seems to me a thou-sand times preferable to the life that is before her.

In the afternoon I rode with Mr. —— to look at the fire in the woods. We did not approach it, but stood where the great volumes of smoke could be seen rising steadily above the pines, as they have now continued to do for upward of a week; the destruction of the pine timber must be something enormous. We then went to visit Dr. and Mrs. G——, and wound up these exercises of civilized life by a call on dear old Mr. C——, whose nursery and kitchen garden are a real refreshment to my spirits. How completely the national character of the worthy canny old Scot is stamped on the care and thrift visible in his whole property, the judicious, successful culture of which has improved and adorned his dwelling in this remote corner of the earth! The comparison, or rather contrast, between himself and his quondam neighbor, Major ——, is curious enough to contemplate. The Scotch tendency of the one to turn every thing to good account, the Irish propensity of the other to leave every thing to ruin, to disorder, and neglect; the careful economy and prudent management of the mercantile man, the reckless profusion and careless extravagance of the soldier. The one made a splendid fortune and spent it in Philadelphia, where he built one of the finest houses that existed there in the old-fashioned days, when fine old family mansions were still to be seen breaking the monotonous uniformity of the Quaker city. The other has resided here on his estate, ameliorating the condition of his slaves and his property, a benefactor to the people and the soil alike—a useful and a good existence, an obscure and tranquil one.

Last Wednesday we drove to Hamilton, by far the finest estate on St. Simon's Island. The gentleman to whom it belongs lives, I believe, habitually in Paris; but Captain F—— resides on it, and, I suppose, is the real overseer of the plantation. All the way along the road (we traversed nearly the whole length of the island) we found great tracts of wood all burnt or burning; the destruction had spread in every direction, and against the sky we saw the slow rising of the smoky clouds that showed the pine forest to be on fire still. What an immense quantity of

L

property such a fire must destroy! The negro huts on
several of the plantations that we passed through were
the most miserable human habitations I ever beheld. The
wretched hovels at St. Annie's, on the Hampton estate,
that had seemed to me the *ne plus ultra* of misery, were
really palaces to some of the dirty, desolate, dilapidated
dog-kennels which we passed to-day, and out of which the
negroes poured like black ants at our approach, and stood
to gaze at us as we drove by.

The planters' residences we passed were only three. It
makes one ponder seriously when one thinks of the mere
handful of white people on this island. In the midst of
this large population of slaves, how absolutely helpless
they would be if the blacks were to become restive! They
could be destroyed to a man before human help could
reach them from the main, or the tidings even of what
was going on be carried across the surrounding waters.
As we approached the southern end of the island we began to discover the line of the white sea-sands beyond the
bushes and fields, and presently, above the sparkling, daz-
zling line of snowy white—for the sands were as white as
our English chalk cliffs—stretched the deep blue sea-line
of the great Atlantic Ocean.

We found that there had been a most terrible fire in
the Hamilton woods—more extensive than that on our
own plantation. It seems as if the whole island had been
burning at different points for more than a week. What
a cruel pity and shame it does seem to have these beautiful masses of wood so destroyed! I suppose it is impossible to prevent it. The " field-hands" make fires to cook
their midday food wherever they happen to be working,
and sometimes through their careless neglect, but sometimes, too, undoubtedly on purpose, the woods are set fire
to by these means. One benefit they consider that they
derive from the process is the destruction of the dreaded

rattlesnakes that infest the woodland all over the island; but really the funeral pyre of these hateful reptiles is too costly at this price.

Hamilton struck me very much—I mean the whole appearance of the place; the situation of the house, the noble water prospect it commanded, the magnificent old oaks near it, a luxuriant vine trellis, and a splendid hedge of yucca gloriosa, were all objects of great delight to me. The latter was most curious to me, who had never seen any but single specimens of the plant, and not many of these. I think our green-house at the North boasts but two; but here they were growing close together, and in such a manner as to form a compact and impenetrable hedge, their spiky leaves striking out on all sides like *chevaux de frise*, and the tall, slender stems, that bear those delicate ivory-colored bells of blossoms, springing up against the sky in a regular row. I wish I could see that hedge in blossom. It must be wonderfully strange and lovely, and must look by moonlight like a whole range of fairy Chinese pagodas carved in ivory.

At dinner we had some delicious green peas, so much in advance of you are we down here with the seasons. Don't you think one might accept the rattlesnakes, or perhaps indeed the slavery, for the sake of the green peas? 'Tis a world of compensations—a life of compromises; you know; and one should learn to set one thing against another if one means to thrive and fare well, *i. e.*, eat green peas on the twenty-eighth of March.

After dinner I walked up and down before the house for a long while with Mrs. F——, and had a most interesting conversation with her about the negroes and all the details of their condition. She is a kind-hearted, intelligent woman; but, though she seemed to me to acquiesce, as a matter of inevitable necessity, in the social system in the midst of which she was born and lives, she did not ap-

pear to me, by several things she said, to be by any means
in love with it. She gave me a very sad character of Mr.
K——, confirming by her general description of him the
impression produced by all the details I have received
from our own people. As for any care for the moral or
religious training of the slaves, that, she said, was a matter that never troubled his thoughts; indeed, his only notion upon the subject of religion, she said, was that it was
something *not bad* for white women and children.

We drove home by moonlight; and as we came toward
the woods in the middle of the island, the fireflies glitter-
ed out from the dusky thickets as if some magical golden
veil was every now and then shaken out into the darkness. The air was enchantingly mild and soft, and the
whole way through the silvery night delightful.

My dear friend, I have at length made acquaintance
with a live rattlesnake. Old Scylla had the pleasure of
discovering it while hunting for some wood to burn. Israel captured it, and brought it to the house for my edification. I thought it an evil-looking beast, and could not
help feeling rather nervous while contemplating it, though
the poor thing had a noose round its neck, and could by
no manner of means have extricated itself. The flat head,
and vivid, vicious eye, and darting tongue, were none of
them lovely to behold; but the sort of threatening whirr
produced by its rattle, together with the deepening and
fading of the marks on its skin, either with its respiration,
or the emotions of fear and anger it was enduring, were
peculiarly dreadful and fascinating. It was quite a young
one, having only two or three rattles in its tail. These,
as you probably know, increase in number by one annu-
ally, so that you can always tell the age of the amiable
serpent you are examining—if it will let you count the
number of joints of its rattle. Captain F—— gave me
the rattle of one which had as many as twelve joints. He

said it had belonged to a very large, snake, which had crawled from under a fallen tree-trunk on which his children were playing. After exhibiting his interesting captive, Israel killed, stuffed, and presented it to me for preservation as a trophy, and made me extremely happy by informing me that there was a nest of them where this one was found. I think with terror of S—— running about with her little socks not reaching half way up her legs, and her little frocks not reaching half way down them. However, we shall probably not make acquaintance with many more of these natives of Georgia, as we are to return as soon as possible now to the North. We shall soon be free again.

This morning I rode to the burnt district, and attempted to go through it at St. Clair's, but unsuccessfully: it was impossible to penetrate through the charred and blackened thickets. In the afternoon I walked round the Point, and visited the houses of the people who are our nearest neighbors. I found poor Edie in sad tribulation at the prospect of resuming her field labor. It is really shameful treatment of a woman just after child-labor. She was confined exactly three weeks ago to-day, and she tells me she is ordered out to field-work on Monday. She seems to dread the approaching hardships of her task-labor extremely. Her baby was born dead, she thinks in consequence of a fall she had while carrying a heavy weight of water. She is suffering great pain in one of her legs and sides, and seems to me in a condition utterly unfit for any work, much less hoeing in the fields; but I dare not interfere to prevent this cruelty. She says she has already had to go out to work three weeks after her confinement with each of her other children, and does not complain of it as any thing special in her case. She says that is now the invariable rule of the whole plantation, though it used not to be so formerly.

I have let my letter lie since I wrote the above, dear
E——; but as mine is a story without beginning, middle,
or end, it matters extremely little where I leave it off or
where I take it up; and if you have not, between my
wood rides and sick slaves, come to Falstaff's conclusion
that I have "damnable iteration," you are patient of sameness. But the days are like each other; and the rides
and the people, and, alas! their conditions, do not vary.

To-day, however, my visit to the Infirmary was marked
by an event which has not occurred before—the death of
one of the poor slaves while I was there. I found, on entering the first ward—to use a most inapplicable term for
the dark, filthy, forlorn room I have so christened—an old
negro called Friday lying on the ground. I asked what
ailed him, and was told he was dying. I approached him,
and perceived, from the glazed eyes and the feeble rattling
breath, that he was at the point of expiring. His tattered
shirt and trowsers barely covered his poor body; his appearance was that of utter exhaustion from age and feeble-
ness; he had nothing under him but a mere handful of
straw that did not cover the earth he was stretched on;
and under his head, by way of pillow for his dying agony,
two or three rough sticks just raising his skull a few
inches from the ground. The flies were all gathering
around his mouth, and not a creature was near him.
There he lay—the worn-out slave, whose life had been
spent in unrequited labor for me and mine, without one
physical alleviation, one Christian solace, one human sympathy, to cheer him in his extremity—panting out the
last breath of his wretched existence like some forsaken,
overworked, wearied-out beast of burden, rotting where
it falls! I bent over the poor awful human creature in
the supreme hour of his mortality; and while my eyes,
blinded with tears of unavailing pity and horror, were
fixed upon him, there was a sudden quivering of the eye-

lids and falling of the jaw—and he was free. I stood up, and remained long lost in the imagination of the change that creature had undergone, and in the tremendous overwhelming consciousness of the deliverance God had granted the soul whose cast-off vesture of decay lay at my feet. How I rejoiced for him; and how, as I turned to the wretches who 'were calling to me from the inner room, whence they could see me as I stood contemplating the piteous object, I wished they all were gone away with him, the delivered, the freed by death from bitter, bitter bondage. In the next room I found a miserable, decrepid old negress, called Charity, lying sick, and I should think near too to die; but she did not think her work was over, much as she looked unfit for farther work on earth; but with feeble voice and beseeching hands implored me to have her work lightened when she was sent back to it from the hospital. She is one of the oldest slaves on the plantation, and has to walk to her field labor, and back again at night, a distance of nearly four miles. There were an unusual number of sick women in the room to-day; among them quite a young girl, daughter of Boatman Quash's, with a sick baby, who has a father, though she has no husband. Poor thing! she looks like a mere child herself. I returned home so very sad and heart-sick that I could not rouse myself to the effort of going up to St. Annie's with the presents I had promised the people there. I sent M—— up in the wood-wagon with them, and remained in the house with my thoughts, which were none of the merriest.

DEAREST E——,—On Friday I rode to where the rattlesnake was found, and where I was informed by the negroes there was a *nest* of them—a pleasing domestic picture of home and infancy that word suggests, not alto-

gether appropriate to rattlesnakes, I think. On horseback
I felt bold to accomplish this adventure, which I certainly
should not have attempted on foot; however, I could discover no sign of either snake or nest—(perhaps it is of the
nature of a mare's nest, and undiscoverable); but, having
done my duty by myself in endeavoring to find it, I rode
off and coasted the estate by the side of the marsh till I
came to the causeway. There I found a new cleared field,
and stopped to admire the beautiful appearance of the
stumps of the trees scattered all about it, and wreathed
and garlanded with the most profuse and fantastic growth
of various plants, wild roses being among the most abundant. What a lovely aspect one side of nature presents
here, and how hideous is the other!

In the afternoon I drove to pay a visit to old Mrs.
A——, the lady proprietress whose estate immediately
adjoins ours. On my way thither I passed a woman called Margaret walking rapidly and powerfully along the
road. She was returning home from the field, having
done her task at three o'clock; and told me, with a mer-
ry, beaming black face, that she was going "to clean up
de house, to please de missis." On driving through my
neighbor's grounds, I was disgusted more than I can express with the miserable negro huts of her people; they
were not fit to shelter cattle—they were not fit to shelter
any thing, for they were literally in holes, and, as we
used to say of our stockings at school, too bad to darn.
To be sure, I will say, in excuse for their old mistress, her
own habitation was but a very few degrees less ruinous
and disgusting. What would one of your Yankee farmers say to such abodes? When I think of the white
houses, the green blinds, and the flower-plots of the villages in New England, and look at these dwellings of
lazy filth and inert degradation, it does seem amazing to
think that physical and moral conditions so widely oppo-

site should be found among people occupying a similar place in the social scale of the same country. The Northern farmer, however, thinks it no shame to work, the Southern planter does; and there begins and ends the difference. Industry, man's crown of honor elsewhere, is here his badge of utter degradation; and so comes all by which I am here surrounded—pride, profligacy, idleness, cruelty, cowardice, ignorance, squalor, dirt, and ineffable abasement.

When I returned home I found that Mrs. F—— had sent me some magnificent prawns. I think of having them served singly, and divided as one does a lobster—their size really suggests no less respect.

Saturday, 31*st*. I rode all through the burnt district and the bush to Mrs. W——'s field, in making my way out of which I was very nearly swamped, and, but for the valuable assistance of a certain sable Scipio who came up and extricated me, I might be floundering hopelessly there still. He got me out of my Slough of Despond, and put me in the way to a charming wood ride which runs between Mrs. W——'s and Colonel H——'s grounds. While going along this delightful boundary of these two neighboring estates, my mind not unnaturally dwelt upon the terms of deadly feud in which the two families owning them are living with each other. A horrible quarrel has occurred quite lately upon the subject of the ownership of this very ground I was skirting, between Dr. H—— and young Mr. W——; they have challenged each other, and what I am going to tell you is a good sample of the sort of spirit which grows up among slaveholders. So read it, for it is curious to people who have not lived habitually among savages. The terms of the challenge that has passed between them have appeared like a sort of advertisement in the local paper, and are to the effect that they are to fight at a certain distance with

L 2

certain weapons—fire-arms, of course; that there is to be on the person of each a white paper, or mark, immediately over the region of the heart, as a point for direct aim; and whoever kills the other is to have the privilege of *cutting off his head, and sticking it up on a pole on the piece of land which was the origin of the debate;* so that, some fine day, I might have come hither as I did to-day, and found myself riding under the shadow of the gory locks of Dr. H—— or Mr. W——, my peaceful and pleasant neighbors.

I came home through our own pine woods, which are actually a wilderness of black desolation. The scorched and charred tree-trunks are still smoking and smouldering; the ground is a sort of charcoal pavement, and the fire is still burning on all sides, for the smoke was rapidly rising in several directions on each hand of the path I pursued. Across this dismal scene of strange destruction, bright blue and red birds, like living jewels, darted in the brilliant sunshine. I wonder if the fire has killed and scared away many of these beautiful creatures. In the afternoon I took Jack with me to clear some more of the wood paths; but the weather is what I call hot, and what the people here think warm, and the air was literally thick with little black points of insects, which they call sand-flies, and which settle upon one's head and face literally like a black net; you hardly see them or feel them at the time, but the irritation occasioned by them is intolerable, and I had to relinquish my work and fly before this winged plague as fast as I could from my new acquaintance the rattlesnakes. Jack informed me, in the course of our expedition, that the woods on the island were sometimes burnt away in order to leave the ground in grass for fodder for the cattle, and that the very beautiful ones he and I had been clearing paths through were not unlikely to be so doomed, which strikes me as a horrible idea.

In the evening poor Edie came up to the house to see me, with an old negress called Sackey, who has been one of the chief nurses on the island for many years. I suppose she has made some application to Mr. G—— for a respite for Edie, on finding how terribly unfit she is for work; or perhaps Mr. ——, to whom I represented her case, may have ordered her reprieve; but she came with much gratitude to me (who have, as far as I know, had nothing to do with it), to tell me that she is not to be sent into the field for another week. Old Sackey fully confirmed Edie's account of the terrible hardships the women underwent in being thus driven to labor before they had recovered from childbearing. She said that old Major —— allowed the women at the rice-island five weeks, and those here four weeks, to recover from a confinement, and then never permitted them for some time after they resumed their work to labor in the fields before sunrise or after sunset; but Mr. K—— had altered that arrangement, allowing the women at the rice-island only four weeks, and those here only three weeks, for their recovery; "and then, missis," continued the old woman, "out into the field again, through dew and dry, as if nothing had happened; that is why, missis, so many of the women have falling of the womb and weakness in the back; and if he had continued on the estate, he would have utterly destroyed all the breeding women." Sometimes, after sending them back into the field at the expiration of their three weeks, they would work for a day or two, she said, and then fall down in the field with exhaustion, and be brought to the hospital almost at the point of death.

Yesterday, Sunday, I had my last service at home with these poor people; nearly thirty of them came, all clean, neat, and decent, in their dress and appearance. S—— had begged very hard to join the congregation, and upon the most solemn promise of remaining still she was admitted; but, in spite of the perfect honor with which she kept her promise, her presence disturbed my thoughts not a little, and added much to the poignancy of the feeling with which I saw her father's poor slaves gathered round me. The child's exquisite complexion, large gray eyes, and solemn and at the same time eager countenance, was such a wonderful piece of contrast to their sable faces, so many of them so uncouth in their outlines and proportions, and yet all of them so pathetic, and some so sublime in their expression of patient suffering and religious fervor: their eyes never wandered from me and my child, who sat close by my knee, their little mistress, their future providence, my poor baby! Dear E——, bless God that you have never reared a child with such an awful expectation: and at the end of the prayers, the tears were streaming over their faces, and one chorus of blessings rose round me and the child—farewell blessings, and prayers that we would return; and thanks so fervent in their incoherency, it was more than I could bear, and I begged them to go away and leave me to recover myself. And then I remained with S——, and for quite a long while even her restless spirit was still in wondering amazement at my bitter crying. I am to go next Sunday to the church on the island, where there is to be service; and so this is my last Sunday with the people.

When I had recovered from the emotion of this scene, I walked out with S—— a little way, but meeting M—— and the baby, she turned home with them, and I pursued my walk alone up the road, and home by the shore. They are threatening to burn down all my woods to make grassland for the cattle, and I have terrified them by telling them that I will never come back if they destroy the woods. I went and paid a visit to Mrs. G——; poor little, well-meaning, helpless woman, what can she do for these poor people, where I, who am supposed to own them, can do nothing? and yet how much may be done, is done, by the brain and heart of one human being in contact with another! We are answerable for incalculable opportunities of good and evil in our daily intercourse with every soul with whom we have to deal; every meeting, every parting, every chance greeting, and every appointed encounter, are occasions open to us for which we are to account. To our children, our servants, our friends, our acquaintances—to each and all every day, and all day long, we are distributing that which is best or worst in existence—influence: with every word, with every look, with every gesture, something is given or withheld of great importance it may be to the receiver, of inestimable importance to the giver.

Certainly the laws and enacted statutes on which this detestable system is built up are potent enough; the social prejudice that buttresses it is almost more potent still; and yet a few hearts and brains well bent to do the work would bring within this almost impenetrable dungeon of ignorance, misery, and degradation, in which so many millions of human souls lie buried, that freedom of God which would presently conquer for them their earthly liberty. With some such thoughts I commended the slaves on the plantation to the little overseer's wife; I did not tell my thoughts to her—they would have scared the poor little woman half out of her senses. To begin with, her bread, her husband's occupation, has its root in slavery; it would be difficult for her to think as I do of it. I am afraid her care, even of the bodily habits and sicknesses of the people left in Mrs. G——'s charge, will not be worth much, for nobody treats others better than they do themselves; and she is certainly doing her best to injure herself and her own poor baby, who is two and a half years old, and whom she is still suckling.

This is, I think, the worst case of this extraordinary

delusion so prevalent among your women that I have ever met with yet; but they all nurse their children much longer than is good for either baby or mother. The summer heat, particularly when a young baby is cutting teeth, is, I know, considered by young American mothers an exceedingly critical time, and therefore I always hear of babies being nursed till after the second summer; so that a child born in January would be suckled till it was eighteen or nineteen months old, in order that it might not be weaned till its second summer was over. I am sure that nothing can be worse than this system, and I attribute much of the wretched ill health of young American mothers to over-nursing; and of course a process that destroys their health and vigor completely must affect most unfavorably the child they are suckling. It is a grievous mistake. I remember my charming friend F—— D—— telling me that she had nursed her first child till her second was born—a miraculous statement, which I can only believe because she told it me herself. Whenever any thing seems absolutely impossible, the word of a true person is the only proof of it worth any thing.

DEAR E——,—I have been riding into the swamp behind the new house; I had a mind to survey the ground all round it before going away, to see what capabilities it afforded for the founding of a garden, but I confess it looked very unpromising. Trying to return by another way, I came to a morass, which, after contemplating, and making my horse try for a few paces, I thought it expedient not to attempt. A woman named Charlotte, who was working in the field, seeing my dilemma, and the inglorious retreat I was about to make, shouted to me at the top of her voice, "You no turn back, missis; if you want to go through, send, missis, send; you hab slave enough, nigger enough, let 'em come, let 'em fetch planks, and make de bridge; what you say dey must do—send, missis, send, missis!" It seemed to me, from the lady's imperative tone in my behalf, that if she had been in my place, she would presently have had a corduroy road through the swamp of prostrate "niggers," as she called her family in Ham, and have ridden over the sand dry-hoofed; and to be sure, if I pleased, so might I, for, as she very truly said, "what you say, missis, they must do." Instead of summoning her sooty tribe, however, I backed my horse out of the swamp, and betook myself to another pretty wood path, which only wants widening to be quite charming. At the end of this, however, I found swamp the second, and out of this having been helped by a grinning, facetious personage, most appropriately named Pun, I returned home in dudgeon, in spite of what dear Miss M—— calls the "moral suitability" of finding a foul bog at the end of every charming wood path or forest ride in this region.

In the afternoon I drove to Busson Hill to visit the people there. I found that both the men and women had done their work at half past three. Saw Tema with her child, that ridiculous image of Driver Bran, in her arms, in spite of whose whity-brown skin she still maintains that its father is a man as black as herself—and she (to use a most extraordinary comparison I heard of a negro girl making with regard to her mother) is as black as "de hinges of hell." Query: Did she really mean hinges, or angels? The angels of hell is a polite and pretty paraphrase for devils, certainly. In complimenting a woman called Joan upon the tidy condition of her house, she answered, with that cruel humility that is so bad an element in their character, "Missis no 'spect to find colored folks' house clean as white folks'." The mode in which they have learned to accept the idea of their own degradation and unalterable inferiority is the most serious impediment that I see in the way of their progress, since assuredly "self-love is not so vile a sin as self-neglecting." In the same way yesterday, Abraham the cook, in speaking of his brother's theft at the rice-island, said "it was a shame even for a colored man to do such things." I labor hard, whenever any such observation is made, to explain to them that the question is one of moral and mental culture—not the color of an integument—and assure them, much to my own comfort, whatever it may be to theirs, that white people are as dirty and as dishonest as colored folks, when they have suffered the same lack of decent training. If I could but find one of these women on whose mind the idea had dawned that she was neither more nor less than my equal, I think I should embrace her in an ecstasy of hopefulness.

In the evening, while I was inditing my journal for your edification, Tema made her appearance with her Bran-brown baby, having walked all the way down from Busson Hill to claim a little sugar I had promised her. She had made her child perfectly clean, and it looked quite pretty. When I asked her what I should give her the sugar in, she snatched her filthy handkerchief off her head; but I declined this sugar-basin, and gave it to her in some paper. Hannah came on the same errand.

After all, dear E——, we shall not leave Georgia so soon as I expected; we can not get off for at least another week. You know, our movements are apt to be both tardy and uncertain. I am getting sick in spirit of my stay here; but I think the spring heat is beginning to affect me miserably, and I long for a cooler atmosphere. Here, on St. Simon's, the climate is perfectly healthy, and our neighbors, many of them, never stir from their plantations within reach of the purifying sea influence. But a land that grows magnolias is not fit for me—I was going to say magnolias and rattlesnakes; but I remember K——'s adventure with her friend the rattlesnake of Monument Mountain, and the wild wood-covered hill half way between Lenox and Stockbridge, which your Berkshire farmers have christened Rattlesnake Mountain. These agreeable serpents seem, like the lovely little humming-birds which are found in your northernmost as well as southernmost states, to have an accommodating disposition with regard to climate.

Not only is the vicinity of the sea an element of salubrity here, but the great masses of pine wood growing in every direction indicate lightness of soil and purity of air. Wherever these fragrant, dry, aromatic fir forests extend, there can be no inherent malaria, I should think, in either atmosphere or soil. The beauty and profusion of the weeds and wild flowers in the fields now is something, too, enchanting. I wish I could spread one of these enameled tracts on the side of one of your snow-covered hills now, for I dare say they are snow-covered yet.

I must give you an account of Aleck's first reading lesson, which took place at the same time that I gave S—— hers this morning. It was the first time he had had leisure to come, and it went off most successfully. He seems to me by no means stupid. I am very sorry he did not ask me to do this before; however, if he can master his alphabet before I go, he may, if chance favor him with the occasional sight of a book, help himself on by degrees. Perhaps he will have the good inspiration to apply to Cooper London for assistance; I am much mistaken if that worthy does not contrive that Heaven shall help Aleck, as it formerly did him, in the matter of reading.

I rode with Jack afterward, showing him where I wish paths to be cut and brushwood removed. I passed the new house, and again circumvented it meditatingly to discover its available points of possible future comeliness, but remained as convinced as ever that there are absolute-

ly none. Within the last two days a perfect border of
the dark blue virginicum has burst into blossom on each
side of the road, fringing it with purple as far as one can
look along it; it is lovely. I must tell you of something
which has delighted me greatly. I told Jack yesterday
that, if any of the boys liked, when they had done their
tasks, to come and clear the paths that I want widened
and trimmed, I would pay them a certain small sum per
hour for their labor; and behold, three boys have come,
having done their tasks early in the afternoon, to apply
for *work* and *wages:* so much for a suggestion not barely
twenty-four hours old, and so much for a prospect of compensation!

In the evening I attempted to walk out when the air
was cool, but had to run precipitately back into the house
to escape from the clouds of sand-flies that had settled on
my neck and arms. The weather has suddenly become in-
tensely hot; at least that is what it appears to me. After I had come in I had a visit from Venus and her daughter, a young girl of ten years old, for whom she begged a
larger allowance of food, as, she said, what she received
for her was totally inadequate to the girl's proper nourishment. I was amazed, upon inquiry, to find that three
quarts of grits a week—that is not a pint a day—was considered a sufficient supply for children of her age. The
mother said her child was half-famished on it, and it seemed to me terribly little.

My little workmen have brought me in from the woods
three darling little rabbits which they have contrived to
catch. They seemed to me slightly different from our
English bunnies; and Captain F——, who called to-day,
gave me a long account of how they differed from the
same animal in the Northern states. I did not like to
mortify my small workmen by refusing their present; but
the poor little things must be left to run wild again, for

we have no conveniences for pets here, besides we are just weighing anchor ourselves. I hope these poor little fluffy things will not meet any rattlesnakes on their way back to the woods.

I had a visit for flannel from one of our Dianas to-day —who had done her task in the middle of the day, yet came to receive her flannel—the most horribly dirty human creature I ever beheld, unless, indeed, her child, whom she brought with her, may have been half a degree dirtier.

The other day, Psyche (you remember the pretty under nurse, the poor thing whose story I wrote you from the rice plantation) asked me if her mother and brothers might be allowed to come and see her when we are gone away. I asked her some questions about them, and she told me that one of her brothers, who belonged to Mr. K——, was hired by that gentleman to a Mr. G——, of Darien, and that, upon the latter desiring to purchase him, Mr. K—— had sold the man without apprising him or any one member of his family that he had done so—a humane proceeding that makes one's blood boil when one hears of it. He had owned the man ever since he was a boy. Psyche urged me very much to obtain an order permitting her to see her mother and brothers. I will try and obtain it for her; but there seems generally a great objection to the visits of slaves from neighboring plantations, and, I have no doubt, not without sufficient reason. The more I see of this frightful and perilous social system, the more I feel that those who live in the midst of it must make their whole existence one constant precaution against danger of some sort or other.

I have given Aleck a second reading lesson with S——, who takes an extreme interest in his newly-acquired alphabetical lore. He is a very quick and attentive scholar, and I should think a very short time would suffice to teach him to read; but, alas! I have not even that short

time. When I had done with my class I rode off with
Jack, who has become quite an expert horseman, and rejoices in being lifted out of the immediate region of snakes
by the length of his horse's legs. I cantered through the
new wood paths, and took a good sloping galop through
the pine land to St. Annie's. The fire is actually still burning in the woods. I came home quite tired with the heat,
though my ride was not a long one.

Just as I had taken off my habit and was preparing to
start off with M—— and the chicks for Jones's in the
wood-wagon, old Dorcas, one of the most decrepid, rheumatic, and miserable old negresses from the farther end
of the plantation, called in to beg for some sugar. She
had walked the whole way from her own settlement, and
seemed absolutely exhausted then, and yet she had to
walk all the way back. It was not otherwise than slightly
meritorious in me, my dear E——, to take her up in the
wagon and endure her abominable dirt and foulness in the
closest proximity, rather than let her drag her poor old
limbs all that way back; but I was glad when we gained
her abode and lost her company. I am mightily reminded occasionally in these parts of Trinculo's soliloquy over
Caliban. The people at Jones's had done their work at
half past three. Most of the houses were tidy and clean,
so were many of the babies. On visiting the cabin of an
exceedingly decent woman called Peggy, I found her, to
my surprise, possessed of a fine large Bible. She told me
her husband, Carpenter John, can read, and that she means
to make him teach her. The fame of Aleck's literature
has evidently reached Jones's, and they are not afraid to
tell me that they can read or wish to learn to do so.
This poor woman's health is miserable; I never saw a
more weakly, sickly-looking creature. She says she has
been broken down ever since the birth of her last child.
I asked her how soon after her confinement she went out

into the field to work again. She answered very quietly, but with a deep sigh, "Three weeks, missis; de usual time." As I was going away, a man named Martin came up, and with great vehemence besought me to give him a Prayer-book. In the evening he came down to fetch it, and to show me that he can read. I was very much pleased to see that they had taken my hint about nailing wooden slats across the windows of their poor huts, to prevent the constant ingress of the poultry. This in itself will produce an immense difference in the cleanliness and comfort of their wretched abodes. In one of the huts I found a broken looking-glass; it was the only piece of furniture of the sort that I had yet seen among them. The woman who owned it was, I am sorry to say, peculiarly untidy and dirty, and so were her children; so that I felt rather inclined to scoff at the piece of civilized vanity, which I should otherwise have greeted as a promising sign.

I drove home, late in the afternoon, through the sweet-smelling woods, that are beginning to hum with the voice of thousands of insects. My troop of volunteer workmen is increased to five—five lads working for my wages after they have done their task-work; and this evening, to my no small amazement, Driver Bran came down to join them for an hour, after working all day at Five Pound, which certainly shows zeal and energy.

Dear E——, I have been riding through the woods all the morning with Jack, giving him directions about the clearings, which I have some faint hope may be allowed to continue after my departure. I went on an exploring expedition round some distant fields, and then home through the St. Annie's woods. They have almost stripped the trees and thickets along the swamp road since I first came here. I wonder what it is for; not fuel surely, nor to make grass-land of, or otherwise cultivate the swamp. I do deplore these pitiless clearings ; and as to this once pretty road, it looks "forlorn," as a worthy Pennsylvania farmer's wife once said to me of a pretty hill-side from which her husband had ruthlessly felled a beautiful grove of trees.

I had another snake encounter in my ride this morning. Just as I had walked my horse through the swamp, and while contemplating ruefully its naked aspect, a huge black snake wriggled rapidly across the path, and I pulled my reins tight and opened my mouth wide with horror. These hideous-looking creatures are, I believe, not poisonous, but they grow to a monstrous size, and have tremendous *constrictive* power. I have heard stories that sound like the nightmare of their fighting desperately with those deadly creatures, rattlesnakes. I can not conceive, if the black snakes are not poisonous, what chance they have against such antagonists, let their squeezing powers be what they will. How horrid it did look, *slithering* over the road ! Perhaps the swamp has been cleared on account of its harboring these dreadful worms.

I rode home very fast, in spite of the exquisite fragrance of the wild cherry blossoms, the carpets and curtains of wild flowers, among which a sort of glorified dandelion glowed conspicuously—dandelions such as I should think grew in the garden of Eden, if there were any at all there. I passed the finest magnolia that I have yet seen ; it was magnificent, and I suppose had been spared for its beauty, for it grew in the very middle of a cotton-field ; it was as large as a fine forest tree, and its huge glittering leaves shone like plates of metal in the sun ; what a spectacle that tree must be in blossom, and I should think its perfume must be smelt from one end of the plantation to the other. What a glorious creature ! Which do you think ought to weigh most in the scale, the delight of such a vegetable, or the disgust of the black animal I had just met a few minutes before? Would you take the one with the other? Neither would I.

I have spent the whole afternoon at home; my "gang" is busily at work again. Sawney, one of them, came to join it nearly at sundown, not having got through his day's task before. In watching and listening to these lads, I was constantly struck with the insolent tyranny of their demeanor toward each other. This is almost a universal characteristic of the manner of the negroes among themselves. They are diabolically cruel to animals too, and they seem to me, as a rule, hardly to know the difference between truth and falsehood. These detestable qualities, which I constantly hear attributed to them as innate and inherent in their race, appear to me the direct result of their condition. The individual exceptions among them are, I think, quite as many as would be found, under similar circumstances, among the same number of white people.

In considering the whole condition of the people on this plantation, it appears to me that the principal hardships fall to the lot of the women—that is, the principal physical hardships. The very young members of the community are of course idle and neglected; the very, very old, idle and neglected too; the middle-aged men do not appear to me overworked, and lead a mere animal existence, in itself not peculiarly cruel or distressing, but involving a constant element of fear and uncertainty, and the trifling evils of unrequited labor, ignorance the most profound (to which they are condemned by law), and the unutterable injustice which precludes them from all the merits and all the benefits of voluntary exertion, and the progress that results from it. If they are absolutely unconscious of these evils, then they are not very ill-off brutes, always barring the chance of being given or sold away from their mates or their young—processes which even brutes do not always relish. I am very much struck with the vein of melancholy, which assumes almost a poetical tone in some of the things they say. Did I tell you of that poor old decrepid creature Dorcas, who came to beg some sugar of me the other day? saying, as she took up my watch from the table and looked at it, "Ah! I need not look at this; I have almost done with time!" Was not that striking from such a poor old ignorant crone?

DEAR E——,—This is the fourth day that I have had a " gang" of lads working in the woods for me after their task hours for pay; you can not think how zealous and energetic they are; I dare say the novelty of the process pleases them almost as much as the money they earn. I must say they quite deserve their small wages.

Last night I received a present from Mrs. F—— of a drum-fish, which animal I had never beheld before, and which seemed to me first cousin to the great Leviathan. It is to be eaten, and is certainly the biggest fish food I ever saw; however, every thing is in proportion, and the prawns that came with it are upon a similarly extensive scale; this magnificent piscatorial bounty was accompanied by a profusion of Hamilton green peas, really a munificent supply.

I went out early after breakfast with Jack hunting for new paths; we rode all along the road by Jones's Creek, and most beautiful it was. We skirted the plantation burial-ground, and a dismal place it looked; the cattle trampling over it in every direction, except where Mr. K—— had had an inclosure put up round the graves of two white men who had worked on the estate. They were strangers, and of course utterly indifferent to the people here; but by virtue of their white skins, their resting-place was protected from the hoofs of the cattle, while

the parents and children, wives, husbands, brothers and
sisters, of the poor slaves, sleeping beside them, might see
the graves of those they loved trampled upon and browsed
over, desecrated and defiled, from morning till night.
There is something intolerably cruel in this disdainful de-
nial of a common humanity pursuing these wretches even
when they are hid beneath the earth.

The day was exquisitely beautiful, and I explored a new
wood path, and found it all strewed with a lovely wild
flower not much unlike a primrose. I spent the afternoon
at home. I dread going out twice a day now, on account
of the heat and the sand-flies. While I was sitting by the
window, Abraham, our cook, went by with some most re-
volting-looking "raw material" (part, I think, of the interior of the monstrous drum-fish of which I have told you).
I asked him, with considerable disgust, what he was going to do with it; he replied, " Oh! we colored people
eat it, missis." Said I, " Why do you say we colored people ?" " Because, missis, white people won't touch what
we too glad of." " That," said I, " is because you are
poor, and do not often have meat to eat, not because you
are colored, Abraham : rich white folks will not touch
what poor white folks are too glad of; it has nothing in
the world to do with color ; and if there were white people here worse off than you (amazing and inconceivable
suggestion, I fear), they would be glad to eat what you
perhaps would not touch." Profound pause of medita-
tion on the part of Abraham, wound up by a considerate
" Well, missis, I suppose so ;" after which he departed
with the horrid-looking offal.

To-day — Saturday—I took another ride of discovery
round the fields by Jones's. I think I shall soon be able
to survey this estate, I have ridden so carefully over it in
every direction; but my rides are drawing to a close, and
even were I to remain here this must be the case, unless

M

I got up and rode under the stars in the cool of the night.
This afternoon I was obliged to drive up to St. Annie's :
I had promised the people several times that I would do
so. I went after dinner and as late as I could, and found
very considerable improvement in the whole condition of
the place ; the houses had all been swept, and some of
them actually scoured. The children were all quite tolerably clean ; they had put slats across all their windows,
and little chicken-gates to the doors to keep out the poultry. There was a poor woman lying in one of the cabins
in a wretched condition. She begged for a bandage, but
I do not see of what great use that can be to her, as long
as she has to hoe in the fields so many hours a day, which
I can not prevent.

Returning home, Israel undertook to pilot me across
the cotton-fields into the pine land ; and a more excruci-
ating process than being dragged over that very uneven
surface in that wood-wagon without springs I did never
endure, mitigated and soothed though it was by the literally fascinating account my charioteer gave me of the
rattlesnakes with which the place we drove through becomes infested as the heat increases. I can not say that
his description of them, though more demonstrative as far
as regarded his own horror of them, was really worse than
that which Mr. G—— was giving me of them yesterday.
He said they were very numerous, and were found in every direction all over the plantation, but that they did not
become really vicious until quite late in the summer ; until then, it appears that they generally endeavor to make
off if one meets them, but during the intense heats of the
latter part of July and August they never think of es-
caping, but at any sight or sound which they may consider inimical they instantly coil themselves for a spring.
The most intolerable proceeding on their part, however,
that he described, was their getting up into the trees, and

either coiling themselves in or depending from the branches.   There is something too revolting in the idea of serpents looking down upon one from the shade of the trees
to which one may betake one's self for shelter in the
dreadful heat of the Southern midsummer; decidedly I
do not think the dog-days would be pleasant here.   The
moccasin snake, which is nearly as deadly as the rattlesnake, abounds all over the island.

In the evening I had a visit from Mr. C—— and Mr.
B——, who officiates to-morrow at our small island church.
The conversation I had with these gentlemen was sad
enough.   They seem good, and kind, and amiable men,
and I have no doubt are conscientious in their capacity of
slaveholders; but to one who has lived outside this dreadful atmosphere, the whole tone of their discourse has a
morally muffled sound, which one must hear to be able to
conceive.   Mr. B—— told me that the people on this
plantation not going to church was the result of a positive order from Mr. K——, who had peremptorily forbidden their doing so, and of course to have infringed
that order would have been to incur severe corporal
chastisement.   Bishop B——, it seems, had advised that
there should be periodical preaching on the plantations,
which, said Mr. B——, would have obviated any necessity
for the people of different estates congregating at any
given point at stated times, which might perhaps be objectionable, and at the same time would meet the reproach which was now beginning to be directed toward
Southern planters as a class, of neglecting the eternal interest of their dependents.   But Mr. K—— had equally
objected to this.   He seems to have held religious teaching a mighty dangerous thing—and how right he was!
I have met with conventional cowardice of various shades
and shapes in various societies that I have lived in, but
any thing like the pervading timidity of tone which I

find here on all subjects, but, above all, on that of the condition of the slaves, I have never dreamed of. Truly slavery begets slavery, and the perpetual state of suspicion and apprehension of the slaveholders is a very handsome offset, to say the least of it, against the fetters and the lash of the slaves. Poor people, one and all, but especially poor oppressors of the oppressed! The attitude of these men is really pitiable; they profess (perhaps some of them strive to do so indeed) to consult the best interests of their slaves, and yet shrink back terrified from the approach of the slightest intellectual or moral improvement which might modify their degraded and miserable existence. I do pity these deplorable servants of two masters more than any human beings I have ever seen—more than their own slaves a thousand times!

To-day is Sunday, and I have been to the little church on the island. It is the second time since I came down to the South that I have been to a place of worship. A curious little incident prefaced my going thither this morning. I had desired Israel to get my horse ready and himself to accompany me, as I meant to ride to church; and you can not imagine any thing droller than his horror and dismay when he at length comprehended that my purpose was to attend divine service in my riding-habit. I asked him what was the trouble; for, though I saw something was creating a dreadful convulsion in his mind, I had no idea what it was till he told me, adding that he had never seen such a thing on St. Simon's in his life—as who should say, such a thing was never seen in Hyde Park or the Tuileries before. You may imagine my amusement; but presently I was destined to shock something much more serious than poor Israel's sense of *les convénances et bienséances*, and it was not without something of an effort that I made up my mind to do so. I was standing at the open window speaking to him about the horses, and telling him to get ready to ride with me, when George, another of the men, went by with a shade or visor to his cap exactly the shape of the one I left behind at the North, and for want of which I have been suffering severely from the intense heat and glare of the sun for the last week. I asked him to hand me his cap, saying, "I want to take the pattern of that shade." Israel exclaimed, "Oh, missis, not to-day; let him leave the cap with you to-morrow, but don't cut pattern on de Sabbath day!" It seemed to me a much more serious matter to offend this scruple than the prejudice with regard to praying in a riding-habit; still, it had to be done. "Do you think it wrong, Israel," said I, "to work on Sunday?" "Yes, missis, parson tell we so." "Then, Israel, be sure you never do it. Did your parson never tell you that your conscience was for yourself and not for your neighbors, Israel?" "Oh yes, missis, he tell we that too." "Then mind that too, Israel." The shade was cut out and stitched upon my cap, and protected my eyes from the fierce glare of the sun and sand as I rode to church.

On our way we came to a field where the young corn was coming up. The children were in the field—little living scarecrows—watching it, of course, as on a week-day, to keep off the birds. I made Israel observe this, who replied, "Oh, missis, if de people's corn left one whole day not watched, not one blade of it remain to-morrow; it must be watched, missis." "What, on the Sabbath-day, Israel?" "Yes, missis, or else we lose it all." I was not sorry to avail myself of this illustration of the nature of works of necessity, and proceeded to enlighten Israel with regard to what I conceive to be the genuine observance of the Sabbath.

You can not imagine any thing wilder or more beautiful than the situation of the little rustic temple in the woods where I went to worship to-day, with the magnificent live oaks standing round it and its picturesque burialground. The disgracefully neglected state of the latter, its broken and ruinous inclosure, and its shaggy, weedgrown graves, tell a strange story of the residents of this island, who are content to leave the resting-place of their dead in so shocking a condition. In the tiny little chamber of a church, the grand old Litany of the Episcopal Church of England was not a little shorn of its ceremonial stateliness; clerk there was none, nor choir, nor organ, and the clergyman did duty for all, giving out the hymn and then singing it himself, followed as best might be by the uncertain voices of his very small congregation, the smallest I think I ever saw gathered in a Christian place of worship, even counting a few of the negroes who had ventured to place themselves standing at the back of the church—an infringement on their part upon the privileges of their betters, as Mr. B—— generally preaches a second sermon to them after the *white* service, to which, as a rule, they are not admitted.

On leaving the church, I could not but smile at the quaint and original costumes with which Israel had so much dreaded a comparison for my irreproachable London riding-habit. However, the strangeness of it was what inspired him with terror; but, at that rate, I am afraid a Paris gown and bonnet might have been in equal danger of shocking his prejudices. There was quite as little affinity with the one as the other in the curious specimens of the "art of dressing" that gradually distributed themselves among the two or three indescribable machines (to use the appropriate Scotch title) drawn up under the beautiful oak-trees, on which they departed in various directions to the several plantations on the island.

I mounted my horse, and resumed my ride and my conversation with Israel. He told me that Mr. K——'s great

objection to the people going to church was their meeting with the slaves from the other plantations; and one
reason, he added, that he did not wish them to do that
was, that they trafficked and bartered away the cooper's
wares, tubs, piggins, etc., made on the estate. I think,
however, from every thing I hear of that gentleman, that
the mere fact of the Hampton people coming in contact
with the slaves of other plantations would be a thing he
would have deprecated. As a severe disciplinarian, he
was probably right.

In the course of our talk, a reference I made to the
Bible, and Israel's answer that he could not read, made
me ask him why his father had never taught any of his
sons to read; old Jacob, I know, can read. What followed I shall never forget. He began by giving all sorts
of childish unmeaning excuses and reasons for never having tried to learn—became confused and quite incoherent
—and then, suddenly stopping, and pulling up his horse,
said, with a look and manner that went to my very heart,
"Missis, what for me learn to read? me have no prospect!" I rode on without venturing to speak to him
again for a little while. When I had recovered from that
remark of his, I explained to him that, though indeed
"without prospect" in some respects, yet reading might
avail him much to better his condition, moral, mental, and
physical. He listened very attentively, and was silent for
a minute; after which he said, "All you say very true,
missis, and me sorry now me let de time pass; but you
know what de white man dat goberns de estate him seem
to like and favor, dat de people find out bery soon and do
it; now Massa K——, him neber favor our reading, him
not like it; likely as not he lick you if he find you reading; or, if you wish to teach your children, him always
say, 'Pooh! teach 'em to read—teach 'em to work.' According to dat, we neber paid much attention to it; but

now it will be different; it was different in former times.
De old folks of my father and mother's time could read
more than we can, and I expect de people will dare to
give some thought to it again now." There's a precious
sample of what one man's influence may do in his own
sphere, dear E——! This man Israel is a remarkably fine
fellow in every way, with a frank, open, and most intelligent countenance, which rises before me with its look of
quiet sadness whenever I think of these words (and they
haunt me), "I have no prospect."

On my arrival at home I found that a number of the
people, not knowing I had gone to church, had come up
to the house, hoping that I would read prayers to them,
and had not gone back to their homes, but waited to see
me. I could not bear to disappoint them, for many of
them had come from the farthest settlements on the estate; and so, though my hot ride had tired me a good
deal, and my talk with Israel troubled me profoundly, I
took off my habit, and had them all in, and read the afternoon service to them. When it was over, two of the
women—Venus and Tressa—asked if they might be permitted to go to the nursery and see the children. Their
account of the former condition of the estate was a cor-
roboration of Israel's. They said that the older slaves on
the plantation had been far better off than the younger
ones of the present day; that Major —— was considerate
and humane to his people; and that the women were especially carefully treated. But they said Mr. K—— had
ruined all the young women with working them too soon
after their confinements; and as for the elder ones, he
would kick them, curse them, turn their clothes over their
heads, flog them unmercifully himself, and abuse them
shamefully, no matter what condition they were in. They
both ended with fervent thanks to God that he had left
the estate, and rejoicing that we had come, and, above all,

that we " had made young missis for them." Venus went
down on her knees, exclaiming, " Oh, missis, I glad now;
and when I am dead, I glad in my grave that you come
to us and bring us little missis."

DEAR E——,—I still go on exploring, or rather surveying the estate, the aspect of which is changing every day
with the unfolding of the leaves and the wonderful profusion of wild flowers. The cleared ground all round the
new building is one sheet of blooming blue of various
tints; it is perfectly exquisite. But in the midst of my
delight at these new blossoms, I am most sorrowfully bidding adieu to that paragon of parasites, the yellow jasmine; I think I must have gathered the very last blossoms of it to-day. Nothing can be more lovely, nothing
so exquisitely fragrant. I was surprised to recognize by
their foliage to-day some fine mulberry-trees by Jones's
Creek; perhaps they are the remains of the silk-worm experiment that Mr. C—— persuaded Major —— to try so
ineffectually. While I was looking at some wild plum
and cherry trees that were already swarming with blight
in the shape of multitudinous caterpillars' nests, an ingenious darkie, by name Cudgie, asked me if I could explain
to him why the trees blossomed out so fair, and then all
" went off into a kind of dying." Having directed his
vision and attention to the horrid white glistening webs,
all lined with their brood of black devourers, I left him to
draw his own conclusions.

The afternoon was rainy, in spite of which I drove to
Busson Hill, and had a talk with Bran about the vile cat-
erpillar blights on the wild plum-trees, and asked him if it
would not be possible to get some sweet grafts from Mr.
C—— for some of the wild fruit-trees, of which there are
such quantities. Perhaps, however, they are not worth

M 2

grafting. Bran promised me that the people should not be allowed to encumber the paths and the front of their houses with unsightly and untidy heaps of oyster-shells. He promised all sorts of things. I wonder how soon after I am gone they will all return into the condition of brutal filth and disorder in which I found them.

The men and women had done their work here by half past three. The chief labor in the cotton-fields, however, is both earlier and later in the season. At present they have little to do but let the crop grow. In the evening I had a visit from the son of a very remarkable man, who had been one of the chief drivers on the estate in Major ——'s time, and his son brought me a silver cup which Major —— had given his father as a testimonial of approbation, with an inscription on it recording his fidelity and trustworthiness at the time of the invasion of the coast of Georgia by the English troops. Was not that a curious reward for a slave who was supposed not to be able to read his own praises? And yet, from the honorable pride with which his son regarded this relic, I am sure the master did well so to reward his servant, though it seemed hard that the son of such a man should be a slave. Maurice himself came with his father's precious silver cup in his hand, to beg for a small pittance of sugar, and for a Prayer-book, and also to know if the privilege of a milch cow for the support of his family, which was among the favors Major —— allowed his father, might not be continued to him. He told me he had ten children "working for massa," and I promised to mention his petition to Mr. ——.

On Sunday last I rode round the woods near St. Annie's, and met with a monstrous snake, which Jack called a chicken-snake; but whether because it particularly affected poultry as its diet, or for what other reason, he could not tell me. Nearer home I encountered another

gliding creature, that stopped a moment just in front of
my horse's feet, as if it was too much afraid of being
trampled upon to get out of the way: it was the only
snake animal I ever saw that I did not think hideous. It
was of a perfectly pure apple-green color, with a delicate
line of black like a collar round its throat; it really was
an exquisite worm, and Jack said it was harmless. I did
not, however, think it expedient to bring it home in my
bosom, though, if ever I have a pet snake, it shall be such
a one.

In the afternoon I drove to Jones's with several supplies of flannel for the rheumatic women and old men.
We have ridden over to Hamilton again, to pay another
visit to the F——'s, and on our way passed an enormous
rattlesnake hanging dead on the bough of a tree. Dead
as it was, it turned me perfectly sick with horror, and I
wished very much to come back to the North immediately, where these are not the sort of blackberries that grow
on every bush. The evening air now, after the heat of
the day, is exquisitely mild, and the nights dry and wholesome, the whole atmosphere indescribably fragrant with
the perfume of flowers; and as I stood, before going to
bed last night, watching the slow revolving light on Sapelo
Island, that warns the ships from the dangerous bar at
the river's mouth, and heard the measured pulse of the
great Atlantic waters on the beach, I thought no more
of rattlesnakes—no more, for one short while, of slavery.
How still, and sweet, and solemn it was!

We have been paying more friendly and neighborly visits, or rather returning them; and the recipients of these
civilized courtesies on our last calling expedition were the
family one member of which was a party concerned in
that barbarous challenge I wrote you word about. Hitherto that very brutal and bloodthirsty cartel appears to
have had no result. You must not, on that account, im-

agine that it will have none.   At the North, were it possible for a duel intended to be conducted on such savage
terms to be matter of notoriety, the very horror of the
thing would create a feeling of grotesqueness, and the antagonists in such a proposed encounter would simply incur an immense amount of ridicule and obloquy.   But
here nobody is astonished and nobody ashamed of such
preliminaries to a mortal combat between two gentlemen,
who propose firing at marks over each other's hearts, and
cutting off each other's heads; and though this agreeable
party of pleasure has not come off yet, there seems to be
no reason why it should not at the first convenient season.
Reflecting upon all which, I rode, not without trepidation,
through Colonel H——'s grounds, and up to his house.
Mr. W——'s head was not stuck upon a pole any where
within sight, however, and as soon as I became pretty
sure of this, I began to look about me, and saw instead a
trellis tapestried with the most beautiful roses I ever beheld, another of these exquisite Southern flowers — the
Cherokee rose.   The blossom is very large, composed of
four or five pure white petals, as white and as large as
those of the finest camellia, with a bright golden eye for
a focus; the buds and leaves are long and elegantly slender, like those of some tea-roses, and the green of the foliage is dark, and at the same time vivid and lustrous; it
grew in masses so as to form almost a hedge, all starred
with these wonderful white blossoms, which, unfortunately, have no perfume.

We rode home through the pine land to Jones's, looked at the new house which is coming on hideously, saw
two beautiful kinds of trumpet honeysuckle already light-
ing up the woods in every direction with gleams of scarlet, and when we reached home found a splendid donation
of vegetables, flowers, and mutton from our kind neighbor Mrs. F——, who is a perfect Lady Bountiful to us.

This same mutton, however—my heart bleeds to say it—disappeared the day after it was sent to us. Abraham the cook declares that he locked the door of the safe upon it, which I think may be true, but I also think he unlocked it again. I am sorry; but, after all, it is very natural these people should steal a little of our meat from us occasionally, who steal almost all their bread from them habitually.

I rode yesterday to St. Annie's with Mr. ——. We found a whole tract of marsh had been set on fire by the facetious negro called Pun, who had helped me out of it some time ago. As he was set to work in it, perhaps it was with a view of making it less damp; at any rate, it was crackling, blazing, and smoking cheerily, and I should think would be insupportable for the snakes. While stopping to look at the conflagration, Mr. —— was accosted by a three parts naked and one part tattered little she slave—black as ebony, where her skin was discoverable through its perfect incrustation of dirt—with a thick mat of frizzly wool upon her skull, which made the sole request she preferred to him irresistibly ludicrous: "Massa, massa, you please to buy me a comb to tick in my head?" Mr. —— promised her this necessary of life, and I promised myself to give her the luxury of one whole garment. Mrs. —— has sent me the best possible consolation for the lost mutton, some lovely flowers, and these will not be stolen.

Saturday, the 13*th.* DEAR E——,—I rode to-day through all my wood paths for the last time with Jack, and I think I should have felt quite melancholy at taking leave of them and him but for the apparition of a large black snake, which filled me with disgust and nipped my other sentiments in the bud. Not a day passes now that I do not encounter one or more of these hateful reptiles; it is curious how much more odious they are to me than the alligators that haunt the mud banks of the river round the rice plantation. It is true that there is something very dreadful in the thick shapeless mass, uniform in color almost to the black slime on which it lies basking, and which you hardly detect till it begins to move. But even those ungainly crocodiles never sickened me as those rapid, lithe, and sinuous serpents do. Did I ever tell you that the people at the rice plantation caught a young alligator and brought it to the house, and it was kept for some time in a tub of water? It was an ill-tempered little monster; it used to set up its back like a cat when it was angry, and open its long jaws in a most vicious manner.

After looking at my new path in the pine land, I crossed Pike Bluff, and, breaking my way all through the burnt district, returned home by Jones's. In the afternoon we paid a long visit to Mr. C——. It is extremely interesting to me to talk with him about the negroes; he has spent so much of his life among them, has managed them so humanely, and apparently so successfully, that his experience is worthy of all attention. And yet it seems to me that it is impossible, or rather, perhaps, for those very reasons it is impossible, for him ever to contemplate them in any condition but that of slavery. He thinks them very like the Irish, and instanced their subserviency, their flattering, their lying, and pilfering, as traits common to the characters of both peoples. But I can not persuade myself that in both cases, and certainly in that of the negroes, these qualities are not in great measure the result of their condition. He says that he considers the extremely low diet of the negroes one reason for the absence of crimes of a savage nature among them; most of them do not touch meat the year round. But in this respect they certainly do not resemble the Irish, who contrive, upon about as low a national diet as civilization is acquainted with, to commit the bloodiest and most frequent outrages with which civilization has to deal. His statement that it is impossible to bribe the negroes to work on their own account with any steadiness may be generally true, but admits of quite exceptions enough to throw doubt upon its being natural supineness in the race rather than the inevitable consequence of denying them the entire right to labor for their own profit. Their laziness seems to me the necessary result of their primary wants being supplied, and all progress denied them. Of course, if the natural spur to exertion, necessity, is removed, you do away with the will to work of a vast proportion of all who do work in the world. It is the law of progress that man's necessities grow with his exertions to satisfy them, and labor and improvement thus continually act and react upon each other to raise the scale of desire and achievement; and I do not believe that, in the majority of instances among any people on the face of the earth, the will to labor for small indulgences would survive the loss of freedom and the security of food enough to exist upon. Mr. —— said that he had offered a bribe of twenty dollars apiece, and the use of a pair of oxen, for the clearing of a certain piece of land, to the men on his estate, and found the offer quite ineffectual to procure the desired result; the land was subsequently cleared as usual task-work under the lash. Now, certainly, we have among Mr. ——'s people instances of men who have made very considerable sums of money by boat-building in their leisure hours, and the instances of almost life-long, persevering, stringent labor, by which slaves have at length purchased their own freedom and that of their wives and children, are on record in numbers sufficient to prove that they are capable of severe sustained effort of the most patient and heroic kind for that great object,

liberty. For my own part, I know no people who dote
upon labor for its own sake; and it seems to me quite natural to any absolutely ignorant and nearly brutish man,
if you say to him, " No effort of your own can make you
free, but no absence of effort shall starve you," to decline
to work for any thing less than mastery over his whole
life, and to take up with his mess of porridge as the alternative. One thing that Mr. —— said seemed to me to
prove rather too much. He declared that his son, object-
ing to the folks on his plantation going about bareheaded,
had at one time offered a reward of a dollar to those who
should habitually wear hats without being able to induce
them to do so, which he attributed to sheer careless indolence; but I think it was merely the force of habit of going uncovered rather than absolute laziness. The universal testimony of all present at this conversation was in
favor of the sweetness of temper and natural gentleness
of disposition of the negroes; but these characteristics
they seemed to think less inherent than the result of diet
and the other lowering influences of their condition; and
it must not be forgotten that on the estate of this wise
and kind master a formidable conspiracy was organized
among his slaves.

We rowed home through a world of stars, the stead-
fast ones set in the still blue sky, and the flashing swathes
of phosphoric light turned up by our oars and keel in the
smooth blue water. It was lovely.

Sunday, 14*th*. My DEAR E——,—That horrid tragedy
with which we have been threatened, and of which I was
writing to you almost jestingly a few days ago, has been
accomplished, and apparently without exciting any thing
but the most passing and superficial sensation in this community. The duel between Dr. H—— and Mr. W——

did not take place, but an accidental encounter in the
hotel at Brunswick did, and the former shot the latter
dead on the spot. He has been brought home and buried
here by the little church close to his mother's plantation;
and the murderer, if he is even prosecuted, runs no risk
of finding a jury in the whole length and breadth of
Georgia who could convict him of any thing. It is horrible.

I drove to church to-day in the wood-wagon, with Jack
and Aleck, Hector being our charioteer, in a gilt guard-
chain and pair of slippers to match as the Sabbatic part
of his attire. The love of dirty finery is not a trait of the
Irish in Ireland, but I think it crops out strongly when
they come out here; and the proportion of their high
wages put upon their backs by the young Irish maidserv-
ants in the North indicates a strong addiction to the female passion for dress. Here the tendency seems to exist in men and women alike; but I think all savage men
rejoice, even more than their women, in personal orna-
mentation. The negroes certainly show the same strong
predilection for finery with their womenkind.

I stopped before going into church to look at the new
grave that has taken its place among the defaced stones,
all overgrown with briers, that lie round it. Poor young
W——! poor widowed mother, of whom he was the only
son! What a savage horror! And no one seems to
think any thing of it, more than of a matter of course.
My devotions were any thing but satisfactory or refreshing to me. My mind was dwelling incessantly upon the
new grave under the great oaks outside, and the miserable mother in her home. The air of the church was perfectly thick with sand-flies; and the disgraceful carelessness of the congregation in responding and singing the
hymns, and the entire neglect of the Prayer-book regulations for kneeling, disturbed and displeased me even more

than the last time I was at church; but I think that was
because of the total absence of excitement or feeling
among the whole population of St. Simon's upon the subject of the bloody outrage with which my mind was full,
which has given me a sensation of horror toward the
whole community. Just imagine—only it is impossible
to imagine—such a thing taking place in a New England
village; the dismay, the grief, the shame, the indignation,
that would fill the hearts of the whole population. I
thought we should surely have some reference to the
event from the pulpit, some lesson of Christian command
over furious passions. Nothing—nobody looked or spoke
as if any thing unusual had occurred; and I left the
church, rejoicing to think that I was going away from
such a dreadful state of society. Mr. B—— remained to
preach a second sermon to the negroes—the duty of submission to masters who intermurder each other.

I had service at home in the afternoon, and my congregation was much more crowded than usual; for I believe
there is no doubt at last that we shall leave Georgia this
week. Having given way so much before when I thought
I was praying with these poor people for the last time, I
suppose I had, so to speak, expended my emotion, and I
was much more composed and quiet than when I took
leave of them before. But, to tell you the truth, this
dreadful act of slaughter done in our neighborhood by
one man of our acquaintance upon another, impresses me
to such a degree that I can hardly turn my mind from it,
and Mrs. W—— and her poor young murdered son have
taken almost complete possession of my thoughts.

After prayers I gave my poor people a parting admo-
nition, and many charges to remember me and all I had
tried to teach them during my stay. They promised with
one voice to mind and do all that "missis tell we;" and
with many a parting benediction, and entreaties to me to

return, they went their way. I think I have done what I could for them—I think I have done as well as I could by them; but when the time comes for ending any human relation, who can be without their misgivings? who can be bold to say, I could have done no more, I could have done no better?

In the afternoon I walked out, and passed many of the people, who are now beginning, whenever they see me, to say " Good-by, missis !" which is rather trying. Many of them were clean and tidy, and decent in their appearance to a degree that certainly bore strong witness to the temporary efficacy of my influence in this respect. There is, however, of course much individual difference even with reference to this, and some take much more kindly and readily to cleanliness, no doubt to godliness too, than some others. I met Abraham, and thought that, in a quiet tête-à-tête, and with the pathetic consideration of my near departure to assist me, I could get him to confess the truth about the disappearance of the mutton; but he persisted in the legend of its departure through the locked door; and as I was only heaping sins on his soul with every lie I caused him to add to the previous ones, I desisted from my inquiries. Dirt and lying are the natural tendencies of humanity, which are especially fostered by slavery. Slaves may be infinitely wrong, and yet it is very hard to blame them.

I returned home, finding the heat quite oppressive. Late in the evening, when the sun had gone down a long time, I thought I would try and breathe the fresh sea air, but the atmosphere was thick with sand-flies, which drove me in at last from standing listening to the roar of the Atlantic on Little St. Simon's Island, the wooded belt that fends off the ocean surges from the north side of Great St. Simon's. It is a wild little sand-heap, covered with thick forest growth, and belongs to Mr. ——. I

have long had a great desire to visit it. I hope yet to be
able to do so before our departure.

I have just finished reading, with the utmost interest
and admiration, J—— C——'s narrative of his escape
from the wreck of the Pulaski: what a brave, and gal-
lant, and unselfish soul he must be! You never read any
thing more thrilling, in spite of the perfect modesty of this
account of his. If I can obtain his permission, and squeeze
out the time, I will surely copy it for you. The quiet, un-
assuming character of his usual manners and deportment
adds greatly to his prestige as a hero. What a fine thing
it must be to be such a man!

DEAR E——,—We shall leave this place next Thursday
or Friday, and there will be an end to this record; meantime I am fulfilling all sorts of last duties, and especially
those of taking leave of my neighbors, by whom the neglect of a farewell visit would be taken much amiss.

On Sunday I rode to a place called Frederica to call on
a Mrs. A——, who came to see me some time ago. I
rode straight through the island by the main road that
leads to the little church.

How can I describe to you the exquisite spring beauty
that is now adorning these woods, the variety of the fresh,
new-born foliage, the fragrance of the sweet, wild per-
fumes that fill the air? Honeysuckles twine round every
tree; the ground is covered with a low, white-blossomed
shrub more fragrant than lilies of the valley. The accac-
nas are swinging their silver censers under the green roof
of these wood temples; every stump is like a classical
altar to the sylvan gods, garlanded with flowers; every
post, or stick, or slight stem, like a Bacchante's thyrsus,
twined with wreaths of ivy and wild vine, waving in the
tepid wind. Beautiful butterflies flicker like flying flowers

among the bushes, and gorgeous birds, like winged jewels, dart from the boughs, and—and—a huge ground snake slid like a dark ribbon across the path while I was stopping to enjoy all this deliciousness, and so I became less enthusiastic, and cantered on past the little deserted church-yard, with the new-made grave beneath its grove of noble oaks, and a little farther on reached Mrs. A——'s cottage, half hidden in the midst of ruins and roses.

This Frederica is a very strange place; it was once a town—*the* town, the metropolis of the island. The English, when they landed on the coast of Georgia in the war, destroyed this tiny place, and it has never been built up again. Mrs. A——'s, and one other house, are the only dwellings that remain in this curious wilderness of dismantled crumbling gray walls compassionately cloaked with a thousand profuse and graceful creepers. These are the only ruins, properly so called, except those of Fort Putnam, that I have ever seen in this land of contemptuous youth. I hailed these picturesque groups and masses with the feelings of a European, to whom ruins are like a sort of relations. In my country, ruins are like a minor chord in music; here they are like a discord; they are not the relics of time, but the results of violence; they recall no valuable memories of a remote past, and are mere encumbrances to the busy present. Evidently they are out of place in America except on St. Simon's Island, between this savage selvage of civilization and the great Atlantic deep. These heaps of rubbish and roses would have made the fortune of a sketcher; but I imagine the snakes have it all to themselves here, and are undisturbed by camp-stools, white umbrellas, and ejaculatory young ladies.

I sat for a long time with Mrs. A——, and a friend of hers staying with her, a Mrs. A——, lately from Florida. The latter seemed to me a remarkable woman; her conversation was extremely interesting. She had been stopping at Brunswick, at the hotel where Dr. H—— murdered young W——, and said that the mingled ferocity and blackguardism of the men who frequented the house had induced her to cut short her stay there, and come on to her friend Mrs. A——'s. We spoke of that terrible crime which had occurred only the day after she left Brunswick, and both ladies agreed that there was not the slightest chance of Dr. H——'s being punished in any way for the murder he had committed; that shooting down a man who had offended you was part of the morals and manners of the Southern gentry, and that the circumstance was one of quite too frequent occurrence to cause any sensation, even in the small community where it obliterated one of the principal members of the society. If the accounts given by these ladies of the character of the planters in this part of the South may be believed, they must be as idle, arrogant, ignorant, dissolute, and ferocious as that mediæval chivalry to which they are fond of comparing themselves; and these are Southern women, and should know the people among whom they live.

We had a long discussion on the subject of slavery, and they took, as usual, the old ground of justifying the system, *where* it was administered with kindness and indulgence. It is not surprising that women should regard the question from this point of view; they are very seldom *just*, and are generally treated with more indulgence than justice by men. They were very patient of my strong expressions of reprobation of the whole system, and Mrs. A——, bidding me good-by, said that, for aught she could tell, I might be right, and might have been led down here by Providence to be the means of some great change in the condition of the poor colored people.

I rode home pondering on the strange fate that has brought me to this place so far from where I was born, this existence so different in all its elements from that of my early years and former associations. If I believed Mrs. A——'s parting words, I might perhaps verify them; perhaps I may yet verify, although I do not believe them. On my return home I found a most enchanting bundle of flowers, sent to me by Mrs. G——; pomegranate blos-soms, roses, honeysuckle, every thing that blooms two months later with us in Pennsylvania.

I told you I had a great desire to visit Little St. Simon's, and the day before yesterday I determined to make an exploring expedition thither. I took M—— and the chil-dren, little imagining what manner of day's work was be-fore me. Six men rowed us in the "Lily," and Israel brought the wood-wagon after us in a flat. Our naviga-tion was a very intricate one, all through sea swamps and marshes, mud-banks and sand-banks, with great white shells and bleaching bones stuck upon sticks to mark the channel. We landed on this forest in the sea by Quash's house, the only human residence on the island. It was larger and better, and more substantial than the negro huts in general, and he seemed proud and pleased to do the honors to us. Thence we set off, by my desire, in the wagon through the woods to the beach; road there was none, save the rough clearing that the men cut with their axes before us as we went slowly on. Presently we came to a deep dry ditch, over which there was no visible means of proceeding. Israel told me if we would sit still he would undertake to drive the wagon into and out of it; and so, indeed, he did, but how he did it is more than I can explain to you now, or could explain to myself then. A less powerful creature than Montreal could never have dragged us through; and when we presently came to a second rather worse edition of the same, I insisted upon getting out and crossing it on foot. I walked half a mile while the wagon was dragged up and down the deep gul-

ly, and lifted bodily over some huge trunks of fallen
trees. The wood through which we now drove was all
on fire, smoking, flaming, crackling, and burning round
us. The sun glared upon us from the cloudless sky, and
the air was one cloud of sand-flies and musquitoes. I
covered both my children's faces with veils and handker-
chiefs, and repented not a little in my own breast of the
rashness of my undertaking. The back of Israel's coat
was covered so thick with musquitoes that one could
hardly see the cloth; and I felt as if we should be
stifled if our way lay much longer through this terrible
wood. Presently we came to another impassable place,
and again got out of the wagon, leaving Israel to manage
it as best he could. I walked with the baby in my arms
a quarter of a mile, and then was so overcome with the
heat that I sat down in the burning wood, on the floor of
ashes, till the wagon came up again. I put the children
and M—— into it, and continued to walk till we came to
a ditch in a tract of salt marsh, over which Israel drove
triumphantly, and I partly jumped and was partly hauled
over, having declined the entreaties of several of the men
to let them lie down and make a bridge with their bodies
for me to walk over. At length we reached the skirt of
that tremendous wood, to my unspeakable relief, and came
upon the white sand-hillocks of the beach. The trees
were all strained crooked, from the constant influence of
the sea-blast. The coast was a fearful-looking stretch of
dismal, trackless sand, and the ocean lay boundless and
awful beyond the wild and desolate beach, from which we
were now only divided by a patch of low, coarse-looking
bush, growing as thick and tangled as heather, and so
stiff and compact that it was hardly possible to drive
through it. Yet in spite of this, several lads who had
joined our train rushed off into it in search of rabbits,
though Israel called repeatedly to them, warning them of

the danger of rattlesnakes. We drove at last down to the smooth sea sand; and here, outstripping our guides, was barred farther progress by a deep gully, down which it was impossible to take the wagon. Israel, not knowing the beach well, was afraid to drive round the mouth of it; and so it was determined that from this point we should walk home under his guidance. I sat in the wagon while he constructed a rough foot-bridge of bits of wood and broken planks for us over the narrow chasm, and he then took Montreal out of the wagon and tied him behind it, leaving him for the other men to take charge of when they should arrive at this point. And so, having mightily desired to see the coast of Little St. Simon's Island, I did see it thoroughly; for I walked a mile and a half round it, over beds of sharp shells, through swamps half knee deep, poor little S—— stumping along with dogged heroism, and Israel carrying the baby, except at one deep *mal passo*, when I took the baby and he carried S——; and so, through the wood round Quash's house, where we arrived almost fainting with fatigue and heat, and where we rested but a short time, for we had to start almost immediately to save the tide home.

I called at Mr. C——'s on my way back, to return him his son's manuscript, which I had in the boat for that purpose. I sent Jack, who had come to meet me with the horses, home, being too tired to attempt riding; and, covered with mud literally up to my knees, I was obliged to lie down ignominiously all the afternoon to rest. And now I will give you a curious illustration of the utter subserviency of slaves. It seems that by taking the tide in proper season, and going by boat, all that horrible wood journey might have been avoided, and we could have reached the beach with perfect ease in half the time; but because, being of course absolutely ignorant of this, I had expressed a desire to go through the wood, not a syllable

N

of remonstrance was uttered by any one; and the men not only underwent the labor of cutting a path for the wagon and dragging it through and over all the impediments we encountered, but allowed me and the children to traverse that burning wood, rather than tell me that by waiting and taking another way I could get to the sea. When I expressed my astonishment at their not having remonstrated against my order, and explained how I could best achieve the purpose I had in view, the sole answer I got even from Israel was, " Missis say so, so me do; missis say me go through the wood, me no tell missis go another way." You see, my dear E——, one had need bethink one's self what orders one gives, when one has the misfortune to be despotic.

How sorry I am that I have been obliged to return that narrative of Mr. C——'s without asking permission to copy it, which I did not do because I should not have been able to find the time to do it! We go away the day after to-morrow. All the main incidents of the disaster the newspapers have made you familiar with—the sudden and appalling loss of that fine vessel laden with the very flower of the South. There seems hardly to be a family in Georgia and South Carolina that had not some of its members on board that ill-fated ship. You know it was a sort of party of pleasure more than any thing else; the usual annual trip to the North for change of air and scene, for the gayeties of Newport and Saratoga, that all the wealthy Southern people invariably take every summer.

The weather had been calm and lovely; and dancing, talking, and laughing, as if they were in their own drawing-rooms, they had passed the time away till they all separated for the night. At the first sound of the exploding boiler Mr. C—— jumped up, and in his shirt and trowsers ran on deck. The scene was one of horrible confusion; women screaming, men swearing, the deck strewn with broken fragments of all descriptions, the vessel leaning frightfully to one side, and every body running hither and thither in the darkness in horror and dismay. He had left Georgia with Mrs. F—— and Mrs. N——, the two children, and one of the female servants of these ladies under his charge. He went immediately to the door of the ladies' cabin and called Mrs. F——; they were all there half dressed; he bade them dress as quickly as possible, and be ready to follow and obey him. He returned almost instantly, and led them to the side of the vessel, where, into the boats, that had already been lowered, desperate men and women were beginning to swarm, throwing themselves out of the sinking ship. He bade Mrs. F—— jump down into one of these boats which was only in the possession of two sailors; she instantly obeyed him, and he threw her little boy to the men after her. He then ordered Mrs. N——, with the negro woman, to throw themselves off the vessel into the boat, and, with Mrs. N——'s baby in his arms, sprang after them. His foot touched the gunwale of the boat, and he fell into the water; but, recovering himself instantly, he clambered into the boat, which he then peremptorily ordered the men to set adrift, in spite of the shrieks, and cries, and commands, and entreaties of the frantic crowds who were endeavoring to get into it. The men obeyed him, and rowing while he steered, they presently fell astern of the ship, in the midst of the darkness, and tumult, and terror. Another boat laden with people was near them. For some time they saw the heart-rending spectacle of the sinking vessel, and the sea strewn with mattresses, seats, planks, etc., to which people were clinging, floating, and shrieking for succor, in the dark water all round them. But they gradually pulled farther and farther out of the horrible chaos of despair, and, with the other boat still consorting with them, rowed on. They watched from a distance the piteous sight of the ill-fated steamer settling down, the gray girdle of light that marked the line of her beautiful saloons and cabins gradually sinking nearer and nearer to the blackness, in which they were presently extinguished; and the ship, with all its precious human freight ingulfed —all but the handful left in those two open boats, to brave the dangers of that terrible coast!

They were somewhere off the North Carolina shore, which, when 'the daylight dawned, they could distinctly see, with its ominous line of breakers and inhospitable perilous coast. The men had continued rowing all night, and as the summer sun rose flaming over their heads, the task of pulling the boat became dreadfully severe; still they followed the coast, Mr. C—— looking out for any opening, creek, or small inlet that might give them a chance of landing in safety. The other boat rowed on at some little distance from them.

All the morning, and through the tremendous heat of the middle day, they toiled on without a mouthful of food —without a drop of water. At length, toward the afternoon, the men at the oars said they were utterly exhausted and could row no longer, and that Mr. C—— must steer the boat ashore. With wonderful power of command, he prevailed on them to continue their afflicting labor. The terrible blazing sun pouring on all their unsheltered heads had almost annihilated them; but still there lay between them and the land those fearful foaming ridges, and the women and children, if not the men themselves, seemed doomed to inevitable death in the attempt to surmount them. Suddenly they perceived that the boat that had kept them company was about to adventure itself in the perilous experiment of landing. Mr. C—— kept his boat's head steady, the men rested on their oars, and watched the result of the fearful risk they were themselves about to run. They saw the boat enter the breakers—they saw her whirled round and capsized, and then they watched, slowly emerging and dragging themselves out of the foaming sea, *some*, and only some, of the people that they knew the boat contained. Mr. C——, fortified with this terrible illustration of the peril that awaited them, again besought them to row yet for a little while farther along the coast, in search of some possible place to take the boat safely to the beach, promising at sunset to give up the search, and again the poor men resumed their toil; but the line of leaping breakers stretched along the coast as far as eye could see, and at length the men declared they could labor no longer, and insisted that Mr. C—— should steer them to shore. He then said that he would do so, but they must take some rest before encountering the peril which awaited them, and for which they might require whatever remaining strength they could command. He made the men leave the oars and lie down to sleep for a short time, and then, giving the helm to one of them, did the same himself. When they were thus a little refreshed with this short rest, he prepared to take the boat into the breakers.

He laid Mrs. N——'s baby on her breast, and wrapped a shawl round and round her body so as to secure the child to it, and said, in the event of the boat capsizing, he would endeavor to save her and her child. Mrs. F—— and her boy he gave in charge to one of the sailors, and the colored woman who was with her to the other, and they promised solemnly, in case of misadventure to the boat, to do their best to save these helpless creatures; and so they turned, as the sun was going down, the bows of the boat to the terrible shore. They rose two of the breakers safely, but then the oar of one of the men was struck from his hand, and in an instant the boat whirled round and turned over. Mr. C—— instantly struck out to seize Mrs. N——, but she had sunk, and, though he dived twice, he could not see her; at last he felt her hair floating loose with his foot, and seizing hold of it, grasped her securely and swam with her to shore. While in the act of doing so, he saw the man who had promised to save the colored woman making alone for the beach; and even then, in that extremity, he had power of command enough left to drive the fellow back to seek her, which he did, and brought her safe to land. The other man kept his word of taking care of Mrs. F——, and the latter never released her grasp of her child's wrist, which bore the mark of her agony for weeks after their escape. They reached the sands, and Mrs. N——'s shawl having been unwound, her child was found laughing on her bosom. But hardly had they had time to thank God for their deliverance when Mr. C—— fell fainting on the beach; and Mrs. F——, who told me this, said that for one dreadful moment they thought that the preserver of all their lives had lost his own in the terrible exertion and anxiety that he had undergone. He revived, however, and crawling a little farther up the beach, they burrowed for warmth and shelter as well as they could in the sand, and lay there till the next morning, when they sought and found succor.

You can not imagine, my dear E——, how strikingly throughout this whole narrative the extraordinary power of Mr. C——'s character makes itself felt—the immediate obedience that he obtained from women whose terror might have made them unmanageable, and men whose selfishness might have defied his control; the wise though painful firmness which enabled him to order the boat away from the side of the perishing vessel, in spite of the pity that he felt for the many, in attempting to succor whom he could only have jeopardized the few whom he was bound to save; the wonderful influence he exercised over the poor oarsmen, whose long protracted labor postponed to the last possible moment the terrible risk of their landing. The firmness, courage, humanity, wisdom, and presence of mind of all his preparations for their final tremendous risk, and the authority which he was able to exercise, while struggling in the foaming water for his own life and that of the woman and child he was saving, over the man who was proving false to a similar sacred charge — all these admirable traits are most miserably transmitted to you by my imperfect account; and when I assure you that his own narrative, full as it necessarily was of the details of his own heroism, was as simple, modest, and unpretending as it was interesting and touching, I am sure you will agree with me that he must be a very rare man. When I spoke with enthusiasm to his old father of his son's noble conduct, and asked him if he was not proud of it, his sole reply was, "I am glad, madam, my son was not selfish."

Now, E——, I have often spoken with you and written to you of the disastrous effect of slavery upon the character of the white men implicated in it; many among themselves feel and acknowledge it to the fullest extent, and no one more than myself can deplore that any human being I love should be subjected to such baneful influences; but the devil must have his due, and men brought up in habits of peremptory command over their fellow-men, and under the constant apprehension of danger, and awful necessity of immediate readiness to meet it, acquire qualities precious to themselves and others in hours of supreme peril such as this man passed through, saving by their exercise himself and all committed to his charge. I know that the Southern men are apt to deny the fact that they do live under an habitual sense of danger; but a slave population, coerced into obedience, though unarmed and half-fed, *is* a threatening source of constant insecurity, and every Southern *woman* to whom I have spoken on the subject has admitted to me that they live in terror of

their slaves.   Happy are such of them as have protectors
like J—— C——.   Such men will best avoid and best encounter the perils that may assail them from the abject
subject, human element, in the control of which their noble faculties are sadly and unworthily employed.

 Wednesday, 17*th April.* I rode to-day, after breakfast,
to Mrs. D——'s, another of my neighbors, who lives full
twelve miles off.   During the last two miles of my expedition I had the white sand hillocks and blue line of the
Atlantic in view.   The house at which I called was a
tumble-down barrack of a dwelling in the woods, with a
sort of poverty-stricken pretentious air about it, like sundry "proud planters'" dwellings that I have seen.   I was
received by the sons as well as the lady of the house, and
could not but admire the lordly rather than manly indifference with which these young gentlemen, in gay guard-
chains and fine attire, played the gallants to me, while
filthy, barefooted, half-naked negro women brought in re-
freshments, and stood all the while fanning the cake, and
sweetmeats, and their young masters, as if they had been
all the same sort of stuff.   I felt ashamed for the lads.
The conversation turned upon Dr. H——'s trial; for there
has been a trial as a matter of form, and an acquittal as a
matter of course; and the gentlemen said, upon my expressing some surprise at the latter event, that there could
not be found in all Georgia a jury who would convict
him, which says but little for the moral sense of "all Georgia."   From this most painful subject we fell into the
Brunswick Canal, and thereafter I took my leave and rode
home.   I met my babies in the wood-wagon, and took
S—— up before me, and gave her a good gallop home.
Having reached the house with the appetite of a twenty-
four miles' ride, I found no preparation for dinner, and not
so much as a boiled potato to eat, and the sole reply to
my famished and disconsolate exclamations was, " Being

that you order none, missis, I not know." I had forgotten to order my dinner, and my *slaves*, unauthorized, had not ventured to prepare any. Wouldn't a Yankee have said, "Wal, now, you went off so uncommon quick, I kinder guessed you forgot all about dinner," and have had it all ready for me? But my slaves durst not, and so I fasted till some tea could be got for me.

THIS was the last letter I wrote from the plantation, and I never returned there, nor ever saw again any of the poor people among whom I lived during this winter but Jack, once, under sad circumstances. The poor lad's health failed so completely that his owners humanely brought him to the North, to try what benefit he might derive from the change; but this was before the passing of the Fugitive Slave Bill, when, touching the soil of the Northern states, a slave became free; and such was the apprehension felt lest Jack should be enlightened as to this fact by some philanthropic Abolitionist, that he was kept shut up in a high upper room of a large empty house, where even I was not allowed to visit him. I heard at length of his being in Philadelphia; and upon my distinct statement that I considered freeing their slaves the business of the Messrs. —— themselves, and not mine, I was at length permitted to see him. Poor fellow! coming to the North did not prove to him the delight his eager desire had so often anticipated from it; nor, under such circumstances, is it perhaps much to be wondered at that he benefited but little by the change—he died not long after.

I once heard a conversation between Mr. O—— and Mr. K——, the two overseers of the plantation on which I was living, upon the question of taking slaves, servants, necessary attendants, into the Northern states; Mr. O—— urged the danger of their being "got hold of," *i. e.*, set

N 2

free by the Abolitionists, to which Mr. K—— very per-
tinently replied, " Oh, stuff and nonsense ; I take care,
when my wife goes North with the children, to send Lucy
with her ; *her children are down here, and I defy all the
Abolitionists in creation to get her to stay North.*" Mr.
K—— was an extremely wise man.

APPENDIX

I WROTE the following letter after reading several leading articles in the *Times* newspaper, at the time of the great sensation occasioned by Mrs. Beecher Stowe's novel of "Uncle Tom's Cabin," and after the Anti-slavery Protest which that book induced the women of England to address to those of America on the subject of the condition of the slaves in the Southern states.

MY DEAR E——,—I have read the articles in the *Times* to which you refer on the subject of the inaccuracy of Mrs. Beecher Stowe's book as a picture of slavery in America, and have ascertained who they were written by. Having done so, I do not think it worth while to send my letter for insertion, because, as that is the tone deliberately taken upon the subject by that paper, my counter statement would not, I imagine, be admitted into its columns. I inclose it to you, as I should like you to see how far from true, according to my experience, the statements of the "*Times*' Correspondent" are. It is impossible, of course, to know why it erects itself into an advocate for slavery; and the most charitable conjecture I can form upon the subject is, that the Stafford House demonstration may have been thought likely to wound the sensitive national views of America upon this subject; and the statement put forward by the *Times*, contradicting Mrs. Stowe's picture, may be intended to soothe their irritation at the philanthropic zeal of our lady Abolitionists. Believe me, dear E——, yours always truly,

F. A. K.

Letter to the Editor of the "TIMES."

SIR,—As it is not to be supposed that you consciously afford the support of your great influence to misstatements, I request your attention to some remarks I wish to make on an article on a book called "Uncle Tom's Cabin as it is," contained in your paper of the 11th. In treating Mrs. Harriet Beecher Stowe's work as an exaggerated picture of the evils of slavery, I beg to assure you that you do her serious injustice: of the merits of her book as a work of art I have no desire to speak; to its power as a most interesting and pathetic story, all England and America can bear witness; but of its truth and moderation as a representation of the slave system in the United States, I can testify with the experience of an eye-witness, having been a resident in the Southern states, and had opportunities of observation such as no one who has not lived on a slave estate can have. It is very true that in reviving the altogether exploded fashion of making the hero of her novel "the perfect monster that the world ne'er saw," Mrs. Stowe has laid herself open to fair criticism, and must expect to meet with it from the very opposite taste of the present day; but the ideal excellence of her principal character is no argument at all against the general accuracy of her statements with regard to the evils of slavery; every thing else in her book is not only possible, but probable, and not only probable, but a very faithful representation of the existing facts: faithful, and not, as you accuse it of being, exaggerated; for, with the exception of the horrible catastrophe, the flogging to death of poor Tom, she has portrayed none of the most revolting instances of crime produced by the slave system, with which she might have darkened her picture, without detracting from its perfect truth. Even with respect to the incident of Tom's death, it must not be said that if such an event is possible, it is hardly probable; for this is unfortunately not true. It is not true that the value of the slave as property infallibly protects his life from the passions of his master. It is no new thing for a man's passions to blind him to his most obvious and immediate temporal interests, as well as to his higher and everlasting ones—in various parts of the world and stages of civilization, various human passions assume successive prominence, and become developed, to the partial exclusion or deadening of others. In savage existence, and those states of civilization least removed from it, the animal passions predominate. In highly cultivated modern society, where the complicated machinery of human existence is at once a perpetually renewed cause and effect of certain legal and moral restraints, which, in the shape of government and public opinion, protect the congregated lives and interests of men from the worst outrages of open violence, the natural selfishness of mankind assumes a different development, and the love of power, of pleasure, or of pelf, exhibits different phenomena from those elicited from a savage under the influence of the same passions. The channel in which the energy and activity of modern society inclines more and more to pour itself is the peaceful one of the pursuit of gain. This is preeminently the case with the two great commercial nations of the earth, England and America; and in either England or the Northern states of America, the prudential and practical views of life prevail so far, that instances of men sacrificing their money interests at the instigation of rage, revenge, and hatred will certainly not abound. But the Southern slaveholders are a very different race of men from either Manchester manufacturers or Massachusetts merchants; they are a remnant of barbarism and feudalism, maintaining itself with infinite difficulty and danger by the side of the latest and most powerful development of commercial civilization.

The inhabitants of Baltimore, Richmond, Charleston, Savannah, and New Orleans, whose estates lie, like the suburban retreats of our city magnates, in the near neighborhood of their respective cities, are not now the people I refer to. They are softened and enlightened by many influences — the action of city life itself, where human sympathy and human respect, stimulated by neighborhood, produce salutary social restraint as well as less salutary social cowardice. They travel to the Northern states and to Europe, and Europe and the Northern states travel to them, and, in spite of themselves, their peculiar conditions receive modifications from foreign intercourse. The influence, too, of commercial enterprise, which in these latter days is becoming the agent of civilization all over the earth, affects even the uncommercial residents of the Southern cities, and, however cordially they may dislike or despise the mercantile tendencies of Atlantic Americans or transatlantic Englishmen, their frequent contact with them breaks down some of the barriers of difference between them, and humanizes the slaveholder of the great cities into some relation with the spirit of his own times and country. But these men are but a most inconsiderable portion of the slaveholding population of the South—a nation, for as such they should be spoken of, of men whose organization and temperament is that of the southern European; living under the influence of a climate at once enervating and exciting; scattered over trackless wildernesses of arid sand and pestilential swamp; intrenched within their own boundaries; surrounded by creatures absolutely subject to their despotic will; delivered over by hard necessity to the lowest excitements of drinking, gambling, and debauchery for sole recreation; independent of all opinion; ignorant of all progress; isolated from all society—it is impossible to conceive a more savage existence within the pale of any modern civilization.

The South Carolinian gentry have been fond of styling themselves the chivalry of the South, and perhaps might not badly represent, in their relations with their dependents, the nobility of France before the purifying hurricane of the Revolution swept the rights of the suzerain and the wrongs of the serf together into one bloody abyss. The planters of the interior of the Southern and Southwestern states, with their furious feuds and slaughterous combats, their stabbings and pistolings, their gross sensuality, brutal ignorance, and despotic cruelty, resemble the chivalry of France before the horrors of the Jacquerie admonished them that there was a limit even to the endurance of slaves. With such men as these, human life, even when it can be bought or sold in the market for so many dollars, is but little protected by considerations of interest from the effects of any violent passion. There is yet, however, another aspect of the question, which is, that it is sometimes clearly *not* the interest of the owner to prolong the life of his slaves; as in the case of inferior or superannuated laborers, or the very notorious instance in which some of the owners of sugar plantations stated that they found it better worth their while to *work off* (*i. e.*, kill with labor) a certain proportion of their force, and replace them by new hands every seven years, than work them less severely and maintain them in diminished efficiency for an indefinite length of time. Here you will observe a precise estimate of the planter's material interest led to a result which you argue passion itself can never be so blind as to adopt. This was a deliberate economical calculation, openly avowed some years ago by a number of sugar planters in Louisiana. If, instead of accusing Mrs. Stowe of exaggeration, you had brought the same charge against the author of the " White Slave," I should not have been surprised; for his book presents some of the most revolting instances of atrocity and crime that the miserable abuse of irresponsible power is capable of producing, and it is by no means written in the spirit of universal humanity which pervades Mrs. Stowe's volumes; but it is not liable to the charge of exaggeration any more than her less disgusting delineation. The scenes described in the " White Slave" *do* occur in the slave states of North America; and in two of the most appalling incidents of the book—the burning alive of the captured runaway, and the hanging without trial of the Vicksburg gamblers— the author of the " White Slave" has very simply related positive facts of notorious occurrence. To which he might have added, had he seen fit to do so, the instance of a slave who perished in the sea-swamps, where he was left bound and naked, a prey to the torture inflicted upon him by the venomous musquito swarms. My purpose, however, in addressing you was not to enter into a disquisition on either of these publications; but I am not sorry to take this opportunity of bearing witness to the truth of Mrs. Stowe's admirable book, and I have seen what few Englishmen can see—the working of the system in the midst of it.

In reply to your " Dispassionate Observer," who went to the South professedly with the purpose of seeing and judging of the state of things for himself, let me tell you that, little as he may be disposed to believe it, his testimony is worth less than nothing; for it is morally impossible for any Englishman going into the Southern states, except as a *resident*, to know any thing whatever of the real condition of the slave population. This was the case some years ago, as I experienced, and it is now likely to be more the case than ever; for the institution is not *yet* approved divine to the perceptions of Englishmen, and the Southerners are as anxious to hide its uglier features from any note-making observer from this side of the water as to present to his admiration and approval such as can by any possibility be made to wear the most distant approach to comeliness.

The gentry of the Southern states are pre-eminent in their own country for that species of manner which, contrasted with the breeding of the Northerners, would be emphatically pronounced " good" by Englishmen. Born to inhabit landed property, they are not inevitably made clerks and counting-house men of, but inherit with their estates some of the invariable characteristics of an aristocracy. The shop is not their element; and the eager spirit of speculation and the sordid spirit of gain do not infect their whole existence, even to their very demeanor and appearance, as they too manifestly do those of a large proportion of the inhabitants of the Northern states. Good manners have an undue value for Englishmen, generally speaking; and whatever departs from their peculiar standard of breeding is apt to prejudice them, as whatever approaches it prepossesses them, far more than is reasonable. The Southerners are infinitely better bred men, according to English notions, than the men of the Northern states. The habit of command gives them a certain self-possession, the enjoyment of leisure a certain ease. Their temperament is impulsive and enthusiastic, and their manners have the grace and spirit which seldom belong to the deportment of a Northern people; but, upon more familiar acquaintance, the vices of the social system to which they belong will be found to have infected them with their own peculiar taint; and haughty, overbearing irritability, effeminate indolence, reckless extravagance, and a union of profligacy and cruelty, which is the immediate result of their irresponsible power over their dependents, are some of the less pleasing traits which acquaintance develops in a Southern character. In spite of all this, there is no manner of doubt that the " candid English observer" will, for the season of his sojourning among them, greatly prefer

their intercourse to that of their Northern brethren. Moreover, without in the least suspecting it, he will be bribed
insidiously and incessantly by the extreme desire and endeavor to please and prepossess him which the whole
white population of the slave states will exhibit—as long
as he goes only as a "candid observer," with a mind not
yet made up upon the subject of slavery, and open to conviction as to its virtues. Every conciliating demonstration of courtesy and hospitable kindness will be extended
to him, and, as I said before, if his observation is permitted (and it may even appear to be courted), it will be to
a fairly bound, purified edition of the black book of slavery, in which, though the inherent viciousness of the whole
story can not be suppressed, the coarser and more offensive passages will be carefully expunged. And now permit me to observe that the remarks of your traveler must
derive much of their value from the scene of his inquiry.
In Maryland, Kentucky, and Virginia, the outward aspect
of slavery has ceased to wear its most deplorable features.
The remaining vitality of the system no longer resides in
the interests, but in the pride and prejudices of the planters. Their soil and climate are alike favorable to the labors of a white peasantry : the slave cultivation has had
time to prove itself there the destructive pest which, in
time, it will prove itself wherever it prevails. The vast
estates and large fortunes that once maintained, and were
maintained by, the serfdom of hundreds of negroes, have
dwindled in size and sunk in value, till the slaves have become so heavy a burden on the resources of the exhausted
soil and impoverished owners of it, that they are made
themselves objects of traffic in order to ward off the ruin
that their increase would otherwise entail. Thus the plan
tations of the Northern slave states now present to the
traveler very few of the darker and more oppressive peculiarities of the system ; and, provided he does not stray

too near the precincts where the negroes are sold, or come across gangs of them on their way to Georgia, Louisiana, or Alabama, he may, if he is a very superficial observer, conclude that the most prosperous slavery is not much worse than the most miserable freedom.

But of what value will be such conclusions applied to those numerous plantations where no white man ever sets foot without the express permission of the owner ? not estates lying close to Baltimore and Charleston, or even Lexington and Savannah, but remote and savage wildernesses like Legree's estate in " Uncle Tom," like all the plantations in the interior of Tennessee and Alabama, like the cotton-fields and rice-swamps of the great muddy rivers of Louisiana and Georgia, like the dreary pine barrens and endless woody wastes of North Carolina.   These, especially the islands, are like so many fortresses, approachable for " observers" only at the owners' will.   On most of the rice plantations in these pestilential regions, no white man can pass the night at certain seasons of the year without running the risk of his life ; and during the day, the master and overseer are as much alone and irresponsible in their dominion over their black cattle, as Robinson Crusoe was over his small family of animals on his desert habitation.   Who, on such estates as these, shall witness to any act of tyranny or barbarity, however atrocious ?   No black man's testimony is allowed against a white, and who, on the dismal swampy rice-grounds of the Savannah, or the sugar-brakes of the Mississippi and its tributaries, or the up-country cotton-lands of the Ocmulgee, shall go to perform the task of candid observation and benevolent inquiry ?

I passed some time on two such estates—plantations where the negroes esteemed themselves well off, and, compared with the slaves on several of the neighboring properties, might very well consider themselves so ; and I will.

with your permission, contrast some of the items of my observation with those of the traveler whose report you find so satisfactory on the subject of the "consolations" of slavery.

And, first, for the attachment which he affirms to subsist between the slave and master. I do not deny that certain manifestations on the part of the slave may suggest the idea of such a feeling; but whether, upon better examination, it will be found to deserve the name, I very much doubt. In the first place, on some of the great Southern estates, the owners are habitual absentees, utterly unknown to their serfs, and enjoying the proceeds of their labor in residences as far remote as possible from the sands and swamps where their rice and cotton grow, and their slaves bow themselves under the eye of the white overseer, and the lash of the black driver. Some of these Sybarites prefer living in Paris, that paradise of American republicans, some in the capitals of the Middle States of the Union, Philadelphia or New York.

The air of New England has a keen edge of liberty, which suits few Southern constitutions; and unkindly as abolition has found its native soil and native skies, that is its birthplace, and there it flourishes, in spite of all attempts to root it out and trample it down, and within any atmosphere poisoned by its influence no slaveholder can willingly draw breath. Some travel in Europe, and few, whose means permit the contrary, ever pass the entire year on their plantations. Great intervals of many years pass, and no master ever visits some of these properties: what species of attachment do you think the slave entertains for him? In other cases, the visits made will be of a few days in one of the winter months, the estate and its cultivators remaining for the rest of the year under the absolute control of the overseer, who, provided he contrives to get a good crop of rice or cotton into the market for his employers, is left to the arbitrary exercise of a will seldom uninfluenced for evil by the combined effects of the grossest ignorance and habitual intemperance. The temptation to the latter vice is almost irresistible to a white man in such a climate, and leading an existence of brutal isolation, among a parcel of human beings as like brutes as they can be made. But the owner who at these distant intervals of months or years revisits his estates, is looked upon as a returning providence by the poor negroes. They have no experience of his character to destroy their hopes in his goodness, and all possible and impossible ameliorations of their condition are anticipated from his advent, less work, more food, fewer stripes, and some of that consideration which the slave hopes may spring from his positive money value to his owner—a fallacious dependence, as I have already attempted to show, but one which, if it has not always predominating weight with the master, never can have any with the overseer, who has not even the feeling of regard for his own property to mitigate his absolutism over the slaves of another man.

There is a very powerful cause which makes the prosperity and well-being (as far as life is concerned) of most masters a subject of solicitude with their slaves. The only stability of their condition, such as it is, hangs upon it. If the owner of a plantation dies, his estates may fall into the market, and his slaves be sold at public auction the next day; and whether this promises a better, or threatens a worse condition, the slaves can not know, and no human being cares. One thing it inevitably brings, the uprooting of all old associations; the disruption of all the ties of fellowship in misery; the tearing asunder of all relations of blood and affection; the sale into separate and far-distant districts of fathers, mothers, husbands, wives, and children. If the estate does not lie in the ex-

treme South, there is the vague dread of being driven
thither from Virginia to Georgia, from Carolina to Alabama, or Louisiana, a change which, for reasons I have
shown above, implies the passing from a higher into a lower circle of the infernal pit of slavery.

I once heard a slave on the plantation of an absentee
express the most lively distress at hearing that his master
was ill. Before, however, I had recovered from my surprise at this warm "attachment" to a distant and all but
unknown proprietor, the man added, "Massa die, what
become of all him people?"

On my arrival on the plantation where I resided, I was
hailed with the most extravagant demonstrations of delight, and all but lifted off my feet in the arms of people
who had never seen me before, but who, knowing me to
be connected with their owners, expected from me some
of the multitudinous benefits which they always hope to
derive from masters. These, until they come to reside
among them, are always believed to be sources of benefi-
cence and fountains of redress by the poor people, who
have known no rule but the delegated tyranny of the
overseer. In these expectations, however, they very soon
find themselves cruelly mistaken. Of course, if the absentee planter has received a satisfactory income from his
estate, he is inclined to be satisfied with the manager of
it; and as subordination to the only white man among
hundreds of blacks must be maintained at any and every
cost, the overseer is justified and upheld in his whole administration. If the wretched slave ever dared to prefer
a complaint of ill usage the most atrocious, the law which
refuses the testimony of a black against a white is not
only the law of the land, but of every man's private dealings; and lying being one of the natural results of slavery,
and a tendency to shirk compelled and unrequited labor
another, the overseer stands on excellent vantage-ground

when he refers to these undoubted characteristics of the system, if called upon to rebut any charge of cruelty or injustice. But pray consider for a moment the probability of any such charge being preferred by a poor creature who has been for years left to the absolute disposal of this man, and who knows very well that in a few days, or months at farthest, the master will again depart, leaving him again for months, perhaps for years, utterly at the mercy of the man against whom he has dared to prefer a complaint. On the estates which I visited, the owners had been habitually absent, and the "attachment" of slaves to such masters as these, you will allow, can hardly come under the denomination of a strong personal feeling.

Your authority next states that the infirm and superannuated slaves no longer capable of ministering to their masters' luxuries, on the estate that he visited, were ending their lives among all the comforts of home, with kindred and friends around them, in a condition which he contrasts, at least by implication, very favorably with the work-house, the last refuge provided by the social humanity of England for the pauper laborer when he has reached that term when "unregarded age is in corners thrown." On the plantation where I lived the Infirmary was a large room, the walls of which were simply mud and laths; the floor, the soil itself, damp with perpetual drippings from the holes in the roof; and the open space which served for a window was protected only by a broken shutter, which, in order to exclude the cold, was drawn so near as almost to exclude the light at the same time. Upon this earthen floor, with nothing but its hard, damp surface beneath him, no covering but a tattered shirt and trowsers, and a few sticks under his head for a pillow, lay an old man of upward of seventy, dying. When I first looked at him I thought, by the glazed stare of his eyes, and the flies that had gathered round his half-open mouth,

that he was dead; but on stooping nearer, I perceived
that the last faint struggle of life was still going on, but
even while I bent over him it ceased; and so, like a worn-
out hound, with no creature to comfort or relieve his last
agony, with neither Christian solace or human succor near
him, with neither wife, nor child, nor even friendly fellow-
being to lift his head from the knotty sticks on which he
had rested it, or drive away the insects that buzzed round
his lips and nostrils like those of a fallen beast, died
this poor old slave, whose life had been exhausted in unrequited labor, the fruits of which had gone to pamper
the pride and feed the luxury of those who knew and
cared neither for his life or death, and to whom, if they
had heard of the latter, it would have been a matter of
absolute though small gain, the saving of a daily pittance
of meal, which served to prolong a life no longer available
to them.

I proceed to the next item in your observer's record.
All children below the age of twelve were unemployed,
he says, on the estate he visited: this is perhaps a questionable benefit, when, no process of mental cultivation
being permitted, the only employment for the leisure thus
allowed is that of rolling, like dogs or cats, in the sand
and the sun.   On all the plantations I visited, and on
those where I resided, the infants in arms were committed
to the care of these juvenile slaves, who were denominated
nurses, and whose sole employment was what they call to
"mind baby." The poor little negro sucklings were cared
for (I leave to your own judgment how efficiently or how
tenderly) by these half-savage slips of slavery—carried by
them to the fields where their mothers were working under the lash, to receive their needful nourishment, and
then carried back again to the "settlement," or collection
of negro huts, where they wallowed unheeded in utter
filth and neglect until the time again returned for their

being carried to their mother's breast. Such was the employment of the children of eight or nine years old, and the only supervision exercised over either babies or " baby-minders" was that of the old woman left in charge of the Infirmary, where she made her abode all day long, and bestowed such samples of her care and skill upon its inmates as I shall have occasion to mention presently. The practice of thus driving the mothers afield, even while their infants were still dependent upon them for their daily nourishment, is one of which the evil as well as the cruelty is abundantly apparent without comment. The next note of admiration elicited from your "impartial observer" is bestowed upon the fact that the domestic servants (*i. e.*, house slaves) on the plantation he visited were *allowed* to live away from the owner's residence, and to marry. But I never was on a Southern plantation, and I never heard of one, where any of the slaves were *allowed* to sleep under the same roof with their owner. With the exception of the women to whose care the children of the planter, if he had any, might be confided, and perhaps a little boy or girl slave, kept as a sort of pet animal, and allowed to pass the night on the floor of the sleeping apartment of some member of the family, the residence of *any* slaves belonging to a plantation night and day in their master's house, like Northern or European servants, is a thing I believe unknown throughout the Southern states. Of course I except the cities, and speak only of the estates, where the house-servants are neither better housed or accommodated than the field-hands. Their intolerably dirty habits and offensive persons would indeed render it a severe trial to any family accustomed to habits of decent cleanliness ; and, moreover, considerations of safety, and that cautious vigilance which is a hard necessity of the planter's existence, in spite of the supposed attachment of his slaves, would never permit the near

O

proximity, during the unprotected hours of the night, of those whose intimacy, with the daily habits and knowledge of the nightly securities resorted to might prove terrible auxiliaries to any attack from without. The city guards, patrols, and night-watches, together with their stringent rules about about negroes being abroad after night, and their well-fortified lock-up houses for all detected without a pass, afford some security against these attached dependents; but on remote plantations, where the owner and his family, and perhaps a white overseer are alone, surrounded by slaves and separated from all succor against them, they do not sleep under the white man's roof, and for politic reasons, pass the night away from their master's abode. The house-servants have no other or better allowance of food than the field-laborers, but have the advantage of eking it out by what is left from the master's table—if possible, with even less comfort in one respect, inasmuch as no time whatever is set apart for their meals, which they snatch at any hour and in any way that they can—generally, however, standing or squatting on their hams round the kitchen fire; the kitchen being a mere out-house or barn with a fire in it. On the estate where I lived, as I have mentioned, they had no sleeping-rooms in the house; but when their work was over, they retired like the rest to their hovels, the discomfort of which had to them all the additional disadvantage of comparison with their owner's mode of living. In all establishments whatever, of course some disparity exists between the accommodation of the drawing-rooms and best bedrooms and the servants' kitchen and attics; but on a plantation it is no longer a matter of degree. The young women who performed the offices of waiting and house-maids, and the lads who attended upon the service of their master's table where I lived, had neither table to feed at nor chair to sit down upon themselves; the "boys" lay all night on the hearth by the kitchen fire, and the women upon the usual slave's bed—a frame of rough boards, strewed with a little moss off the trees, with the addition perhaps of a tattered and filthy blanket. As for the so-called privilege of marrying—surely it is gross mockery to apply such a word to a bond which may be holy in God's sight, but which did not prevent the owner of a plantation where my observations were made from selling and buying men and their so-called wives and children into divided bondage, nor the white overseer from compelling the wife of one of the most excellent and exemplary of his master's slaves to live with him; nor the white wife of another overseer, in her husband's temporary absence from the estate, from barbarously flogging three *married* slaves within a month of their confinement, their condition being the result of the profligacy of the said overseer, and probably compelled by the very same lash by which it was punished. This is a very disgusting picture of married life on slave estates; but I have undertaken to reply to the statements of your informant, and I regret to be obliged to record the facts by which alone I can do so. "Work," continues your authority, "began at six in the morning; at nine an hour's rest was allowed for breakfast, and by two or three o'clock the day's work was done." Certainly this was a pattern plantation, and I can only lament that my experience lay amid such far less favorable circumstances. The negroes among whom I lived went to the fields at daybreak, carrying with them their allowance of food, which toward noon, and not till then, they ate, cooking it over a fire which they kindled as best they could where they were working; their *second* meal in the day was at night, after their labor was over, having worked at the *very least* six hours without rest or refreshment since their noonday meal—properly so called, indeed, for it was meal and nothing else, or a

preparation something thicker than porridge, which they
call hominy. Perhaps the candid observer, whose report
of the estate he visited appeared to you so consolatory,
would think that this diet contrasted favorably with that
of potato and buttermilk fed Irish laborers. But a more
just comparison surely would be with the mode of living of the laboring population of the United States, the
peasantry of Ohio, Pennsylvania, and Massachusetts, or
indeed with the condition of those very potato and buttermilk fed Irishmen when they have exchanged their
native soil for the fields of the Northern and North-
western states, and when, as one of them once was heard
to say, it was of no use writing home that he got meat
three times a day, for nobody in Ireland would believe
it. The next item in the list of commendation is the
hospital, which your informant also visited, and of which
he gives the following account: "It consisted of three
separate wards, all clean and well ventilated: one was for
lying-in women, who were invariably allowed a month's
rest after their confinement." Permit me to place beside this picture that of a Southern Infirmary, such as I
saw it, and taken on the spot. In the first room that
I entered I found only half of the windows, of which
there were six, glazed; these were almost as much obscured with dirt as the other windowless ones were darkened by the dingy shutters which the shivering inmates
had closed in order to protect themselves from the cold.
In the enormous chimney glimmered the powerless embers of a few chips of wood, round which as many of
the sick women as had strength to approach were cowering, some on wooden settles (there was not such a thing
as a chair with a back in the whole establishment), most
of them on the ground, excluding those who were too ill
to rise; and these poor wretches lay prostrate on the
earth, without bedstead, bed, mattress, or pillow, with no

covering but the clothes they had on and some filthy rags
of blanket in which they endeavored to wrap themselves
as they lay literally strewing the floor, so that there was
hardly room to pass between them. Here, in their hour of
sickness and suffering, lay those whose health and strength
had given way under unrequited labor—some of them, no
later than the previous day, had been urged with the lash
to their accustomed tasks—and their husbands, fathers,
brothers, and sons were even at that hour sweating over
the earth whose increase was to procure for others all the
luxuries which health can enjoy, all the comforts which can
alleviate sickness. Here lay women expecting every hour
the terror and agonies of childbirth, others who had just
brought their doomed offspring into the world, others
who were groaning under the anguish and bitter disappointment of miscarriages—here lay some burning with
fever, others chilled with cold and aching with rheumatism, upon the hard cold ground, the draughts and damp
of the atmosphere increasing their sufferings, and dirt,
noise, stench, and every aggravation of which sickness is
capable combined in their condition. There had been
among them one or two cases of prolonged and terribly
hard labor; and the method adopted by the ignorant old
negress, who was the sole matron, midwife, nurse, physician, surgeon, and servant of the Infirmary, to assist them
in their extremity, was to tie a cloth tight round the throats
of the agonized women, and by drawing it till she almost
suffocated them she produced violent and spasmodic strug-
gles, which she assured me she thought materially assisted the progress of the labor. This was one of the Southern Infirmaries with which I was acquainted; and I beg to
conclude this chapter of contrasts to your informant's consolatory views of slavery by assuring you once more very
emphatically that they have been one and all drawn from
estates where the slaves esteemed themselves well treat-

ed, were reputed generally to be so, and undoubtedly, as far as my observation went, were so, compared with those on several of the adjoining plantations.

With regard to the statement respecting the sums of money earned by industrious negroes, there is no doubt that it is perfectly correct. I know of some slaves on a plantation in the extreme South who had received, at various times, large sums of money from a shopkeeper in the small town near their estate for the gray moss or lichen collected from the evergreen oaks of Carolina and Georgia, upon which it hangs in vast masses, and after some cleaning process becomes an excellent substitute for horse-hair, for bed, chair, and sofa-stuffing. On another estate, some of the slaves were expert boat-makers, and had been allowed by their masters to retain the price (no inconsiderable one) for some that they had found time to manufacture after their day's labor was accomplished. These were undoubtedly privileges; but I confess it appears to me that the juster view of the matter would be this: if these men were industrious enough, out of their scanty leisure, to earn these sums of money, which a mere exercise of arbitrary will on the part of the master allowed them to keep, how much more of remuneration, of comfort, of improvement, physical and mental, might they not have achieved, had the due price of their daily labor merely been paid to them? It seems to me that this is the mode of putting the case to Englishmen, and all who have not agreed to consider uncertain favor an equivalent for common justice in the dealings of man with man. As the slaves are well known to toil for years sometimes to amass the means of rescuing themselves from bondage, the fact of their being able and sometimes allowed to earn considerable sums of money is notorious. But now that I have answered one by one the instances you have produced, with others—I am sure as accurate, and I believe as common—of an entirely opposite description, permit me to ask you what this sort of testimony amounts to. I allow you full credit for yours, allow me full credit for mine, and the result is very simply a nullification of the one by the other statement, and a proof that there is as much good as evil in the details of slavery; but now, be pleased to throw into the scale this consideration, that the principle of the whole is unmitigated abominable evil, as by your own acknowledgment you hold it to be, and add, moreover, that the principle being invariably bad beyond the power of the best man acting under it to alter its execrable injustice, the goodness of the detail is a matter absolutely dependent upon the will of each individual slaveholder, so that though the best can not make the system in the smallest particular better, the bad can make every practical detail of it as atrocious as the principle itself; and then tell me upon what ground you palliate a monstrous iniquity, which is the rule, because of the accidental exceptions which go to prove it. Moreover, if, as you have asserted, good preponderates over evil in the practice, though not in the theory of slavery, or it would not maintain its existence, why do you uphold to us, with so much complacency, the hope that it is surely, if not rapidly approaching its abolishment? Why is the preponderating good, which has, as you say, proved sufficient to uphold the institution hitherto, to become (in spite of the spread of civilization and national progress, and the gradual improvement of the slaves themselves) inadequate to its perpetuation henceforward? Or why, if good really has prevailed in it, do you rejoice that it is speedily to pass away? You say the emancipation of the slaves is inevitable, and that through progressive culture the negro of the Southern states daily approaches more nearly to the recovery of the rights of which he has been robbed. But whence do you draw this happy augury, except from

the hope, which all Christian souls must cherish, that God
will not permit much longer so great a wickedness to
darken the face of the earth ?   Surely the increased stringency of the Southern slave-laws, the more than ever vig-
ilant precautions against all attempts to enlighten or educate the negroes, the severer restrictions on manumission,
the thrusting forth out of certain states of all free persons
of color, the atrocious Fugitive Slave Bill, one of the latest
achievements of Congress, and the piratical attempt upon
Cuba, avowedly, on the part of all Southerners, abetting
or justifying it because it will add slave territory and
600,000 slaves to their possessions—surely these do not
seem indications of the better state of things you antici-
pate, except, indeed, as the straining of the chain beyond
all endurable tightness significantly suggests the probability of its giving way.

I do not believe the planters have any disposition to
put an end to slavery, nor is it perhaps much to be wondered at that they have not.   To do so is, in the opinion
of the majority of them, to run the risk of losing their
property, perhaps their lives, for a benefit which they pro،
fess to think doubtful to the slaves themselves.   How far
they are right in anticipating ruin from the manumission
of their slaves I think questionable, but that they do so is
certain, and self-impoverishment for the sake of abstract
principle is not a thing to be reasonably expected from
any large class of men.   But, besides the natural fact that
the slaveholders wish to retain their property, emancipation is, in their view of it, not only a risk of enormous pe-
cuniary loss, and of their entire social status, but involves
elements of personal danger, and, above all, disgust to inveterate prejudices, which they will assuredly never encounter.   The question is not alone one of foregoing great
wealth or the mere means of subsistence (in either case
almost equally hard); it is not alone the unbinding the

hands of those who have many a bloody debt of hatred
and revenge to settle; it is not alone the consenting suddenly to see by their side, upon a footing of free social
equality, creatures toward whom their predominant feeling is one of mingled terror and abhorrence, and who,
during the whole of their national existence, have been,
as the earth, trampled beneath their feet, yet ever threatening to gape and swallow them alive. It is not all this
alone which makes it unlikely that the Southern planter
should desire to free his slaves: freedom in America is not
merely a personal right; it involves a political privilege.
Freemen there are legislators. The rulers of the land are
the majority of the people, and in many parts of the Southern states the black free citizens would become, if not at
once, yet in process of time, inevitably voters, landholders,
delegates to state Legislatures, members of Assembly—
who knows?—senators, judges, aspirants to the presidency of the United States. You must be an American, or
have lived long among them, to conceive the shout of de-
risive execration with which such an idea would be hailed
from one end of the land to the other.

That the emancipation of the negroes need not necessarily put them in possession of the franchise is of course
obvious; but, as a general consequence, the one would follow from the other; and at present certainly the slaveholders are no more ready to grant the political privilege
than the natural right of freedom. Under these circumstances, though the utmost commiseration is naturally excited by the slaves, I agree with you that some forbear-
ance is due to the masters. It is difficult to conceive a
more awful position than theirs: fettered by laws which
impede every movement toward right and justice, and utterly without the desire to repeal them—dogged by the
apprehension of nameless retributions—bound beneath a
burden of responsibility for which, whether they acknowl-

edge it or not, they are held accountable by God and men
—goaded by the keen consciousness of the growing reprobation of all civilized Christian communities, their existence presents the miserable moral counterpart of the physical condition of their slaves; and it is one compared with
which that of the wretchedest slave is, in my judgment,
worthy of envy.

<hr />

Letter to C. G., Esq.

BEFORE entering upon my answer to your questions,
let me state that I have no claim to be ranked as an Abolitionist in the American acceptation of the word, for I
have hitherto held the emancipation of the slaves to be
exclusively the business and duty of their owners, whose
highest moral interest I thought it was to rid themselves
of such a responsibility, in spite of the manifold worldly
interests almost inextricably bound up with it.

This has been my feeling hitherto with regard to the
views of the Abolitionists, which I now, however, heartily
embrace, inasmuch as I think that from the moment the
United States government assumed an attitude of coercion and supremacy toward the Southern states, it was
bound, with its fleets and armies, to introduce its polity
with respect to slavery, and wherever it planted the standard of the Union, to proclaim the universal freedom which
is the recognized law of the Northern United States. That
they nave not done so has been partly owing to a super-
stitious but honorable veneration for the letter of their
great charter, the Constitution, and still more to the hope
they have never ceased to entertain of bringing back the
South to its allegiance under the former conditions of the
Union, an event which will be rendered impossible by any
attempt to interfere with the existence of slavery.

The North, with the exception of an inconsiderable mi-

nority of its inhabitants, has never been at all desirous of
the emancipation of the slaves. The Democratic party,
which has ruled the United States for many years past,
has always been friendly to the slaveholders, who have,
with few exceptions, been all members of it (for, by a
strange perversion both of words and ideas, some of the
most democratic states in the Union are Southern slave
states, and in the part of Georgia where the slave population is denser than in any other part of the South, a county
exists bearing the satirical title of *Liberty County*). And
the support of the South has been given to the Northern
Democratic politicians upon the distinct understanding
that their "domestic institution" was to be guaranteed to
them.

The condition of the free blacks in the Northern states
has of course been affected most unfavorably by the slavery of their race throughout the other half of the Union;
and, indeed, it would have been a difficult matter for
Northern citizens to maintain toward the blacks an attitude of social and political equality as far as the borders
of Delaware, while immediately beyond they were pledged
to consider them as the "chattels" of their owners, animals no more noble or human than the cattle in their
masters' fields.

How could peace have been maintained if the Southern
slaveholders had been compelled to endure the sight of
negroes rising to wealth and eminence in the Northern
cities, or entering as fellow-members with themselves the
halls of that Legislature to which all free-born citizens are
eligible? They would very certainly have declined with
fierce scorn, not the fellowship of the blacks alone, but
of those white men who admitted the despised race of
their serfs to a footing of such impartial equality. It
therefore was the instinctive, and became the deliberate
policy of the Northern people, once pledged to maintain

slavery in the South, to make their task easy by degrading the blacks in the Northern states to a condition contrasting as little as possible with that of the Southern slaves. The Northern politicians struck hands with the Southern slaveholders, and the great majority of the most enlightened citizens of the Northern states, absorbed in the pursuit of wealth and the extension and consolidation of their admirable and wonderful national prosperity, abandoned the government of their noble country and the preservation of its nobler institutions to the slaveholding aristocracy of the South—to a mob of politicians by trade, the vilest and most venal class of men that ever disgraced and endangered a country—to foreign emigrants, whose brutish ignorance did not prevent the Democratic party from seizing upon them as voters, and bestowing on the Irish and German boors just landed on their shores the same political privileges as those possessed and intelligently exercised by the farmers and mechanics of New England, the most enlightened men of their class to be found in the world.

The gradual encroachment of the Southern politicians upon the liberties of the North, by their unrelaxing influence in Congress and over successive cabinets and presidents, was not without its effect in stimulating some resistance on the part of Northern statesmen of sufficient intelligence to perceive the inevitable results toward which this preponderance in the national councils was steadily tending; and I need not remind you of the rapidity and force with which General Jackson quelled an incipient rebellion in South Carolina, when Mr. Calhoun made the tariff question the pretext for a threatened secession in 1832, of the life-long opposition to Southern pretensions by John Quincy Adams, of the endeavor of Mr. Clay to stem the growing evil by the conditions of the Missouri Compromise, and all the occasional attempts of individuals of more conscientious convictions than their fellow-citizens on the subject of the sin of slavery, from Dr. Channing's eloquent protest on the annexation of Texas, to Mr. Charles Sumner's philippic against Mr. Brooks, of South Carolina.

The disorganization of the Democratic party, after a cohesion of so many years, at length changed the aspect of affairs, and the North appeared to be about to arouse itself from its apathetic consent to Southern domination. The Republican party, headed by Colonel Fremont, who was known to be an anti-slavery man, nearly carried the presidential election six years ago, and then every preparation had been made in the South for the process of secession, which was only averted by the election of Mr. Buchanan, a pro-slavery Southern sympathizer, though born in Pennsylvania. Under his presidency, the Southern statesmen, resuming their attitude of apparent friendliness with the North, kept in abeyance, maturing and perfecting by every treasonable practice, for which their preponderating share in the cabinet afforded them facilities, the plan of the violent disruption of the Union, upon which they had determined whenever the Republican party should have acquired sufficient strength to elect a president with Northern views. Before, however, this event occurred, the war in Kansas rang a prophetic peal of warning through the land; and the struggle there begun between New England emigrants bent on founding a free state, and Missouri border ruffians determined to make the new territory a slaveholding addition to the South, might have roused the whole North and West to the imminence of the peril by which the safety of the Union was threatened.

But neither the struggle in Kansas, nor the strange and piteous episode which grew out of it, of John Brown's attempt to excite an insurrection in Virginia, and his execution by the government of that state, did more than startle the North with a nine days' wonder out of its apathetic indifference. The Republican party, it is true, gained adherents, and acquired strength by degrees; and Mr. Buchanan's term of office approaching its expiration, it became apparent that the Democratic party was about to lose its supremacy, and the slaveholders their dominion; and no sooner was this evident than the latter threw off the mask, and renounced their allegiance to the Union. In a day—in an hour almost—those stood face to face as mortal enemies who were citizens of the same country, subjects of the same government, children of the same soil; and the North, incredulous and amazed, found itself suddenly summoned to retrieve its lost power and influence, and assert the dignity of the insulted Union against the rebellious attempt of the South to overthrow it.

But it was late for them to take that task in hand. For years the conduct of the government of the United States had been becoming a more desperate and degraded *jobbery*, one from which day by day the Northern gentlemen of intelligence, influence, and education withdrew themselves in greater disgust, devoting their energies to schemes of mere personal advantage, and leaving the commonweal with selfish and contemptuous indifference to the guidance of any hands less nice and less busy than their own.

Nor would the Southern planters—a prouder and more aristocratic race than the Northern merchants—have relished the companionship of their fellow-politicians more than the latter, but *their* personal interests were at stake, and immediately concerned in their maintaining their predominant influence over the government; and while the Boston men wrote and talked transcendentalism, and became the most accomplished of *œstetische* cotton-spinners and railroad speculators, and made the shoes and cowhides of the Southerners, the latter made their laws (I believe New Jersey is really the great cowhide factory); and the New York men, owners of the fastest horses and finest houses in the land, having made a sort of Brummagem Paris of their city, were the bankers and brokers of the Southerners, while the latter were the legislators.

The grip the slaveholders had fastened on the helm of the state had been tightening for nearly half a century, till the government of the nation had become literally theirs, and the idea of their relinquishing it was one which the North did not contemplate, and they would not tolerate.

If I have said nothing of the grievances which the South has alleged against the North—its tariff, made chiefly in the interest of the Northeastern manufacturing states, or its inconsiderable but enthusiastic Massachusetts and Pennsylvania Abolition party, it is because I do not believe these causes of complaint would have had the same effect upon any but a community of slaveholders, men made impatient (by the life-long habit of despotism) not only of all control, but of any opposition. Thirty years ago Andrew Jackson—a man of keen sagacity as well as determined energy—wrote of them that they were bent upon destroying the Union, and that, whatever was the pretext of their discontent, that was their aim and purpose. "To-day," he wrote, "it is the tariff, by-and-by it will be slavery." The event has proved how true a prophet he was. My own conviction is that the national character produced and fostered by slaveholding is incompatible with free institutions, and that the Southern aristocracy, thanks to the pernicious influences by which they are surrounded, are unfit to be members of a Christian republic. It is slavery that has made the Southerners rebels to their government, traitors to their country, and the originators of the bloodiest civil war that ever disgraced humanity and civilization. It is for their sinful complicity in slavery, and their shameful abandonment of all their duties as citizens, that the Northerners are paying in the blood of their men, the tears of their women, and the treasure which they have till now held more precious than their birthright. They must now not merely impose a wise restriction upon slavery, they must be prepared to extinguish it. They neglected and despised the task of moderating its conditions and checking its growth; they must now suddenly, in the midst of unparalleled difficulties and dangers, be ready to deal summarily with its entire existence. They have loved the pursuit of personal prosperity and pleasure more than their country; and now they must spend life and living to reconquer their great inheritance, and win back at the sword's point what Heaven had forbidden them to lose. Nor are we, here in England, without part in this tremendous sin and sorrow; we have persisted in feeding our looms, and the huge wealth they coin, with the produce of slavery. In vain our vast Indian territory has solicited the advantage of becoming our free cotton plantation; neither our manufacturers nor our government would venture, would wait, would spend or lose, for that purpose; the slave-grown harvest was ready, was abundant, was cheap—and now the thousand arms of our great national industry are folded in deplorable inactivity; the countless hands that wrought from morn till night the wealth that was a world's wonder are stretched unwillingly to beg their bread; and England has never seen a sadder sight than the enforced idleness of her poor operatives, or a nobler one than their patient and heroic endurance.

And now you ask me what plan, what scheme, what project the government of the United States has formed for the safe and successful emancipation of four millions

of slaves, in the midst of a country distracted with all the
horrors of war, and the male population of which is engaged in military service at a distance from their homes?
Most assuredly none. Precipitated headlong from a state
of apparent profound security and prosperity into a series
of calamitous events which have brought the country to
the verge of ruin, neither the nation or its governors have
had leisure to prepare themselves for any of the disastrous
circumstances they have had to encounter, least of all for
the momentous change which the President's proclamation announces as imminent : a measure of supreme importance, not deliberately adopted as the result of philanthropic conviction or far-sighted policy, but (if not a mere
feint of party politics) the last effort of the incensed spirit
of endurance in the North — a punishment threatened
against rebels, whom they can not otherwise subdue, and
which a year ago half the Northern population would
have condemned upon principle, and more than half re-
volted from on instinct.

The country being in a state of war necessarily compli-
cates every thing, and renders the most plausible suggestions for the settlement of the question of emancipation
futile, because from first to last now it will be one tremendous chapter of accidents, instead of a carefully considered and wisely prepared measure of government.
But, supposing the war to have ceased, either by the success of the Northern arms or by the consent of both bel-
ligerents, the question of manumission in the Southern
states when reduced to the condition of territories or re-
stored to the sway of their own elected governors and
Legislatures, though difficult, is by no means one of insuperable difficulty ; and I do not believe that a great nation
of Englishmen, having once the will to rid itself of a danger and a disgrace, will fail to find a way. The thing,
therefore, most to be desired now is, that Americans may

unanimously embrace the purpose of emancipation, and, though they have been reluctantly driven by the irresistible force of circumstances to contemplate the measure, may henceforward never avert their eyes from it till it is accomplished.

When I was in the South many years ago I conversed frequently with two highly intelligent men, both of whom agreed in saying that the immense value of the slaves as property was the only real obstacle to their manumission, and that whenever the Southerners became convinced that it was their interest to free them they would very soon find the means to do it. In some respects the conditions are more favorable than those we had to encounter in freeing our West India slaves. Though the soil and climate of the Southern states are fertile and favorable, they are not tropical, and there is no profuse natural growth of fruits or vegetables to render subsistence possible without labor; the winter temperature is like that of the Roman States; and even as far south as Georgia and the borders of Florida, frosts severe enough to kill the orange-trees are sometimes experienced. The inhabitants of the Southern states, throughout by far the largest portion of their extent, must labor to live, and will undoubtedly obey the beneficent law of necessity whenever they are made to feel that their existence depends upon their own exertions. The plan of a gradual emancipation, preceded by a limited apprenticeship of the negroes to white masters, is of course often suggested as less dangerous than their entire and immediate enfranchisement. But when years ago I lived on a Southern plantation, and had opportunities of observing the miserable results of the system on every thing connected with it—the souls, minds, bodies, and estates of both races of men, and the very soil on which they existed together—I came to the conclusion that immediate and entire emancipation was not only an act of imperative right, but would be the safest and most profitable course for the interests of both parties. The gradual and inevitable process of ruin which exhibits itself in the long run on every property involving slavery, naturally suggests some element of decay inherent in the system; the reckless habits of extravagance and prodigality in the masters, the ruinous wastefulness and ignorant incapacity of the slaves, the deterioration of the land under the exhausting and thriftless cultivation to which it is subjected, made it evident to me that there were but two means of maintaining a prosperous ownership in Southern plantations: either the possession of considerable capital wherewith to recruit the gradual waste of the energies of the soil, and supply by all the improved and costly methods of modern agriculture the means of profitable cultivation (a process demanding, as English farmers know, an enormous and incessant outlay of both money and skill), or an unlimited command of fresh soil, to which the slaves might be transferred as soon as that already under culture exhibited signs of exhaustion. Now the Southerners are for the most part men whose only wealth is in their land and laborers—a large force of slaves is their most profitable investment. The great capitalists and moneyed men of the country are Northern men; the planters are men of large estates but restricted means: many of them are deeply involved in debt, and there are very few who do not depend from year to year for their subsistence on the harvest of their fields and the chances of the cotton and rice crops of each season.

This makes it of vital importance to them to command an unrestricted extent of territory. The man who can move a "gang" of able-bodied negroes to a tract of virgin soil is sure of an immense return of wealth; as sure as that he who is circumscribed in this respect, and limited to the cultivation of certain lands with cotton or tobacco by slaves, will in the course of a few years see his estate gradually exhausted and unproductive, refusing its increase, while its black population, propagating and multiplying, will compel him eventually, under penalty of starvation, to make *them* his crop, and substitute, as the Virginians have been constrained to do, a traffic in human cattle for the cultivation of vegetable harvests.

The steady decrease of the value of the cotton-crop, even on the famous sea-island plantations of Georgia, often suggested to me the inevitable ruin of the owners within a certain calculable space of time, as the land became worn out, and the negroes continued to increase in number; and had the estate on which I lived been mine, and the laws of Georgia not made such an experiment impossible, I would have emancipated the slaves on it immediately, and turned them into a free tenantry, as the first means of saving my property from impending destruction. I would have paid them wages, and they should have paid me rent. I would have relinquished the charge of feeding and clothing them, and the burden of their old, young, and infirm; in short, I would have put them at once upon the footing of free hired laborers. Of course such a process would have involved temporary loss, and for a year or two the income of the estate would, I dare say, have suffered considerably; but, in all such diversions of labor or capital from old into new channels and modes of operation, there must be an immediate sacrifice of present to future profit, and I do not doubt that the estate would have recovered from the momentary necessary interruption of its productiveness, to resume it with an upward instead of a downward tendency, and a vigorous impulse toward progress and improvement substituted for the present slow but sure drifting to stagnation and decay.

As I have told you, the land affords no spontaneous produce which will sustain life without labor. The negroes, therefore, must work to eat; they are used to the soil and climate, and accustomed to the agriculture, and there is no reason at all to apprehend—as has been suggested—that a race of people singularly attached to the place of their birth and residence would abandon in any large numbers their own country, just as the conditions of their existence in it were made more favorable, to try the unknown and (to absolute ignorance) forbidding risks of emigration to the sterner climate and harder soil of the Northern states.

Of course, in freeing the slaves, it would be necessary to contemplate the possibility of their becoming eventual proprietors of the soil to some extent themselves. There is as little doubt that many of them would soon acquire the means of doing so (men who amass, during hours of daily extra labor, through years of unpaid toil, the means of buying themselves from their masters, would soon justify their freedom by the intelligent improvement of their condition), as that many of the present landholders would be ready and glad to alienate their impoverished estates by parcels, and sell the land which has become comparatively unprofitable to them, to its enfranchised cultivators. This, the future ownership of land by negroes, as well as their admission to those rights of citizenship which every where in America such ownership involves, would necessarily be future subjects of legislation; and either or both privileges might be withheld temporarily, indefinitely, or permanently, as might seem expedient, and the progress in civilization which might justify such an extension of rights. These, and any other modifications of the state of the black population in the South, would require great wisdom to deal with, but their immediate transformation from bondsmen to free might, I think, be accomplished with little danger or difficulty, and with certain increase of prosperity to the Southern states.

On the other hand, it is not impossible that, left to the unimpeded action of the natural laws that govern the existence of various races, the black population, no longer directly preserved and propagated for the purposes of slavery, might gradually decrease and dwindle, as it does at the North, where, besides the unfavorable influence of a cold climate on a race originally African, it suffers from its admixture with the whites, and the amalgamation of the two races, as far as it goes, tends evidently to the destruction of the weaker. The Northern mulattoes are an unhealthy, feeble population, and it might yet appear that even under the more favorable influence of a Southern climate, whenever the direct stimulus afforded by slavery to the increase of the negroes was removed, their gradual extinction or absorption by the predominant white race would follow in the course of time.

But the daily course of events appears to be rendering more and more unlikely the immediate effectual enfranchisement of the slaves: the President's proclamation will reach with but little efficacy beyond the mere borders of the Southern states. The war is assuming an aspect of indefinite duration; and it is difficult to conceive what will be the condition of the blacks, freed *de jure* but by no means *de facto*, in the vast interior regions of the Southern states, as long as the struggle raging all round their confines does not penetrate within them. Each of the combatants is far too busily absorbed in the furious strife to afford thought, leisure, or means either effectually to free the slaves or effectually to replace them in bondage; and, in the mean time, their condition is the worst possible for the future success of either operation. If the North succeeds in subjugating the South, its earliest business will be to make the freedom of the slaves real as well as nominal, and as little injurious to themselves as possible. If, on the other hand, the South makes good its pretensions to a separate national existence, no sooner will the disseverment of the Union be an established fact than the slaveholders will have to consolidate once more the system of their "peculiar institution," to reconstruct the prison which has half crumbled to the ground, and rivet afresh the chains which have been all but struck off. This will be difficult: the determination of the North to restrict the area of slavery by forbidding its ingress into future territories and states has been considered by the slaveholders a wrong, and a danger justifying a bloody civil war; inasmuch as, if under those circumstances they did not abolish slavery themselves in a given num ber of years, it would infallibly abolish them by the in- crease of the negro population, hemmed with them into a restricted space by this *cordon sanitaire* drawn round them. But, bad as this prospect has seemed to slave- holders (determined to continue such), and justifying— as it may be conceded that it does from their point of view—not a ferocious civil war, but a peaceable separa- tion from states whose interests were declared absolute- ly irreconcilable with theirs, the position in which they will find themselves if the contest terminates in favor of secession will be undoubtedly more difficult and terrible than the one the mere anticipation of which has driven them to the dire resort of civil war. All round the South- ern coast, and all along the course of the great Mississippi, and all across the northern frontier of the slave states, the negroes have already thrown off the trammels of slavery. Whatever their condition may be—and doubtless, in many respects, it is miserable enough—they are to all intents and purposes free. Vast numbers of them have joined the Northern invading armies, and considerable bodies of them have become organized as soldiers and laborers, un- der the supervision of Northern officers and employers; most of them have learned the use of arms, and possess them ; all of them have exchanged the insufficient slave diet of grits and rice for the abundant supplies of animal food, which the poorest laborer in that favored land of cheap provisions and high wages indulges in to an extent unknown in any other country. None of these slaves of yesterday will be the same slaves to-morrow. Little essential difference as may yet have been effected by the President's proclamation in the interior of the South in the condition of the blacks, it is undoubtedly known to them, and they are waiting in ominous suspense its accomplishment or defeat by the fortune of the war; they are watching the issue of the contest of which they well know themselves to be the theme, and at its conclusion, end how it will, they must be emancipated or exterminated. With the North not only not friendly to slavery, but henceforward bitterly hostile to slaveholders, and no more to be reckoned upon as heretofore, it might have been infallibly by the Southern white population in any difficulty with the blacks (a fact of which the negroes will be as well aware as their former masters)—with an invisible boundary stretching from ocean to ocean, over which they may fly without fear of a master's claim following them a single inch—with the hope and expectation of liberty suddenly snatched from them at the moment it seemed within their grasp—with the door of their dungeon once more barred between them and the light into which they were in the act of emerging, is it to be conceived that these four millions of people, many thousands of whom are already free and armed, will submit without a struggle to be again thrust down into the hell of slavery ? Hitherto there has been no insurrection among the negroes, and observers friendly and inimical to them have alike drawn from that fact conclusions unfavorable to their appreciation of the freedom apparently within their grasp; but they are waiting to see what the North will really achieve for them. The liberty offered them is hitherto anomalous, and uncertain enough in its conditions; they probably trust it as little as they know it; but slavery they *do* know; and when once they find themselves again delivered over to *that* experience, there will not be ONE insurrection in the South—there will be an insurrection in every state, in every county, on every plantation—a struggle as fierce as it will be futile—a hopeless effort of hopeless men, which will baptize in blood the new American nation, and inaugurate its birth among the civilized societies of the earth, not by the manumission, but the massacre of every slave within its borders.

Perhaps, however, Mr. Jefferson Davis means to free the negroes. Whenever that consummation is attained, the root of bitterness will have perished from the land; and when a few years shall have passed, blunting the hatred which has been excited by this fratricidal strife, the Americans of both the Northern and Southern states will perceive that the selfish policy of other nations would not have so rejoiced over their division, had it not seemed, to those who loved them not, the proof of past failure and the prophecy of future weakness.

Admonished by its terrible experiences, I believe the nation will reunite itself under one government, remodel its Constitution, and again address itself to fulfill its glorious destiny. I believe that the country sprung from ours—of all our just subjects of national pride the greatest—will resume its career of prosperity and power, and become the noblest as well as the mightiest that has existed among the nations of the earth.

P

THE END.